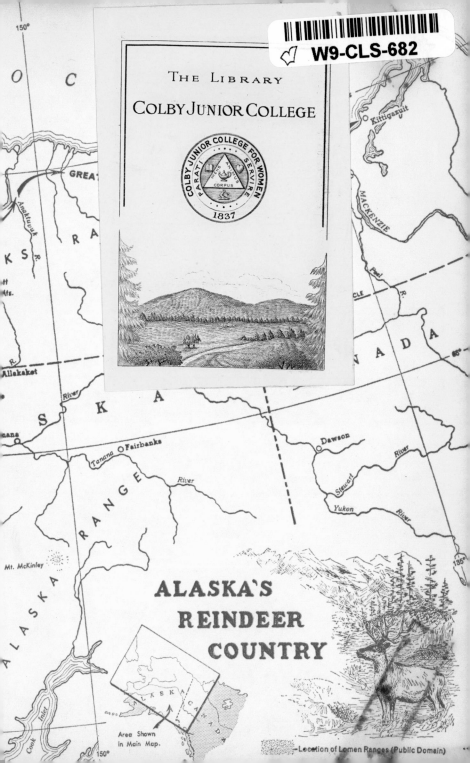

ALASKA'S
REINDEER
COUNTRY

Area Shown
in Main Map.

Location of Lomen Ranges (Public Domain)

FIFTY YEARS
IN ALASKA

FIFTY YEARS IN ALASKA

CARL J. LOMEN

Foreword by Richard E. Byrd
Rear Admiral, USN (ret.)

David McKay Company, Inc.

New York

*To my wife, Laura, after
twenty-five happy years together*

ACKNOWLEDGMENTS

WHILE I enjoyed writing this book, it was to me, an American businessman, a monumental task. I should perhaps never have finished it had it not been for the encouragement and help of my family and friends. I owe them much.

My wife Laura checked the manuscript, making many corrections and suggestions. Sister Helen and my brothers Harry and Ralph, all of whom lived much of this book, were a constant inspiration.

I am also indebted to others. Mrs. Mabel Walker Willebrandt assisted in rendering order out of chaos. Lyman Ellsworth, already a successful author when I first met him in Seattle, collaborated with me on part of the manuscript. And in addition, my heartfelt thanks goes to Miss Anna Feley of Granite Falls, Minnesota, Miss Ruth Reat of Vashon, Washington, Mrs. Percy N. Shepheard, Mrs. Marie Rogalski and Miss Lulu Fairbanks of Seattle, Washington, Mr. Robert B. Walkinshaw and Mr. Clinton Austin of Seattle, Washington, Mr. Paul Ivanoff of Eek, Alaska, and Mr. Hal G. Vermes of New York City. Finally, I would like to extend my sincere appreciation to the many good friends I have among the Eskimo and Lapps who were so faithful in working with me in the development of the reindeer business.

C. J. L.

FOREWORD

DURING the spring of 1925 I was very busy making preparations for a new venture—that of performing the aerial work for the MacMillan Arctic Expedition. Then one day in May in the office of the Secretary of the Navy, Mr. Wilbur, I met Carl Lomen. That meeting was of special interest to me when I learned that he was one of the Lomens of Nome, who had spent many years in the North Country and had pioneered in the reindeer industry of Alaska. The Lomens were expert in the technique of winter travel by both dogs and reindeer, and had adapted the arctic dress of the Eskimo—parkas, fur pants, mukluks, mittens, and sleeping bags—for the use of arctic travelers, drawing on their large herds for choice skins for such purposes. The admirable nature of these products bore eloquent testimony to the Lomen mastery of the art of polar travel.

Returning with MacMillan in the fall, I felt that a flight from Spitzbergen to the North Pole and back was feasible. I got in touch with my Alaska friend, requesting that he have made for my pilot, Floyd Bennett, and me complete fur outfits for such a flight, together with a small hickory sled to carry in the plane should there be a forced landing necessitating an ice trip back to civilization.

The trip proved successful; the winter clothing perfect for the purpose. Later Carl and his brothers supplied my first two Antartic Expeditions with reindeer-fur clothing, sleeping bags, and much of our foot gear.

Now I learn that after these many years, Carl has written for publication his story and that of the Alaska reindeer industry, and I am delighted to contribute a foreword to the book of a man who has lived a most varied and interesting life in northwestern Alaska for a half century, and whose experiences and recollections of a pioneer country will prove of great interest and value to the American people.

RICHARD E. BYRD
Rear Admiral, USN (Ret.)

INTRODUCTION

PERHAPS I was destined to spend nearly a half-century with reindeer in Alaska. In 1900, when I first heard of this gentle animal, my interest was aroused. Maybe it was in my blood, as both of my parents were Norwegian. My father, Judge G. J. Lomen, had the spirit of adventure in him. In 1923 he received the Order of St. Olaf from King Haakon of Norway in recognition of his assistance to Captain Roald Amundsen in his polar expeditions.

Reindeer became for me both a hobby and a business. When I went to Alaska, it was a pioneer industry in a pioneer country. Our family gave it our best. When the going was rough and funds were low, we maintained the load through our other enterprises. We sincerely believed that we were helping in the building of a new industry, one which would prove valuable to Alaska and also contribute to the economy of the United States.

I was born in Minnesota, but Alaska was to become my adopted home. Most Americans do not realize the vastness of the northernmost member of our democracy. It is almost 600,000 square miles in area, twice that of Texas, and one fifth the size of the United States. Nome is 500 miles farther west than Honolulu; and the greatest breadth of Alaska is comparable in distance to that between Cuba and Greenland.

When I first saw it, Alaska was a district without a local legislature and without representation in Congress. In 1906 it was granted a congressional delegate who had speaking privileges but no vote. Alaska was made a territory in 1912.

Our family is no longer in the reindeer business though our roots and hearts are still in Alaska. Today my younger brother Ralph and I operate the Lomen Commercial Company, an Alaskan corporation, with offices at Nome and Seattle. There are no dock facilities on the shores of the northern Bering Sea, therefore, during the five months from June to October, when there is open navigation, ships anchor off shore from one to ten miles. Our main business is that of lighterage discharging and loading of freight from and to the steamers anchored in the roadstead. Our lighters and barges are towed by tugs. Our crews, as well as the longshoremen ashore, are largely Eskimo. We perform this service at Nome, Teller, Lost River, Tin City, Golovin, and Moses Point, all on the Bering Sea. We are agents at Nome for the Standard Oil Company of California and transport oil, gasoline, machinery, and general merchandise up and down the Alaskan coast.

While this is an interesting business it does not, at least to me, hold the fascination of my many years spent with the reindeer. It will, I feel certain, be a surprise to most readers that reindeer are not indigenous to Alaska and had to be imported across the Bering Sea from Siberia.

That was part of the adventure, and I am happy to have had some share in it. Even though we were finally forced out of the reindeer business by government officialdom, I have no regrets. It was a rich and often thrilling experience. I hope that the reader, through my memories, will also be imbued with the spirit of adventure.

CARL J. LOMEN

FIFTY YEARS
IN ALASKA

1.

THE TIME was 1900, and I was nineteen. It was a crisp, cold winter's day, and I was sitting in my father's comfortable law office in St. Paul, Minnesota. Preparing to enter law school at the University of Minnesota, I was learning the ropes by working for my father meanwhile.

I could not have known, by the wildest stretch of the imagination, that this quiet day, this lazy hour, was the most crucial in my life. My career had already been mapped out for me. Like my father, I, too, would become an attorney at law. And the law, as any young law clerk who has pored over the thick volumes of *Shepard's Citations* can testify, is often a very dull business.

While Father was otherwise engaged, I chatted with a visitor, Henry Anderson of Minneapolis. All over the world the imaginations of men had been fired by the great gold rush of 1897–98 in the Klondike. Anderson had been a member of that mad horde that scrambled for gold in Alaska. As I listened, fascinated by his colorful tales, he told me of his experiences while searching for the elusive yellow dust. Now, he said, he was going to Nome.

I was so tantalized by his vivid descriptions that the next day I went to the local library and took out several books about Alaska. I soon learned how different life was there as compared to staid St. Paul and Father's sleepy law office. They were worlds apart. In those days young Americans thought of Alaska as the youth of today think of the planet Mars.

I went to the railroad offices and stuffed my pockets with colorful folders about the great gold fields where every man had the opportunity to make a fortune. After reading them I'd casually drop them on my father's desk. It wasn't long before I saw that the gleam in my eye was reflected in his own.

Father was a hard-working attorney at law in his mid-forties striving to raise and educate a large family. There were eight of us altogether: Dad and Mother, George, twenty-one, Harry, seventeen, Ralph, thirteen, Alfred, ten, Helen, six, and myself.

One day Dad called me into his private office and carefully closed the door.

"Carl," he said, "I see that you have been bitten by the goldbug. Are you really determined to go to Alaska this summer?"

"Yes, Dad," I replied.

"Do you realize what this step may mean?" he pointed out. "It means giving up everything with which you have been familiar since childhood: a good home, security, an education, and a career in an honorable profession. Alaska is a rough, tough country, still primitive, ungoverned, and uncultured."

"I know," I said. "There'll be hardships, privation, but there'll be adventure. And, after all, it's only a vacation."

Father took my hand in his, and there was a look on his face I had not seen before.

"Carl," he whispered, "I'll go with you!"

"But Dad!" I exclaimed, shocked by this sudden turn of events. "You've got Mother and the family to think of. Your roots are in St. Paul. You have built up a good practice. You would be losing a lot, while I have nothing to lose."

"Mother and the children," he said, "have always been well taken care of. Besides, they'll be out at Bald Eagle Lake for the summer and your uncle George will keep an eye on them."

4

"Mother won't let you go," I said.

"I know how to convince her," he assured me. "Remember, I haven't had a real vacation in twenty years and I'm certainly entitled to one."

I nodded my head in agreement.

"And this, Carl, is what will clinch it," he continued. "You are my excuse for going to Alaska. You are set on going; but you are only nineteen, and Mother would never hear of your going alone. So your father goes with you!"

That logic would convince twelve good men and true, and it seemed to me that it would also convince Mother. After all, Dad was a good lawyer.

Very little was known about Alaska by our family and friends, though they had all heard of the tragedies of the Yukon and Klondike trails and considered it suicidal for Dad and me to attempt such a long trip into the far north. We explained that Henry Anderson, who had spent the preceding year there, was now taking his family, including a four-year-old daughter.

Mother, who had a practical philosophy, was equal to the emergency and finally gave her consent. My four brothers were naturally envious of me and looked forward to the day when they could follow Father. Curiously, nobody thought of it as a vacation trip. And it wasn't, for it lasted more than forty years.

Almost everyone we knew came to the Union Depot in St. Paul on May 12, 1900, to wish us Godspeed and see us off. Mother was tearful, my four brothers laughed and joked, and my little sister Helen cried.

Seattle, "The Gateway to the North," was crowded with gold seekers, and ships for Alaska were leaving every day. We were unable to find hotel accommodations but eventually succeeded in getting the use of the parlor in a private home on the understanding that we would not come in before 10 P.M.

5

and would be out by 8 A.M. That was no hardship for us, as we had to book passage on a boat and meanwhile wanted to see the bustling town.

On May 23 we boarded the S.S. *Garonne*, once known as "The Mistress of the Seas." Now all she was able to do was to plug along at a steady eight knots. She barely made that modest speed as the ship was crowded with 850 passengers, a crew of more than 100, and 63 stowaways.

Our stateroom was hardly first class, as called for by our tickets, but at least it was one of the few with two berths. Other passengers were not so fortunate, and the passageways were lined with standees. Our trip proved strenuous. The old ship heaved and pitched. So did most of the passengers, many of them being landlubbers. Father and I found places to sit on a bench in the smoking room, which ran athwart the ship. Running the length of the room, several card tables were fastened to the floor. Bright brass cuspidors were strategically placed here and there.

One day at sea a sharp voice suddenly cut through the friendly comradeship of the saloon.

"Look out!" it cried. "We're headin' into a storm!"

An immense rolling wave smashed over the good ship *Garonne*. Now "The Mistress of the Seas" had met her master. She heeled over at a dangerous angle, and the passengers held their breath as they waited for her to swing back and list to an even more alarming angle.

As the ship rolled, those of us sitting on the benches slid down, then back again. Card players, their game momentarily forgotten, clutched at the tables. But as the vessel pitched and tossed, the tables broke from their moorings and sailed down the room, helter-skelter. Everybody ran for the doors, slipping and falling. The well-filled cuspidors overturned, tobacco juice slicking the heaving floor. There were shouts, curses, and cries of injury. Pandemonium turned into near

6

panic. But after a couple of hours of anxiety the S.S. *Garonne* safely rode out the storm.

Two hundred miles south of Nome we encountered solid ice and spent a week maneuvering for a lead. But the pack was a virtually impenetrable mass of ice cakes five to twenty feet thick. They heaved and ground against each other with the incessant action of the sea. The old *Garonne* followed lead after lead, only to run into a dead end and be forced to retreat.

The ice floes churned as the ship stood on end, hesitated for an eternal instant, and then plunged terrifyingly into a deep trough. "The Mistress of the Seas" groaned in the agony of her dotage as she struggled against the fury of the elements. The engines jerked and shuddered as the propellers caught the sea and then were helplessly thrust heavenward again. They slipped, then roared, as the vessel dived, rolled, and climbed interminably. The *Garonne* seemed to be gasping for her last breath.

Eventually the storm spent itself and fled over the horizon. Again the ship began the burdensome task of working her way through the ice floes. On June 3, 1900, we were anchored in mid-ocean. The S.S. *Olympia* was at anchor two miles distant. The next day the captain's log read: "Steamed up to the ice pack at 4 A.M. Found heavy ice and freshening NW wind and southerly set of water. At 5:30 A.M. we returned and anchored two miles north of previously recorded position."

Two small boats out of San Francisco joined us. Soon there were seven ships driven close together by the anger of the ice. Late in the evening of June 5 we all stood south.

Another two days and we were in sight of Cape Romanzoff, where we'd been a week ago. The thermometer was at freezing, and a lively snowstorm frosted our whiskers. On June 9 we signaled the steam schooner *Rainier* just out of Dutch Harbor, and she reported eleven ships at that port waiting their turn to coal up.

The next day we moved northward and were rammed by an ice floe. We pulled anchor and steamed south again. Then we dropped anchor north of Nunivak Island. A soft gray flannel fog enveloped us, and suddenly the ship was rammed by another large floe. Up anchor and we headed south once more, this time for Dutch Harbor, as the *Garonne*'s coal supply was running dangerously low.

While at anchor near the Aleutians the crew got out fishing tackle and, to alleviate the anxiety and boredom, we became disciples of Izaak Walton. Dad, unfortunately, caught nothing, but I managed to land a fine white cod weighing nearly twenty-five pounds, which was later served to us at the captain's table. After the fog lifted we proceeded cautiously and anchored at Dutch Harbor at 10:45 P.M. on June 13.

We spent a week in Dutch Harbor, during which time we visited the quaint little village of Unalaska, where we saw an old Greek Orthodox church erected during the Russian occupation. We made courtesy calls to other ships, and held athletic contests: baseball, tug of war, foot races, and pole vaulting. We had clambakes on the shore and climbed nearby mountains.

After coaling up, we got under way again though it was blowing a gale. The captain was hesitant, but the passengers were driven on by the beckoning of the Golden Sands of Nome.

Amateur poets aboard the *Garonne* vied with one another to record our voyage. From the bulletin board I copied the work of a bard who had facetiously signed himself "Lynn Seed Oil." Here is his parody recorded for the ages:

> I've wandered for days o'er the seas, Maggie,
>> And watched the midnight sun;
> Our whiskers have hit the breeze, Maggie,
>> And we've had all kinds of fun.
> But now we are nearing the shore, Maggie,

And our trouble soon begins,
Without wood or oil or coal, Maggie,
 To warm our frozen shins.

The mills of the gods grind slow, Maggie,
 And so does the good ship *Garonne;*
We stuck in the ice and snow, Maggie,
 One hundred miles from Nome.
So we played our national game, Maggie,
 In the far-off Aleutian Isles,
And could not win the same, Maggie,
 You could hear the catcalls for miles.

We met the *Skookum* there, Maggie,
 With the *Hoot Mon* and *Billy the Mug;*
She left us, but 'twasn't fair, Maggie,
 To be beaten by that old tub.
We're now on the high seas, Maggie,
 And no place to inquire;
But as we hit the breeze, Maggie,
 We may beat her to the wire.

Green waves marched out of the north in a succession of white-topped combers that hurled themselves against the *Garonne,* making her stagger drunkenly. It was obvious that the "old soak" had had one too many. This time, however, we encountered very little ice and, the wind finally dying down, we anchored at last in the roadstead off Nome the early evening of June 23, 1900.

2.

MY HEART sank as Dad and I stood on the deck of the *Garonne* and peered toward the distant Alaskan shore.

"What a barren-looking country!" I exclaimed.

"Man will go anywhere for treasure," he replied.

Flat lowland stretched as far as we could see along the coast line. There was not a tree in sight. In the distance loomed jagged mountain peaks covered with snow. Thousands of new white tents were pitched on the littered beach. As we silently gazed at this American pioneer outpost, I was swept with homesickness. If I had known that I was to spend half my life in this uncivilized territory, I am certain that I would have booked passage back to the States.

We were anchored one and a half miles off the beach. The weather was perfect and the sea like a millpond. The sun set just before 11 P.M. and rose again at 1:15 A.M. Many ships were at anchor, and their whistles tooted all through the night. Hundreds of sled dogs ashore added to the din with their howling. I later learned that the dogs of the North seldom bark; instead, they point their noses at the sky and howl dismally.

Early the following morning Henry Anderson came out in a small boat and picked us up. Instead of landing on the beach, he entered the mouth of the Snake River and rowed upstream to his camp, which consisted of several tents on frames and with board floors. We stayed with the Andersons for a few days until we set up our own tent some distance away.

Later in the day Dad and I wandered along the Nome beach, getting our first feel of the country. In places the sand was piled to a height of ten feet with freight and, right at the water's edge, pieces of heavy machinery lay rusting from the salt water.

The first discovery of gold near Nome was in the fall of 1898. Only a few people managed to reach the scene of the strike before winter set in. A thousand more poured in when the 1899 season for prospecting opened up. Now, in 1900, came the big rush. Forty thousand people arrived from all parts of the world. The beach on which they landed bordered a timberless tundra. The word "tundra" had always intrigued me, suggesting something foreign, a touch of the Russian, perhaps. Now I learned at firsthand what it was really like: vast, treeless, largely level plains, with a mucky topsoil and permanently frozen subsoil, supporting a dense growth of mosses and lichens, grasses, dwarf shrubs, willows and alder, and many varieties of flowers. Beyond "city limits" tundra characterizes the arctic regions in both hemispheres.

In Nome people thronged the main street, rushing here and there, seemingly without purpose. Board shacks mushroomed. As the sun burrowed into the ground the narrow, muddy street turned into a quagmire. For miles in all directions the tundra was dotted with tents, jammed so close together along the beach that their guy ropes crossed. Occupants were limited to the ground covered by their tents. The "Consent" city government erected a few crude latrines—four posts enclosed in burlap—and passed an ordinance requiring people to use them. Tickets were sold for ten cents apiece, or three for a quarter.

Cramped in the narrow area surrounding the forty-odd "gambling hells" that had sprung up in the center of town

11

were many more tents. Stovepipe chimneys were everywhere, all breathing out a slow black smoke that settled in a dank fog over everything, biting at a man's throat and making his nose run.

The confusion was appalling. Machinery, hay and grain, hardware, provisions, liquor, tents, pianos, mirrors, bar fixtures, household furniture were piled in the open. Warehouses were unknown. Transportation by wagon along the beach cost ten dollars an hour; and the wagons barely moved in the seemingly bottomless mud.

Only the fortunate few slept on floors. The others borrowed a board or huddled on a pile of moss on the open tundra. The mind of every man was inflamed by the burning hope of untold millions simply waiting to be scratched out of the earth by the first lucky hand. In this vigorous atmosphere the gunsmith and blacksmith outthrove the haberdasher; and saloonkeepers prospered more than the average miner.

We learned that three days prior to our arrival one of the most spectacular gun fights in Nome's history had occurred. A man named Hank Lucas was in possession of a townsite lot. Another man came along and ordered him to clear out. When Lucas firmly refused, the trespasser drew his gun and fired. Hank fell to the ground but, though mortally wounded, he had sufficient strength left to draw and return the fire, instantly killing his aggressor. A few minutes later Lucas also was dead.

Lucas was a Kentuckian. Later that year it became the unhappy duty of a friend of ours, the attorney for Lucas's estate, to go to Kentucky and acquaint Hank's widowed mother with the mournful news. The attorney was as gentle as the occasion allowed.

Hank's mother listened intently. For a moment or two she was silently thoughtful. Then she quietly remarked:

"I never could have believed that Hank would ever let anyone get the drop on him."

One enterprising merchant shipped a milk cow to Nome on an early boat that season. It was astounding the amount of milk that cow gave. It finally got to the point where the owner was actually delivering fifty gallons of milk every day from that solitary cow! Then his customers got wise to the fact that they were paying for a little fresh cow's milk plus a lot of condensed milk and plenty of water at the fancy price of two dollars a gallon.

The milk business dried up and so did the cow. But this so-called dairy farmer was undaunted. Figuring to make a little more profit, he butchered the lean cow and sold the meat to one of the restaurants in Nome that did a land-office business. The proprietor had just finished carving one hind-quarter into huge steaks when in came a burly miner from the creeks, ravenous as a wolf. He was a giant of a man with massive sloping shoulders, his face a bramble of iron-gray whiskers. Upon him was the smell of whisky gone sour and sweat earned at the end of a long-handled miner's No. 2 shovel. He stared at the fresh meat, which he hadn't seen for months, and ordered the restaurant owner to cook up the largest steak in the house. One slice had been carved from a section clear across the widest part of the hindquarter.

"I'll take that one!" he demanded, pointing.

"It's much too big for one man," the proprietor objected. "It won't go in the frying pan."

"Cook it on top of the stove," the miner insisted. "I'm danged hongry and I want that steak!"

Shaking his head dubiously, the cook prepared the steak. It was so huge that, when served on the largest platter, it stuck out over the ends.

With a grin of anticipation, the sourdough salted the immense steak and then attacked it with gusto. The knife the restaurant had supplied did not prove sharp enough to please him so he yanked a sheath knife from his belt and commenced sawing away. But the tough meat resisted the strength of his muscled right arm. Finally he succeeded in hacking off a large chunk that he stuffed into his mouth. Now it was evident that the miner possessed a pair of ill-fitting false teeth, which clacked noisily up and down. The more he chewed, the more rubbery the meat seemed to become.

A bewildered expression replaced the satisfied smile he had worn when he first attacked the steak. Again he sawed away with his sheath knife until he had liberated another portion. Once again he chewed lustily but without result, for the meat proved to be as durable as leather. Jumping up in disgust, the miner walked up to the proprietor, who was taking in the scene with a smile.

"How much do I owe you for that steak?" the sourdough demanded.

"Fifteen dollars."

"What?" the miner raged.

"That meat," the owner pointed out, "was big enough for four steaks."

"Take it out of that!" The miner thumped a poke of gold dust on the counter.

The proprietor weighed out fifteen dollars in gold dust. The customer grabbed his poke, shoved it into his pocket, and then picked up the steak, platter and all. Going to the door, he kicked his inedible meal out into the muddy street, and followed it, cursing.

The first discovery of gold at Nome was made in September 1898 by a party of five men who had come up the coast to investigate the report of gold found at Sinuk (now Sinrock). Bad weather forced them to land at the mouth of a river—later named Snake River—where Nome was built. Jafet Lindeberg, a Norwegian, and Eric O. Lindbloom and John Brynteson, Swedes, were to become famous as the "Three Lucky Swedes." The other two members of the party were Dr. A. N. Kittilsen, a physician to the Eskimo employed by the Bureau of Education, and Gabe Price, who represented the interests of that fine old California miner, Charles D. Lane.

Jafet Lindeberg, living in Norway and anxious to reach Alaska, had hired out as one of the foremen to accompany the government reindeer expedition from Norway to Alaska in 1898. He purchased his release from government service shortly after the expedition landed at Unalakleet, and became a prospector and miner.

Eric O. Lindbloom was a tailor by trade. Living in San Francisco, one day he was accosted by two men who inquired:

"Are you a sailor?"

"Yes," Lindbloom replied, thinking they had said "tailor."

"Come with us then; we have a job for you."

They entered one of the saloons on the San Francisco water front.

"Have a drink," one of the men invited.

When Lindbloom returned to consciousness, he found that he had been shanghaied and was at sea on board an American whaling vessel headed for the Arctic Ocean. Weeks later they put in at Port Clarence Bay, Alaska, for fresh water. Lindbloom deserted ship and, being supplied with two pack reindeer by the local minister, he speedily headed for the hills. Circling inland, he managed to reach Golovin, where he joined up with the other two lucky Swedes to prospect for gold. This trio later formed the Pioneer Mining and Ditch Company, the largest and most successful in the Nome district, which produced in excess of $23,000,000 in gold. They were prime factors in the development and economic success of Northwestern Alaska.

News of the gold strike did not get around until some time after the discovery was made. But when it did, bearded men loaded their sleds in the nighttime, tightened their belts and the thongs of their snowshoes, and melted like ghosts into the darkness in the race to be first at the new gold fields.

Gaunt, ragged, and travel-worn, a stream of hardy adventurers surged down the Yukon River: by dog team, bicycle, or on foot, in winter; by raft and hastily improvised boats in summer. They arrived to find the land, from beach to rolling upland, already occupied by Swedes, Finns, and Laplanders. Many of this early group were Lapp reindeer men hired by the United States Government to act as instructors to the Eskimo in the care of the reindeer herds.

These Lapps were not, of course, citizens. And newcomers from the States, knowing that aliens could not legally file on a mining claim, jumped those on which appeared a name that looked Norwegian, Finn, or Lapp. Jafet Lindeberg's claims were jumped. Prior to the arrival of the newcomers he, like many other members of the reindeer expedition, had declared before a United States commissioner his intention of becoming an American citizen, thus, in effect, legalizing his claims. That resourceful commissioner hatched out "declared" citizens like an incubator hatching out chicks.

Now the battle was on. Numerous claims were jumped, the richer claims so repeatedly that the tangle was frightful. Then a point of law was discovered that had never occurred to the greedy miners. This was that the question of ownership by an alien could not be raised against the claimant by anyone except the United States Government. As an attorney, Dad found plenty of legal work in Nome. And that was one reason why he and I had no vacation.

The preceding winter Congress had drafted and passed "The Alaska Code," both civil and criminal, organizing Alaska as a district, dividing it into four judicial divisions, and providing for the appointment of federal judges, marshals, and United States attorneys for each.

For the Second Judicial Division, wherein Nome was located, President McKinley appointed Arthur H. Noyes of Minneapolis as judge. On July 19, 1900, Judge Noyes and other members of the court and official family arrived in

Nome. They were given a most cordial welcome by local leaders, all designed to point to the need of a court and the related exercise of that civil authority that is vested in the court.

It soon appeared, however, that a new and powerful figure had also arrived on the steamer: Alexander H. McKenzie by name, a politician and "kingmaker" from the Dakotas. McKenzie was ostensibly the president of the Alaska Gold Mining Company. But it developed that he had larger plans than merely managing the affairs of a mining company— especially one without any mining claims.

McKenzie set up a plan, with the connivance of the court, whereby all the richer claims in the area were to be thrown into receivership and he be appointed as receiver. Shortly the miners were saying that "both God and Washington" were far away. As McKenzie's plan was aided and abetted by the court, claim after claim was tied up, with McKenzie or one of his henchmen named as receiver, and instructions from the court to carry on operation of the seized properties. As the receiver was under bond of only $5,000, and many claims produced from $10,000 to $15,000 a day in gold dust, this maneuver became one of the biggest and boldest attempted "steals" the country had ever witnessed.

Nome bristled with attorneys. Sixty-four were sworn in as members of the bar on the very first day the court, sat, Dad being one of them. Before the close of the season 127 lawyers had been admitted to practice. Many of these worked closely with McKenzie and his gang in taking away miners' claims with legal prestidigitation. Several times Dad was warmly invited to join "the ring," but he always firmly refused. As a result, he was not invited to their "social functions," and saw them only when he faced them as opposing counsel in the Court.

Mine operators were soon aware that all was not as it should be. Judge Noyes had a reputation as a man of undoubted fine mentality, with a classical education and refined tastes. McKenzie was also recognized as a "big" man, mentally as well as physically, but domineering, with few scruples, and a grim determination to control mining throughout the Nome area. However, it became more and more clear that a judge could be bought and the law perverted. In a very short time the United States Government was given a black eye by this heinous conspiracy that was defrauding so many honest miners.

Such was the situation in Nome, Alaska, in the summer of 1900. No law and order. No protection for the honest prospector. No decent living quarters. No food at reasonable prices. No conveniences and comforts of any kind. Weather that would wear the patience of a clergyman. And home thousands of miles away.

3.

THAT FIRST summer in Alaska I had frequent twinges of homesickness. I guess Dad did, too, though he was handling so many cases involving title to mining claims that he didn't have much time to think of home. But occasionally of an evening he'd have a breathing spell and we'd sit on the bunks in our tent and reminisce about Mother and the folks back in St. Paul. We wrote them regularly, though not too often, as Dad was doing a land-office business and I was a "green-horn" prospector lured by the yellow gold that usually turned out to be found on the next man's claim.

As a youngster of nineteen I was having the time of my life. I was too green to recognize a prospect if I fell over one, but I considered myself a prospector, nevertheless. Most of the men who came to Nome in 1900 were in the same category. In time we picked up the rudiments of prospecting for gold from the sourdoughs who had trekked down the Yukon River.

Those who went North during this period were, in the main, brave men. Most of them were poor, too, or they would not have struggled against the privation and danger. They worked killingly at a thankless task, never faltering, yet often failing. Some laid down their lives along the bleak shores of Bering Strait, overcome by cold winds and driving snows, scurvy and other diseases of a primitive environment.

United States federal laws stipulated that a sixty-foot strip of land along the Nome beach could not be subject to location. Miners, therefore, were limited to the area covered by a tent or tents, and the space under actual occupancy.

I had my fling at mining on the beach. Teaming up with a fine fellow named Alex Allen, I traveled some thirty miles west of Nome. Alex had been assistant physical director of the YMCA at Rochester, New York, and was no more of a miner than I.

We had a small wooden contraption, called a "rocker," some three and a half feet high, with a hopper on top and two burlap-covered frames leading down from it. On the lower section of the rocker there was a copper plate on which quicksilver was spread to amalgamate any fine gold that might wash down over it. Using a copper plate, we were forced to clean it every day with a solution of cyanide of potassium. A silver plate made daily cleaning unnecessary, but it was unobtainable at Nome. Some beach miners went to the trouble of lining their lower plate with silver dollars.

The square wooden frame of the hopper was open at the top, with a thin sheet of iron on the bottom, perforated like a sieve with holes about a quarter inch in diameter. A gallon tin can affixed to a heavy stick was used as a dipper.

Two men usually worked together, taking turns at the rocker. First you dropped a shovelful of sand or gravel into the hopper, then you dipped water over it until all the fine material was washed down, meanwhile rocking the equipment back and forth by means of a wooden handle fastened to the side. At intervals you removed the hopper to empty the coarser material, and repeated the process endlessly. While one of us operated the rocker, the other brought up the best pay dirt to be found in the vicinity. Any gold collecting on the burlap was washed off into a pan. Then the amalgam on the plate was burned off to evaporate the quicksilver. This was known as "retorted gold."

I think that one of history's strangest sights was that witnessed by the equally startled Eskimo and reindeer of the Bering Strait area as multitudes of white men and a few adventurous women, bitten by the goldbug, ranged up and down many miles of the beaches on both sides of Nome, ripping up the tundra in a frantic search for wealth beyond their dreams.

With the onslaught of the first storm of the season the beach miners had to give up their digging while the seas swept the shores clean. As soon as the storm had passed, the miners rushed back to the beach, but they were seldom able to find the holdings they had been working. Several storms so mixed up the sand that beach mining became profitless; and the prospectors packed their equipment and moved elsewhere. Yet in the summer of 1900 some $2,000,000 in gold was snatched from the beach sands; and a few of the more experienced miners took in upward of $1,000 a day with their rockers.

One stormy night our diggings were washed out by the sea and, after trying several other locations, Alex and I concluded that we were too far west for "pay dirt," and we returned to Nome.

A macabre note was to be found in connection with the graveyard that had been staked out at the western edge of Nome, where the dead were buried in shallow graves dug in the perpetually frozen earth. When it was discovered that Mother Nature had provided golden shrouds for the bodies buried there, the very graves were tunneled out with little respect given to the corpses.

Miners pursued "pay dirt" up and down the streets of Nome, ripping them up as they went along, sometimes even tearing down buildings that were under construction. Here at last in America was found a city whose streets were literally paved with gold!

Now I was a prospector, right enough, though I hadn't found enough gold to rate a notice on the back page of my home-town newspaper. Out into the hills I would go, sometimes alone, with my pack on my back, no tent, but with a primus stove, tarpaulin, and blanket. We miners usually worked all night, but it was no hardship as it was light around the clock. We slept during the warmth of the day. Everything was new and strange to me and, like any nineteen-year-old, I enjoyed it to the fullest.

One day, approaching a small pond, I saw my first swan. This beautiful creature, whiter than milk, paddled busily to outdistance me, breasting the water, carrying its graceful neck nobly. It sped to the opposite bank and, awkwardly flopping ashore, paused there to regard me. As I went on, it proudly took to the water again.

I made the discovery that the back country formed into fantastic shapes, like forts and battlements in a mythical kingdom. Here was a vast and lonesome land, big, barren, and yet majestic. It played tricks with a man's mind, tightening the belly and the heart.

I also found out about sub-Arctic insects, "nosee-ums" or mosquitoes, and black gnats. Insects swarmed out of the tundra moss in streams that ran like wisps of smoke, growing into circles that wheeled around a man's head. It did no good to fight them. Destroy a hundred and a thousand mobilized to take their place. They were not so bad along the ocean beaches; but inland, especially where there was no wind, they were a continual torment.

On these prospecting trips I had my first sample of the Arctic wind. A cold bully of a wind, strangely enough it drove not from the polar regions but from the coast and Siberia. It would let up for a moment, then come on again stronger than before. Lancing through stout clothing as though it were cheesecloth, it raised goose pimples on the skin, even when the sun shone brightly. The north wind blew across Seward

Peninsula incessantly, though during the short summer season it was usually mild.

Shortly after we were established in our two-tent home on Belmont Point, Nome, Dad secured options on two placer mining claims some dozen or so miles away, on tributaries of the Snake River. We arranged for two men, whom we had met on the *Garonne,* to join me on a trip to prospect the claims.

We assembled our equipment: picks, shovels, blankets, gold pans, food, and cooking utensils. When all was ready, we struck out across the tundra, each with a fifty-pound pack strapped to his shoulders. Dad accompanied us for a couple of miles and then turned back to our home and the lawbook he was studying: the new civil and criminal code of Alaska, adopted by Congress the preceding winter. During our first year in Alaska, Dad checked that book from cover to cover.

We established our first camp, without tent or tarpaulins, on Balto Creek, where we spent several days digging shafts and panning the gravel for gold. We found some but not enough to call it "pay." The Balto was a very small creek with all wash gravel. There were some trout in the stream, which we caught and ate. The mosquitoes were so thick that we got very little sleep.

I was careful in my panning and saved the colors found, wrapping each prospect in a piece of paper. One evening we were visited by two miners who had been in the Klondike.

"How you making out, boys?" they asked.

"Oh, so-so," I said, producing our slim prospects.

"Want to see some real gold?" one of them offered.

"We sure do," I declared.

He dug into a hip pocket and took out a heavy poke. Opening it, he poured the contents into one of our pans. We stared at the nuggets ranging in value from a few dollars to around fifty dollars each.

"That's Klondike gold," I guessed.

"Right enough."

"Gosh," I exclaimed. "I hope I make a strike like that someday."

I'm still hoping.

We broke camp and moved across the valley to Boulder Creek. This time we worked at night and slept during the day, as it was a bit warmer and the mosquitoes a little less maddening. After a week's trial, and failing to make a strike, we turned back toward Nome, as our supplies were running short. This was just another of many prospecting trips that resulted in no prospects.

When I got back to our tent home, I found a message from Henry Anderson. It said that a stampede was on, and he had left Dad and a companion about fifteen miles up the Sinook River. Henry had returned to Nome for more supplies and food and wanted me to take my rocker and accompany him to Dad's camp. While I packed, a man stopped by and asked me to tell Dad to come back as soon as possible as he wished to retain him in an important mining case.

We went up the coast in a fifteen-foot Columbia River fishing boat. In our party were my friends Alex Allen and Jim Ford. Jim was an intercollegiate pole-vaulting champion. Arriving at the mouth of the Cripple River the first afternoon, we decided to spend the night there. As we came close to the beach, Jim, with pike pole in hand, jumped ashore, but the boat swung back to the opposite bank of the river. I offered to push the boat across for him but he said that he would vault over, the river being some twenty feet wide at that point. Jim took a run and planted his pole in the water; but it struck a stone and he landed in the middle of the river, getting a thorough ducking.

A couple of days later Jim had a much closer call. Rummaging around in the boat for refreshment, he raised the hopper of my rocker and saw a mineral water bottle. Knowing that Dad and I had a case of mineral water for drinking purposes, he uncorked the bottle and lifted it to his lips. Happening to turn toward him at that moment, I saw what he was doing and struck the bottle from his hand.

"My God!" I cried. "That's cyanide of potassium!"

But Jim didn't hear me, for he had fallen to the ground unconscious. Alex and I worked over him for a half-hour before he regained consciousness. Fortunately, he had not touched the bottle with his lips but had evidently inhaled a good dose of the deadly fumes. He apparently suffered no aftereffects and was lucky to be alive.

The following morning we reached Dad and his companion, and none too soon. For the past three days they had been without food except for unsalted corn meal. Jim and I got a roaring fire going, and Alex, who was an excellent camp cook, prepared a big meal in short order. While it was plain prospectors' fare, it was a pleasure to watch Dad and his friend dig into it as if they were being served at the Waldorf-Astoria. After the inner man was fully satisfied, I told Dad about the mining case that required his immediate attention, and before we bedded down for the night, he and his companion were headed downstream.

Just as I had fallen deep in sleep something landed on me, and I awoke with a start to find that I was wrestling with Henry Anderson. He had come over to our camp and jumped me in the hope that I would think I was being hugged by a bear.

"Hey," I protested, "it's the middle of the night!"

"Scared of bears, aren't you?" He laughed.

"You're worse than a bear," I said. "Anyway, what's up?"

"Bad news, sonny."

I sat up quickly. "Has something happened to Dad"

"Nope."

"What, then?"

"We met some sourdoughs just out of Nome," he explained, "and they say the strike is a fake."

"Shucks," I said in disgust. "My first stampede and it turns out to be another unfounded rumor."

"Never mind, Carl." Henry chuckled. "There'll be more, and the miners, even though they've been fooled a hundred times, will still stampede."

"Hope springs eternal..." I commented drowsily, and went back to sleep.

4.

I AM NO Santa Claus, but reindeer became my business. Fate plays such tricks upon us all that I cannot offer any reasonable explanation for my having spent nearly half a century in this unique, exciting, and often dangerous enterprise. I can only present the facts and let the reader sprinkle them with as much salt as he pleases.

When an American child thinks of reindeer, he thinks of Santa Claus. It is an immediate reference for adults as well. Most people know nothing else about them. It is news to the average person that at the dawn of history there was a "Reindeer Age." In 1900, still in my teens, I hardly knew a reindeer from an elk.

One beautiful day that summer I saw my first herd of reindeer. I was prospecting for gold along the beach some thirty miles west of Nome. I'd just had a sparse lunch and was going up the beach when, to my astonishment, I saw ahead of me a herd of several hundred reindeer. I was scared and stopped dead in my tracks. I was alone and unarmed in a treeless country, with the Bering Sea on one side, open tundra on the other. I had no knowledge of reindeer habits and wondered if these strange animals would suddenly attack me. Then I spotted an Eskimo herder on the far side of the animals and felt somewhat safer. The reindeer didn't seem to be paying any particular attention to me, so I edged my way cautiously past them and went on about my business. But my curiosity had been permanently aroused.

The reindeer, an antlered "herbivorous, graminiverous, gregarious, semimigratory, ruminant and ungulate mammal" is among the earliest and best friends man has ever had. Its coexistence with man dates back some twenty thousand years. I made a rather thorough study of the reindeer, and the thought came to me that surely these two mammals should become better acquainted.

Reindeer are members of the deer family (Cervidae), of the species *Rangifer tarandus*. The caribou of North America are actually reindeer.

The reindeer is the most widely distributed mammal in the world and, within its own realm, the most useful. Wild reindeer have furnished the hunter with a fascinating sport and often with a livelihood. Domestic reindeer provide their owners with food, clothing, fuel, and bone and horn implements. As a beast of burden they have been as useful to the nomads of the North as the "ship of the desert," the camel, to the wandering Bedouins of the Sahara and the Gobi.

When, in the early nineteenth century, the white man began to hunt the whale, walrus, and seal in the Bering Sea and Arctic Ocean, he became a competitor of the Eskimo. With superior equipment he soon put the Eskimo at a helpless disadvantage. Fortunately, the United States Government awakened to the necessity of providing these wards with a means of livelihood in lieu of what they had lost.

Recommendations that reindeer be introduced into Alaska for the benefit of its native population had been made first back in 1872, by Henry W. Elliott, and in 1885 by Dr. Charles Townsend (later director of the New York Aquarium). But the real pioneer, who grasped the full possibilities of what the reindeer could do to better the conditions of the Alaskan Eskimo, was Dr. Sheldon Jackson, a Presbyterian missionary.

Dr. Jackson was also the educational agent in Alaska for the Department of the Interior.

Since the purchase of Alaska from Russia in 1867, the United States Government had been very lax in assuming any responsibility toward its new wards, the Indian, Eskimo, and Aleut, though it did make a slight gesture of good will by providing a rather primitive school system for them, developing it through co-operation with the several church boards already established in the North.

In one of his early reports Dr. Jackson wrote:

To establish schools among starving people would be of little service. The proper method of relief is suggested by the wild nomad tribes on the Siberian side of Bering Sea. They have had an unfailing food supply in their large herds of domestic reindeer. Why not introduce this domestic reindeer on the American side, and thus provide a new and adequate food supply? It will do more than preserve life. It will preserve the self-respect of these people and advance them in the scale of civilization. It will change them from hunters to herders. It will also utilize the hundreds of thousands of square miles of moss-covered tundra of arctic and sub-arctic Alaska and make these now useless and barren wastes conducive to the wealth and prosperity of the United States.

The one asset in northern and western Alaska recognized by the Federal Government during the twenty-five years following its purchase was the fur seal of the Pribilof Islands in the Bering Sea. Watching over and guarding that asset was the United States Coast Guard, then known as the Revenue Marine Service. This always-efficient service became the great friend of the natives on both sides of the Bering Sea and of the few whites who had the hardihood to attempt to live in Alaska at that time. The ships of the service, making annual cruises into the Bering Sea and Arctic Ocean, made it possible for Dr. Jackson to visit the missions and schools. Stops were made at Siberian as well as Alaskan villages, bringing relief to anyone who required it.

It was obvious that the Siberian native had one great advantage over his Alaskan cousins—ownership of domesticated reindeer. Dr. Jackson foresaw the benefits that would accrue if this animal could be purchased in Siberia and transported to Alaska, and he applied to Congress for the necessary funds.

This effort, made through the Act of August 30, 1890, failed to pass Congress. Unwilling to drop the matter, Dr. Jackson appealed for aid from the general public, through the press of the eastern states. The proposal to introduce domesticated reindeer into Alaska excited widespread interest, and contributions totaling $2,146 were received. But the work entailed was new and untried, and many things could be learned only by actual experience.

The wild-deer-men of Siberia were very superstitious. Would they sell their live reindeer? Would the animals stand up under ship transportation? If safely transported, would the Eskimo on the Alaskan side, or their vicious sled dogs, destroy them?

The cutter *Bear* and its officers were well and favorably known to the Siberian deer owners because of their many kindnesses. Captain M. A. Healey, skipper of the *Bear,* enjoyed the confidence of the Siberians. In the summer of 1891 he was able to make arrangements for the purchase of animals the following season. To solve the question—whether reindeer could be transported alive—sixteen head were taken to Amaknek Island in the harbor of Unalaska, a sea voyage of more than 1,000 miles.

A reindeer experimental station was established on the north shore of Port Clarence Bay, and during the summer of 1892 the *Bear* transported 171 reindeer from Siberia to the new station, where they were successfully landed on July 4.

Dr. Jackson was active, sincere, and enthusiastic. Congress made small appropriations and each year, up to and including

1902, additional deer were purchased in Siberia and transported across Bering Sea to Port Clarence Bay.

To protect the Eskimo, Government regulations prohibited white men from owning female reindeer, a wise precaution during the early days of the industry. The Eskimo gained his livelihood by hunting and fishing. He had had no experience with domestic livestock, therefore, a few Siberian deer men were brought over to instruct the Alaska Eskimo in the care of the animals; but somehow they failed in their mission and were returned to their homes. From northern Norway, during 1894, a few Lapp reindeer men were brought over, and they proved a success.

Dr. Jackson's real opportunity came during the fall of 1897 when it was reported that the miners at Circle City on the upper Yukon River had insufficient food, and there would be starvation in that camp prior to the opening of navigation in the spring of 1898 unless food could be brought in. He now decided to kill two birds with one well-aimed stone. He would provide the miners with food and throw the spotlight of national public opinion upon the reindeer question by securing sled deer and Lapp drivers in Norway, transporting them to and across the United States to Seattle, thence by steamer to some point in southeastern Alaska. The animals could then be driven across country to Circle City and butchered, thus furnishing a food supply for the miners. At the same time this plan would bring to Alaska additional and much-needed expert Lapp reindeer men, to assist in the development of the Alaskan herds.

Congress approved Dr. Jackson's plan, appropriated the funds, and instructed him, under an arrangement between the Secretary of War and the Department of the Interior, to proceed to Norway to purchase reindeer and supplies. As disbursing agent for the expedition, Lieutenant D. B. Devore, United States Army, accompanied him.

By great good luck Mr. William Kjellman, assistant superintendent of the Port Clarence Reindeer Station, was in Norway, having just returned to their homes four Lapp families whose contracts with the government had expired. Dr. Jackson cabled Kjellman to engage all the help he could use to expedite the purchase of reindeer and the securing of Lapp colonists.

On January 12, 1898, Dr. Jackson and Lieutenant Devore reached Hammerfest, Norway, the northernmost city in the world. They proceeded to Bosekop, where they met Mr. Kjellman, who reported he had secured the reindeer drivers, reindeer equipment, and the deer, and it was arranged that they should assemble at Bosekop. At this juncture a severe blizzard swept the country for many days, reaching its peak on January 28.

In the United States Government publication, *Introduction of Domesticated Reindeer into Alaska,* dated 1898, Dr. Jackson says:

The hotel at Bosekop, a strong log building with a substantial stone foundation, in a sheltered spot, trembled under the furious blasts of wind and snow. At midday, houses a block away could not be seen through the driving snow. All traffic was suspended in the street and yet on the mountains, where the cold was much greater and the wind swept with the force of a hurricane, were four herds of reindeer and between one and two hundred men, women, and children in open sleds, facing the blizzard, as on different roads and widely separated sections they converged on Bosekop. I asked the mayor of the village what the prospects were of the Lapps getting through. He shook his head and said, "Nothing can face a storm like this for any length of time and live."

I doubt whether men of any race except the Lapps, cradled in the snow and inured from childhood to such hardships, could have done so, or that any animal other than the reindeer could have brought them safely over the storm-swept and treeless mountains.

About noon, going to the window, I scraped off the frost with a knife. I saw faintly, through the whirling snow, a solitary reindeer coming up the street, and soon after could make out a man with a sled. It was Mr. Kjellman, in great fur coat, covered with snow, his face and whiskers encased in a coating of ice. He had left Bosekop a few days before to meet the herders.

Toward evening a Lapp arrived and announced that Mr. Mathis Risa, with a band of ninety deer, had arrived from Maci and gone into camp in the mountains back of the village.

Two days later Mr. Carl Suhr and Mr. Samuel Kemi, with four men and 114 deer, arrived from Bautojok, 165 miles distant; and Mr. M. Kjelsberg and Mr. Per Rist from Kautokeino arrived with 44 Lapps and 252 reindeer. A messenger also announced that Mr. O. Paulsen, with 25 Lapps and 90 reindeer, had arrived from Karasjok. The three parties, with their herds, starting from places a hundred miles apart and journeying by different routes, had reached the rendezvous within a few hours of each other.

On February 1st, the little village of Bosekop awoke from its Arctic night to unusual stir and activity as the Lapps and deer came pouring in long lines over the hill into the village, filling the market square. The hundreds of Lapps in their bright-colored, picturesque national dress, those that were going away and those that had come to see them off, greeting old friends and meeting new ones, the unpacking of sleds and preparations for embarkation, made a picture never to be forgotten. By night everything was ready for the arrival of the steamship.

All this was accomplished within one month from the time the appropriation had been made by Congress.

The expedition landed in New York on the steamer *Manitoban*, February 27, 1898, with 113 Lapps, men, women, and children, 538 head of reindeer, 418 sleds, 411 sets of harness, and a large quantity of reindeer moss as forage for the deer.

In their square "pillow" hats and quaint costumes trimmed in yellow, green, and red, the Lapps made a very colorful scene, and their trip across the United States attracted a great deal of attention. After a short stay at Port Townsend in the state of Washington, to rest both animals and people, the expedition proceeded to Haines, in southeastern Alaska.

However, by this time word had reached the States that Circle City had sufficient food and there was no longer any danger of starvation. Therefore, the expedition was divided: some men and deer went off across country, toward the Yukon; the remainder went westward, through Unimak Pass, thence northward to Unalakleet, a small village on Norton Sound. Thus were reindeer and their herders transported from the old to the new world.

5.

FOLLOWING my summer of prospecting, on the beach and up several of the Snake River tributaries, I returned to Nome. We had planned—and faithfully promised Mother—only to vacation in Alaska. Now October was approaching and the last of the sailings out of Nome until spring. Dad, however, had been retained in some important mining litigation—only one case of which I have mentioned—and if there is anything slower than molasses, it's the law.

What to do? If we left on the last steamer, it would cost Dad a pretty penny. He was working harder but he was making more money than he had made in St. Paul. He saw to it that his family was well provided for. Mother was undoubtedly unhappiest of all. They were both entering middle age, and she wanted her husband by her side. But the last boat left and we were isolated in Alaska. Mother, as always, took it philosophically.

Dad had rented two rooms in the Discovery Building for combined office space and living quarters. The first floor was occupied by a saloon—some people preferred to call them "gentlemen's clubs"—and the upper floor by law offices. The building was of the flimsiest construction, being just a single thickness of boards without benefit of construction paper either inside or out. As winter set in it got so cold that the saloon closed its doors. One by one the law offices were frozen out. Finally Dad and I were the only occupants left. In order to survive in the freezing weather, we began dressing in furs and Eskimo footwear.

Our living quarters lacked all the comforts of home. The "apartment" fronted on D Street and comprised two rooms. The front one had a skimpy rug on the floor. Here there were a bookcase, a rack to hold legal blanks, and a small potbellied stove that strove valiantly but unsuccessfully to fight off the bitter cold. There was also a table on which dishes, when not in use, were piled and covered with a cloth. In various corners stood an iron safe, a trunk—used as a settee by visitors—a catch-all table, a coal sack, a five-gallon kerosene or coal-oil can, a steamer chair, and four kitchen chairs.

The door to the bedroom was only three and a half feet high and to enter it we had to bend over double and crawl under Dad's stationary bunk. My bunk was at right angles to Dad's. There was only one chair in the room. The other two walls were lined with boxes—mostly of food—piled three feet high. To add to the confusion there were our folded summer tents, kindling, a woodpile, a trunk, and other odds and ends.

To say that our rooms were cold is putting it very mildly indeed. A bucket of water, only a foot from the red-hot stove, would be covered with a skim of ice. On the morning of December 8, 1900, my diary tells me, the temperature in our bedroom was just twelve degrees above zero. We did not consider the extreme cold a hardship, however, as we were on our way to becoming "sourdoughs," an honored title earned by those who witnessed the ice come in the fall and go out in the spring.

All things considered, the winter passed pleasantly enough. We had weekly mail service by steamer from Seattle to southern Alaska, thence to Nome by dog team, a distance of about 1,200 miles. The first mail of the winter reached Nome on February 5, 1901. I can still recall my deep disappointment when I reached the post office and found a notice on the bulletin board reading: "Half of mail frozen; office open tomorrow." The mail sled, we found out later, had broken through the ice on a river en route, and the mail had to be thawed out before it could be sorted and distributed. It always warmed the heart to hear from home.

People entered with lively enthusiasm into the social life of the camp. Public dances were held nightly. There were amateur theatricals and a minstrel show. Gambling was wide open. But though there were several hundred gamblers, dance-hall girls, and saloon hangers-on, Nome was about as orderly as one could expect in a boom town above the 64th latitude.

The first boat of the new year arrived May 24. It was the *Jeanie,* a whaler. She brought a few passengers and newspapers from Seattle, San Francisco, and New York, a welcome addition to the limited reading matter available in Nome. The *Jeanie* anchored at the edge of the shore ice, two miles from the beach, giving the passengers the unusual experience of debarking on an ice field. The first piece of news I picked up was that General Fred Funston had captured Aguinaldo in the Philippines.

Six days later the *Nome City* arrived. But the big day was June 16, when five ships hove into view. I went out to them in a dory with a friend, and we picked up five stowaways at a dollar a head. The steamers brought some 2,000 passengers, in addition to the mail, fresh foods, fruits, and vegetables. Dad and I greeted many friends we had made the previous year who had returned for another try at striking pay dirt.

Meanwhile, in Washington, D.C., the lawmakers in their idealistic dream state did not realize that a concentrated effort was under way to legalize the actions of arbitrary men who had jumped the claims of hard-working miners in the Nome area. The Norwegian Lapps did not as yet know the extent of their rights as prospective citizens of the United States. Consequently, they were being bulldozed unmercifully by the political gang of pirates formed for the specific purpose of looting the gold fields.

There was one thing the looters did not bargain for. This was the willingness of the original discoverers to spend their hard-earned money to fight for their rights. But since Judge Noyes himself was actually one of the "gang," it was an uphill struggle.

A great gold strike was made on Daniels Creek, sixty miles east of Nome. In places the gold lay barely six inches under the surface of the tundra. An Eskimo village was located there, and the miners ruthlessly tunneled from the beach right up under their rude huts, toppling them over. This unceremonious treatment naturally brought yells of protest from the bewildered natives. Poverty-stricken, these Eskimos had unwittingly dragged their skin boats for centuries over a golden horde. As usual, the ambitious McKenzie and his henchmen jumped these claims and systematically milked them after they were thrown into receivership.

The first claim to become involved with the new Judge Noyes court was Discovery, on Anvil Creek. According to plan, McKenzie was appointed receiver. Injunctions were granted and he was placed in possession of many valuable properties. By order of the court the receiver was also granted possession of all personal property found on the claims. McKenzie impounded the gold dust, sluice boxes, mining implements, tents, provisions, even the cooking utensils, before proceeding with the operation of the claims.

The defendants in these cases were represented by able counsel. Dad was not one of them, as he was engaged in other legal matters. First an effort was made to have the injunctions dissolved, but this move was quickly overruled. Application was then made to the Circuit Court of Appeals, four thousand miles away in San Franciso. There being no telegraph or wireless, the fastest means of communication— as well as transportation—was a ten- to twelve-knot ship.

A writ of supersedeas was issued by the Circuit Court and returned to Nome. When it became evident that neither Judge Noyes nor Alexander McKenzie intended to obey the order of the Appellate Court, another long and costly sea voyage became necessary. This time defense counsel was rowed out to the waiting ship secretly in the dead of night, whereupon the vessel heaved anchor, sailing for San Francisco under full speed. Time was short, as the open season for navigation would end in late October. Fortunately, the steamer made a speedy voyage.

The court acted with celerity, and this time two deputies of the Circuit Court boarded the ship with the defense attorney, armed with a warrant for McKenzie's arrest on a charge of contempt. He was taken into custody at Nome and removed to San Francisco, where he was found guilty and sentenced to one year's imprisonment in the Alameda County jail.

Bond offers totaling $1,000,000 were made for McKenzie. It became clear that he had powerful friends at Washington. Even President McKinley was besieged with pleas to turn him loose. So great was McKenzie's influence in high places that he was granted a presidential pardon after serving only a few weeks of his sentence.

There still remained Judge Noyes in jurisdiction over the court at Nome. Though the miners had been patient and long-suffering, now they'd had enough. Vigilantes were assembled and plans laid to hang the judge or anyone else "who needed it." The vigilantes were business and professional men, law-abiding citizens all. But in the face of many abuses they had decided it was high time that justice be served.

The Bar Association met on August 15, 1901, and petitioned the President of the United States, requesting that he remove Judge Noyes and immediately appoint his successor.

The charges in the petition left no doubt of the state of affairs, setting forth:

> ... that the Honorable Arthur H. Noyes, the present judge of the district court for the Second Division of the District of Alaska, is vacillating and dilatory, weak and partial, negligent, carelessly and absolutely incompetent; that he has lost the confidence and respect of the attorneys of the bar of his court and of the residents of his judicial district; that his orders and decrees are violated and treated with open contempt; that the interposition of a fearless, competent and honest judge is urgently required at Nome to prevent further riot and bloodshed, to relieve the congested calendar, to preserve law and order and to protect life, liberty and property.

Throughout the division conditions were in such a state that miners were afraid to work their property, knowing it would be taken from them by legal action. Judge Noyes even went so far as to solicit lawsuits for his secretary—certainly a cynical concept of justice inasmuch as such suits would be tried in his own court.

The one man of the official retinue who eluded control by the "ring" was George V. Borchsenius, clerk of the District Court. Mr. Borchsenius had with him his wife and son. Dad and I were frequent dinner guests in their home and soon came to realize the increasing gravity of conditions at Nome.

Mr. Borchsenius was well aware that the "gang" was most anxious to get rid of him and that in all probability active steps would be taken as soon as the last boat sailed south. Then he would be left high and dry without other means of communication except for the mail which, as I have said, had to travel 1,200 miles via dog team.

One day, while there was still a steamer in the roadstead, Mr. Borchsenius strode into Judge Noyes's chambers and laid his cards on the table.

"Judge Noyes," he emphatically declared, "if you permit the last steamer to sail from Nome this fall and then discharge me as court clerk, I will kill you just as surely as you are now sitting in that chair!"

Mr. Borchsenius obviously meant just exactly what he said and he was not discharged from office—not, that is, until the arrival of the first steamers seven months later, in the spring of 1901. He proceeded to Washington at once and in the fall of that year he returned to Nome, having been reappointed to his original post by President McKinley.

Over the years it was to be our good fortune to have many pleasant relationships with the native people. As I remember it, our first service for the Eskimo was on Daniel's Creek. A "squaw man" came to see Dad regarding the encroachments being made on the villagers by the miners. Father advised that the natives had certain possessory or "domicile" rights. The squaw man carried this information back to his wife's people and, when the miners heard of it, they lost no time in approaching the villagers and purchasing such rights. That was one of the first effective moves touching on the "Aboriginal Rights" of the natives of Alaska.

One summer's day in 1901 I was mining a few miles out of Nome, on No. 2 Specimen Gulch, when I saw an army lieutenant and twenty or so men headed in my direction. The officer came up to me and asked how to get to Glacier Creek. I explained that it was over the next divide, and then down Snow Gulch for about a mile.

A few days later I learned of a riot on Glacier Creek. A group of irate citizens had commandeered the locomotive and flat cars of the local railroad and proceeded to Glacier Creek, where they threw off the jumpers who had taken possession of a valuable claim. The word got around that justice was on the march.

Shortly after that incident Judge Noyes left for San Francisco to answer contempt charges in the Circuit Court. He was tried and fined $1,000. Judges Ross and Morrow both remarked on the seriousness of the crimes committed and the inadequacy of the punishment.

In an editorial the *Nome Gold Digger* commented in part:

Judge Noyes will long be remembered in Nome as an anomaly. Too honorable to be a scoundrel, too much of a scoundrel to be an honorable man; too strong to be a pliant tool; too weak to protect his own honor; brilliant and brainy, with many of the mental graces of a Chesterfield, but a fool.

It was later learned that the total value of the gold dust extracted by McKenzie during his regime as receiver amounted to nearly $600,000. This money was eventually returned to its rightful owners. And so ended an infamous era in the turbulent history of Alaska.

6.

AS THE winter of 1901 approached, again the family problem arose. Mother wanted Dad and me to come back home, while my brothers were champing at the bit to make the exciting trip to Alaska. It was truly a house divided. And, as before, Dad's law practice settled the matter—by no means satisfactorily to all but irrevocably nevertheless. As it happened, Dad was handling an important lawsuit that was set for trial the day following the scheduled departure of the last steamer of the year from Nome. Dad threw up his hands helplessly. I was secretly pleased, as Alaska was now in my blood; and dear Mother was much too far away to grab us by the nape of the neck and shake some sense into her errant spouse and adventurous offspring. Now we were really sourdoughs and mighty proud of it.

The mining season was over, winter set in, and I spent much of my time—when you're young you have an eternity— getting acquainted with the Lapps who had come over with the expedition from Norway in 1898. They impressed me with their intelligence and friendliness. I met the Nilimas, Baltos, Hattas, Nillukas, Vests, Kjelsbergs, Boynos, Klemetsens, Bahrs, Bals, and Bangos, to name a few. Every time I visited with these expert deer men my interest in reindeer grew stronger.

Under Dr. Jackson the Reindeer Service developed an apprenticeship system whereby young, progressive Eskimo were engaged to tend the reindeer under Lapp instruction. In

43

addition to his maintenance, each young man was given a few animals every year. At the end of the five-year apprenticeship period he was graduated to ownership, with some forty head of reindeer; and as an owner he could, if necessary, employ an apprentice himself.

The Lapps, under their contracts with the Government, had the right to request a loan of 100 head of reindeer, usually 75 females and 25 bulls. They would hold them for a period of three to five years, and then return a like number and kind to the Government, retaining the increase. Similar arrangements were made between the various missions and the Government.

The contract entered into with the Lapps prior to their departure from Norway was an interesting document that began:

All the undersigned admit and make known by these presents they have hired themselves as reindeer herders, drivers, tamers, and to teach the Eskimo in Alaska in reindeer raising in all its details, and furthermore, to carry out such work as our superiors put over us by the United States Government may require, also to look out for the reindeer during transport to Alaska. Furthermore, we bind ourselves to behave ourselves orderly and decently and to show discipline, and also to depart from our houses the 28th of January next, from which date this contract goes into effect.

The following portion of the contract was a great inducement for the Lapps to leave their native land herds for a new country:

Should any of the undersigned, after two years' service, desire his salary to be paid in reindeer instead of money, such payment shall take place. The price for reindeer shall then be counted according to the price at that time prevailing, or what is paid in the common market. Even so shall every one of the hired men, if he is deemed qualified by appointed government officials, have the right to a loan of 100 reindeer for three or five years, as will later be determined, without lease or rent, in such a way that only the original number shall be returned to the government, and all offspring or surplus belongs to the leaser, all other things as with reference to residence, etc., in accordance with and under such conditions as may be stipulated in the contract of lease. Such loan of reindeer can, however, not take place until after a two years' period.

Dr. Jackson had expended a great deal of thought on the reindeer projects. It was also quite obvious that he intended the Lapps to be prime factors as private owners in the expanding reindeer industry.

From 1892 to 1902, the period during which mother stock—1,280 head—was bought from Siberian deer men, Port Clarence Bay on Seward Peninsula, the nearest harbor to northeast Siberia, was selected as the receiving center for the reindeer. As the work expanded, Teller Reindeer Station on Port Clarence Bay became the base of supply from which, winter after winter, herds were sent out over northern Alaska to establish new centers of the reindeer industry.

In these formative years Dr. Jackson was fortunate in having some able and courageous assistants. During 1890 the American Missionary Association (Presbyterian) established a station at Cape Prince of Wales, Alaska, westernmost village on the North American continent; assigned to it were H. R. Thornton and William T. Lopp as teachers.

This was a very difficult project for two young men, as the Eskimo of Wales were a wild people who had never known any discipline. The natives could not comprehend the purpose or language of the teachers, and the teachers could not understand the people. For the first several months the missionary teachers ate, worked, and slept with loaded guns always at hand.

To make matters more difficult and dangerous for them, an epidemic of grippe broke out in the village, resulting in twenty-six deaths. The Eskimo attributed this to the presence of white men. During the epidemic a number of slates, which the village children had been allowed to take home at night to write on, were returned by order of the *shaman* (medicine man), who stated that much of the sickness in the village was due to the slates and the "bad medicine" pictures that the children drew on them. Through tact and good management hostilities were prevented, and gradually confidence was established between the natives and their teachers.

Early in January 1903 Mr. Lopp and his wife made the long trip to Point Hope by dog team to visit the several Eskimo settlements that dotted the coast. In each village he told the natives of the work of Dr. Jackson and Captain Healey, skipper of the United States Marine Service cutter *Bear*, in bringing reindeer from Siberia to Alaska. Later some of these northern Eskimo traveled to Port Clarence Bay to see the work undertaken for their benefit. All of them were enthusiastic and requested that deer be sent to them as soon as possible.

Mr. Lopp was appointed superintendent of the reindeer station at Port Clarence Bay during 1893 and with Mrs. Lopp moved to that place, leaving the Thorntons in charge of the mission at Cape Prince of Wales.

Soon after a tragedy occurred at the Cape. Mr. Thornton expelled two young Eskimo men from the school for disorderly conduct. They lost face in the village and brooded over it. And one night they returned to the schoolhouse and murdered Mr. Thornton.

The older Eskimo men hunted down the two young murderers, shooting one on the beach as he attempted to run away. They captured the other, who admitted the crime. Knowing that he, too, would be shot, he requested the privilege of choosing the plot in the cemetery where he was to rest for eternity. The group marched up the hill to the cemetery where the boy selected his burial place. He stretched himself on his back to locate the most comfortable spot. He would sit up and remove a stone or smooth out a place, then try it again. Finally, the exertion made him thirsty. He asked for a drink, so the party went down to a small creek where the youthful murderer slaked his thirst. Back up the hill, and again the boy stretched out, found the most comfortable position, and said, "All right." Then the guns spoke and justice was done.

The Reindeer Service under Dr. Jackson performed well and its accomplishments grew. The reindeer from northeastern Siberia were the "mother stock" of the Alaskan herds. The Lapps brought over from Norway were sufficient in number and competent. The missionary stationed at the headquarters of the new enterprise was Rev. T. L. Brevig of the Lutheran Church, an able and efficient leader who contributed much to the success of the work.

During 1900 a plan was made to attempt to secure a shipment of the superior "Tunguse" reindeer from the neighborhood of the Okhotsk Sea, to improve the present Alaskan stock, which were a smaller type of animal. Lieutenant E. P. Bertholf of the United States Marine Service was detailed by the Secretary of the Treasury to proceed to St. Petersburg, Russia, to clear with the Imperial Government the purchase of reindeer and then proceed on the long trip across Siberia to the Okhotsk. After weary weeks of strenuous travel Lieutenant Bertholf had lengthy negotiations with the Tunguse deer men. Finally, he loaded several hundred reindeer on board a steamer at Ola and transported them to Port Clarence Bay, where, in the spring of 1901, 254 were landed.

At this time Alfred Nilima, one of the Lapps who accompanied the expedition from Norway, exercised his rights under the contract he held with our Government and requested a loan of 100 deer. The selection had to be made from the animals at Port Clarence Station, and the only available deer there were the newcomers from the Okhotsk, a thin, long-legged group of deer in poor physical condition because of the rough trip from Ola.

Nilima was dubious. Would these sorry animals prove difficult to herd? Would they be good meat animals? There was no choice, so Nilima's hundred head, together with another hundred loaned to the Friends' Mission, were driven to Kotzebue, 200 miles to the north and east, and arrived at their new home in December 1901. During succeeding years these Tunguse reindeer developed into the finest stock in all Alaska, and it became a Lapp's or Eskimo's proud boast to claim Tunguse blood in his driving deer.

In 1902 the last importation of reindeer from Siberia took place, when Dr. William Hamilton, Assistant Agent of Education in Alaska and later Assistant Commissioner of the Federal Bureau of Education, assisted by Captain Francis Tuttle of the *Bear,* secured thirty head of reindeer from the vicinity of Cape Ilpinski at the entrance to Baron Korf Bay. The Russians thereupon withdrew all permits for the exportation of reindeer from their domain.

The withdrawal of the permits would have been tragic had it occurred a few years earlier. Fortunately the original 1,280 imported, together with an increase of 1,654 fawns in 1902, and 2,214 born in previous years—making a total of 5,148 reindeer in the herds—were sufficient to form a sizable nucleus for the new industry.

The venturesome, versatile, and friendly Lapps proved a valuable addition to the population of Alaska. They were facile linguists and had a good working knowledge of four languages: their own Lappish, Finnish, Norwegian, and Swedish. It did not take them long to add both English and Eskimo to their vocabulary.

The Lapps say that a house smothers a man once he has the smell, look, and feel of the tundra country in his blood. To them a house is close and shut in and full of little smells that are alien to their sensitive nostrils. They say a man with

48

a roof over his head and four walls shutting him in cannot see the sky or feel the wind or even know the time of night by looking overhead. Herders of reindeer for countless generations, cradled in the snow and suckled on reindeer milk, they love the out-of-doors. Nomadic by instinct, they are the perfect people for the work they love, far surpassing the Eskimo in the affection they have for the reindeer.

Here is an example of the understanding of reindeer possessed by the Lapps. During one of his first years in Alaska, Andrew Bahr, to become famous as the leader of the great reindeer trek from Alaska to Canada, which I will tell about later, had been commissioned by the Government to care for a small herd of reindeer, alone and far from any neighbor. Instructions of the officials miscarried and six months passed before it was realized that no relief had been provided for. Many things could happen to a solitary man in an isolated section of Arctic Alaska and the officials were much concerned. Relief was sent in, and it was found that Andrew had remained at his post and had kept the animals in good condition. To have left for help might well have caused the loss of the herd. But Bahr stuck it out under the most adverse conditions, realizing that his highest duty was to protect the reindeer.

Andrew had been born among the reindeer in Norway. He had no peer among the deer men of Alaska in so far as an understanding of the animal was concerned. He felt that he understood the "language" of the reindeer, and that the animals understood him. Sometimes I was almost forced to believe that he did "savvy" their talk, since he could accomplish more with the animals than anyone else I ever knew.

The reindeer do indeed seem to talk to each other, their call being a peculiar grunt or bark, sounding something like "uhrr." This call is continually audible in a large herd as the fawns call their mothers and vice versa. It is also heard when the buck is calling or "belling" the does. The male reindeer is polygamous and during the rutting season he gathers his harem. This is the time of love and hate. The bucks fight many duels over the does, sometimes to the death. At that season the clatter of horns is continually heard. The antlers of the battling deer occasionally become interlocked in such a fashion that the animals cannot separate themselves. If human help does not arrive, they both starve.

Andrew Bahr always seemed to be able to pacify his reindeer herd, even in the rutting season, far better than the other herders.

"Sometimes when I am driving a deer," he said to me one day, "it becomes frightened. I walk up to it, place my arm about its neck and, pointing to the willows, say, 'There is no bear over there.'

" 'Yes,' answers the reindeer, 'there is a bear over there.'

" 'No,' I repeat, 'there is no bear over there, and when I am with you, you don't have to be afraid, for I will take care of you.' "

I recall his telling me once, some years later, that he was "just as big a man as President Coolidge." I asked him how he figured that out, and he said, "Mr. Coolidge has a job and does it well; I have a job and I do it well; both the same."

Another Lapp for whom I had great admiration was Johan Petter Johansen Stalogargo, a mouthful of a name, to be sure. Before coming to Alaska from Norway he had the distinction of being the most northerly mail carrier in the world, having for eight years carried the mail from Bosekop to North Cape, Norway, a distance of more than 100 miles. He covered most of this distance on foot. When he left for Alaska the Norwegian Government discontinued the route, as no one else could be found to carry the mail over such difficult terrain.

During 1900 a number of mail contracts were let by the United States Government for western Alaska, and mails were carried by reindeer. One of the routes—St. Michael—Eaton—

Golovin–Kotzebue—required three round trips a year. Stalogargo was employed as carrier and successfully negotiated these trips, 1,240 miles each, with reindeer and through a wilderness without roads or trails of any kind. On another route, Eaton to Nome, round trip 480 miles, Nils Klementsen, also a Lapp, negotiated the four trips in from eleven and a half to fourteen days each. The efficiency of the reindeer for transportation and the expertness of the Lapp drivers are graphically shown by these examples of reliability and endurance.

Visiting with Stalogargo one afternoon in our office, I suggested he should not travel alone on such hazardous trips during the winter season. I pointed out that an accident that would be of no particular consequence if he had a companion along might prove fatal if he were alone. Stalogargo threw back his head and roared with laughter at my cautious attitude. I realized that, to him, my advice was most amusing. Nevertheless, a short time later, on a mail run from Nome to Candle, by way of Teller, Cape Prince of Wales, Shishmaref, and Deering, the fearless mailman lost his life.

The tracks in the snow told the story. He had picketed his reindeer, pitched his shelter tent, and started a fire to warm up a mess of beans. Then he had evidently gone out to look for his fur mittens—later found near the reindeer— and lost his bearings in the blinding storm. His body was found more than twenty-five miles from his camp, face down, his hands tucked up under his armpits as he stoically awaited inevitable death.

Within their own habitat the reindeer undoubtedly were domesticated centuries before any records were made. The Lapp language is generally limited in the number of its words yet those pertaining to both wild and domestic reindeer are numerous and rich. To the Lapp the reindeer herd itself is known as *alo* or *aello,* meaning subsistence, sustenance. The words reindeer in English, *renadyr* in Norwegian, and *renn-*

tier in German, all are derived from the Lappish word *reino* (pasture), and deer, *dyr, tier* (animal, hence meaning *an animal that pastures*).

Perhaps the earliest reference made to reindeer is the Cervus, mentioned by Julius Caesar, in which "males and females have antlers." Tacitus (A.D. 55–120), and Procopius (fifth-century Byzantine historian) refer to the Finns (Lapps) of Thule (Norway) as "hunters, who dress themselves in skins, fastened together with the sinews of beasts, that cover their whole bodies." Paulus Warnefridi, a Langobard author of the eighth century, writing of the Finns (our modern Lapps), says: "Among them is an animal which is not much unlike a stag. I have seen a dress made of the hide of this animal bristling with hairs. It was made like a tunic and reached to the knees."

The aborigines of the North do not seem greatly to have changed the style of their dress since the foregoing was written a thousand and more years ago. The description of the tunic might well apply to the modern Eskimo parka. However, obvious references to reindeer do not indicate their domestication. The first historical record of the domestication of reindeer among any people is, according to Berthald Laufer, to be found in the Chinese annals of the Liang dynasty. Laufer tells us, in a monograph published in the Memoirs of the American Anthropological Association:

In A.D. 449, the Buddhist monk Huei Shen returned to King-Chow, the capital of the Liang, and gave a fabulous account of the mythical country of Fu-Sang, far off in the Northeastern ocean. As to means of conveyance, he reported, "the people there have vehicles drawn by horses, oxen and stags." They raise deer in the manner that oxen are raised in China, and make cream from their milk.

The allusion to domesticated reindeer is unmistakable. Laufer concludes that Huei Shen's account of the reindeer in connection with horses and cattle has doubtless hailed from the Baikal region, where, alone, the breeding of all these animals, in combination, occurs, particularly among the present Soyot.

Laufer also calls attention to the annals of the T'ang dynasty (618–906) containing mention of a reindeer-breeding tribe, the Wu-huan, then settled in a region east or southeast of Lake Baikal: "In their country there are trees, but grass is lacking, while there is plenty of moss. The inhabitants have neither sheep nor horses, but keep reindeer in the manner of horses or cattle. They are trained to draw sledges. Reindeer skins, moreover, are utilized as material for clothing."

The earliest reference to tame or domestic reindeer from Western sources is contained in the famous narrative of the Norseman, Othere (Ottar), of whom we know comparatively little except that he served at the Court of King Alfred; that he came from the farthest North; was born in Halogaland, Norway; in 890 made a voyage rounding the North Cape, entered the White Sea, and touched the shore of the Kola Peninsula. An account of his expedition is noted by Alfred the Great in his translation of the *Hormista* of Paulus Orosius, as follows:

He [Othere] was a very rich man in those possessions in which their wealth consists, that is in wild animals. He still had when he came to the King six hundred tame deer unsold. These deer they call reindeer: six of them were decoy deer, these are much prized among the Finns, because they capture the wild deer with them.

The reindeer has often been compared with the camel. Not because these animals have much in common; rather, perhaps, because they are so different. Each of these animals, however commonplace in their respective realms, becomes the object of romantic interest when transported to other climes where they are seen only as an object of curiosity.

To define the boundaries of where reindeer are found is not easily done. Their extent differs in various countries and has changed from age to age. While the wild reindeer of Asia, in their winter migrations, touch upon the realms of the lion and the Bengal tiger, the wild reindeer, or caribou of North America, in their summer migrations, touch upon the realms of the musk ox and the polar bear.

Paradoxical as it may seem, the treeless, frozen wastes and tundras furnish rich pastures. The *Cladonia rangiferina,* or reindeer moss, other lichens, grasses, and shrubs grow there in abundance and constitute the winter and summer foods that the reindeer most relish.

The size of reindeer differs according to locale, age, and sex. Generally speaking, a large, full-grown reindeer stands about four and one-half feet high, measures six to seven feet in length from tip of nose to tail, and weighs at three or four years of age about 300 pounds on the hoof. Its coat or pelage is generally a chocolate brown in summer but lighter in winter. Some reindeer are white, others spotted. During our early studies of the reindeer we considered the white and spotted animals somewhat inferior until at the Reindeer Fair it was a white reindeer that won the blue ribbon for pulling the heaviest load—more than 2,300 pounds. The hair under the throat, belly, stubby tail, on the muzzle, and immediately above the hoofs is white or nearly so. Below the throat of the males the hair is very long and tufted, hanging like a pendant mane.

The pelage of the reindeer keeps it warm in bitter cold. The strong legs and sharp hoofs of the animal enable it to dig out the snow-covered foods that its remarkable olfactory powers enable it to detect. Its broad hoofs support it on soft snow or boggy ground. Its coat of hollow, chambered, buoyant hair makes the reindeer a good swimmer. No other quadruped swims with its body so much out of water. Its coat is a natural life preserver.

Nature has been exceptionally partial to reindeer. They have wonderful powers of orientation—an instinct similar to the homing pigeon. They seem to cultivate a love for their home pastures and for their kind. Their homing instinct enables them, when far removed, unerringly to return to their home. It is not strange that Nature, considering the perfection exhibited in the reindeer, should finish by giving it a crown of antlered glory.

The branched appendages to the skull of the reindeer, called antlers, though not so large or so heavy as those of some of the other of the deer family, are very large in proportion to the size of the animal, and are its most outstanding feature. As with fingerprints, no two sets of antlers are exactly alike. Antlers differ in size; some are more branched than others, having as many as sixty points; they are not always symmetrical, the beams, prongs, tines, and palmation differing in each case. The reindeer is unique in that antlers are common to both sexes but considerably smaller and lighter in the female than in the male. Both have brow as well as bez tines.* While growing and in the velvet, the antlers present a much more massive appearance than after the velvet has shed. During the peeling-off process, the reindeer frequently rub their antlers with their hoofs, or against stones, willows, and trees. While shedding, the velvet often hangs from the antlers in bloody shreds. When the velvet has all peeled off, the antlers are full grown. It is then that the rut, or mating time, begins.

It is believed that the antlers are secondary sexual characteristics. In the months of August and September, "when the frost nips crisply and blood runs hot in the veins of the reindeer and stirs up both love and hate," the buck gathers his harem about him. But he must fight to secure it. This is

---

* Brow tines and bez tines, two of each, are secondary horns that slope down from the base of the antlers proper. Brow tines are the central ones, bez tines outside of brow tines.

where the evolutionary rule of "survival of the fittest" comes into full play and has much to do with the improvement as well as the perpetuation of the race. "Faint heart ne'er won fair lady" is a motto that the reindeer express in action if not in words.

The antlers are shed annually—the bucks, steers, does, and fawns shed them in that order. Nature here seems to afford providential protection to the weak against the strong. The mothers and their fawns are able to secure forage that would otherwise be difficult to obtain. With ice covering the snow, it is the still-antlered animals that break the crust and paw down to the moss. It is amusing to observe the fawn, with its sharp prongs, drive away the larger and, at this season, "bald-headed" animal, securing for itself the patch of moss.

Next to the antlers, the feet and the hoofs of the reindeer present the most interesting and unique characteristics. The hoof is large and very broad in proportion to the size of the animal. The cleft between the toes extends far up and allows great spread of lateral expansion, thus exposing a large bearing surface. Each hoof is surrounded with an abundance of coarse, stiff hairs extending down to the cleft. The hind, or accessory, hoofs (little toes, dew claws) of this animal, unlike those of other deer, are functional and of real use. They are larger than the dew claws of any other quadruped of its size, and more lateral, adding much to the bearing surface of the foot. In winter the frog of the hoofs is almost entirely absorbed, leaving the edges of the hoofs quite concave, each division of the undersurface presenting the appearance of a mussel shell. The shell continues to grow while the frog does not fill up again until spring, when the new antlers bud out. With this singular conformation of the foot—its great lateral spread, its four toes, and the additional assistance afforded by the long, stiff bristles that grow downward from the fetlock, curving upward between the divisions—the reindeer is able to proceed over crusted snow or swampy ground with an ease unparalleled by any other animal.

In reindeer the sense of smell is more strongly developed than is the sense of sight; they scent approaching danger more frequently than they see it. It is this olfactory power that enables the animals to detect mosses and lichens lying buried under the snow.

The doe gives birth to one fawn each year, two only in rare cases. Strong and early-born fawns sometimes breed in the year of their birth, bearing fawn when yearlings. The does continue to breed until ten or twelve years of age. It is a peculiarity of the reindeer that it has no gall bladder, a fact common to all Cervidae.

These are the salient facts about the animal that became, to me, the most interesting creature on earth. I was to learn more, much more, about them over the years. I found them to be dependable and faithful servants of man. I tried to treat them with intelligence and kindness and they reciprocated in full. It was man, not the reindeer, who generated my woes.

7.

OUR THIRD FALL in Alaska I helped to transport a typhoid patient with whom I had been placer mining during the summer season. We were six days en route. Several days after our arrival at Nome I came down with the dread disease. Dad put my ill companion and me on a steamer and watched over us anxiously during the long, rough trip to Seattle. There I spent more than two months in a hospital with Dad constantly by my side.

When I was at last well enough to travel, we took the train to St. Paul. The whole family met us at the railroad station and it was a joyful homecoming after nearly three years of separation. Mother and Helen cried, and our eyes were wet, too.

I, of course, had many stories that I was bursting to tell, and my brothers and sister listened eagerly. I didn't have to embroider my tales because in Alaska what appears to be an exaggeration turns out to be the truth. When my brothers were skeptical, I challenged them to come to Nome and see for themselves.

We had been home but a few hours when Dad poured a glass of brandy and handed it to me. Without hesitation I drank it neat, while Mother stared at me, shocked.

"I was afraid," she exclaimed, "that Carl would get into bad habits in that awful north country. It's no place for a young boy."

"Calm yourself, my dear," Dad placated her. "I assure you that he hasn't gone to the devil."

"But he swallowed that brandy as if it was water!"

Dad and I broke into laughter, and Mother looked at us in astonishment.

"Tell her, Carl," Dad said to me.

"Wal, I'll confess everything, folks," I began with a wink at Dad. "We gold miners is a rootin', tootin' bunch of hard-bitten men. Dad and me is sourdoughs and mighty proud of it. To be a sourdough, y'know, you got to drink every other man in the saloon under the table. Pour me another two fingers of that there brandy, Pop!"

Mother looked as though she were going to faint so Dad rushed to the rescue.

"Carl's only teasing," he hastily explained. "He's not a drinking man, by any means. But while he was in the hospital he was given a preparation of peptonoid, glycerine, and brandy every day. So he's just carrying out the doctor's orders."

Mother sighed with relief while my brothers looked at me rather disappointedly, it seemed.

Meanwhile, we caught up with what had happened during our absence. George had a good job, and Harry, the "inventor" of the family, had developed the principle of the "chainless bicycle" prior to its patent by others. Ralph, through his own efforts, had secured an appointment as page for a session of the State Senate and was now in high school. Alfred and Helen were attending public school. Ralph and Alfred were members of the Bald Eagle Yacht Club, winning the pennant in their class.

Everyone in the family was, fortunately, healthy, happy, and content. But naturally the question came up as to whether Dad and I were planning to go back to Alaska, and there were many long discussions about it. Following our departure from St. Paul three years before, when it was learned that we would not return that fall, Dad's office was closed and his large law library sold. So there was nothing to keep him in St. Paul. Meanwhile, he had secured an interest in a valuable mining claim on Ophir Creek some sixty miles from Nome, where I had been part of the crew during the summer of 1902. I had already planned to return to the claim upon the opening of navigation the following spring.

I fully regained my health and was offered a tempting position in St. Paul. But it seemed to me that my long stay in Alaska and the valuable experience I had gained would be wasted if I stayed in the States. So on the first steamer leaving Seattle in June of 1903 I returned to Nome, and Dad followed me a month later.

Alaska was in Dad's blood, too. And he knew from previous experience that there would always be law cases that would carry over into the winter. As we didn't want to go through another long absence from the rest of the family, it was arranged that they would move to Alaska. Mother had guessed our intentions and desires and was prepared for this major event. Arrangements were made for them to embark at Seattle on the S. S. *Oregon,* the last steamer of the season. George liked his job in St. Paul and was also at the time busily courting an attractive young lady so he did not join us until three years later. But all the rest packed up and started the long trek to Nome.

Dad rented a house on a corner directly across the street from the Federal Court House, and retained his offices and living quarters on the main street of Nome. There was no telegraph or radio and no means of knowing just when a ship would arrive. On the rear of our office building a ladder was fastened that reached to the roof. Each morning before breakfast I would climb up and scan the waters of the Bering Sea. On the twenty-second of October I gazed over the roof and

60

almost fell from my precarious perch—there was the *Oregon* riding at anchor in the roadstead!

I whooped down the ladder and Dad and I ran to the beach. A large dory came toward us and Mother and her chicks piled out into our arms. Now all together at last, with the exception of George, we were the largest and, at least momentarily, the noisiest family in Nome.

Apparently our vivid descriptions had failed to draw an adequate picture of the town and its surroundings. We marched down the main street, passing Eskimo women with babies on their backs, miners with packs, teams of horses, stovepipes protruding from the rooftops, for there was not a brick chimney anywhere. Mother laughed all the way home, glad to have her brood together again and unfearful of whatever might lie ahead in this pioneer country.

Our house was nicely furnished—for Nome, that is—and food was now plentiful. Soon we were well established and happy in our new home. Mother took Nome and all of Alaska in her stride. Almost at once our neighbors and friends came to meet Mother and the rest of the "greenhorns."

On Halloween we were startled as heavy five-gallon cans rolled down our roof. My brothers ran out and were immediately adopted by the younger crowd of Nome. All that winter Mother played the perfect hostess to the many people Dad and I knew. It was an active household where any friend was always welcome.

Our home became open house for the young people in Nome. Almost automatically Mother would add a place, or two or three, at the dinner table. On Sunday evenings after church we brought our friends home to visit and gather around the piano and sing to my sister Helen's accompaniment. On such occasions Alfred and our pet dog Oolik might be persuaded to stage a wrestling match.

Alfred would remove his coat and vest, get down on his hands and knees, and invite Oolik to "come on!" Oolik, recognizing the preliminaries, was both willing and ready. Coming out cautiously, first he would circle Alfred, maneuvering for position. Alfred, constantly shifting and feinting, would finally reach suddenly for one of Oolik's forelegs. Growling ostentatiously, quick as a flash Oolik would swing his leg back out of reach, then rush in to seize Alfred by the neck, releasing his hold only when Alfred again caught his foreleg and flipped him over, still growling. They were both very fast. Alfred used popular wresting holds, half and full Nelsons being his favorites. It was a continuous performance, with no "falls" called until Alfred was ready to quit.

Oolik had the distinction of being able to trace his ancestry halfway around the globe. Silla, his mother, was a cross between a Norwegian elkhound and a Greenland Eskimo dog. She was born on Nansen's ship *Fram,* in Jones Sound, during Captain Otto Sverdrup's Arctic voyage. Later she was given to Captain Roald Amundsen and was the only dog to negotiate the Northwest Passage on board the *Gjoa,* 1903–1906.

Silla was a courageous fighter. One afternoon while the *Gjoa* was locked in the ice a polar bear was sighted, headed for open water. The crew rushed for their guns, but Silla was ahead of them. She jumped the rail and was off after the bear. It had just reached open water when Silla made her jump, seizing the bear by its stubby tail. The bear pivoted sharply, flinging Silla into the sea. By that time Lieutenant Hansen, Amundsen's second in command, fired, wounding the bear. Silla, furious at having been tossed into the sea, crawled out onto the ice and rushed for the bear's throat. One blow of the bear's forepaw and Silla was knocked unconscious, but a second bullet from Hansen's rifle put an end to the fight.

Captain Amundsen presented Silla to my father, and she was bred to a very fine St. Lawrence Island Eskimo dog named Oolik. As Silla passed away shortly after the birth of Oolik II, he was raised on a bottle and grew up in the Lomen household. He was an aristocrat and not far removed from the wild. He had intelligence, beauty, and courage, and resented familiarity from strangers who were attracted to him. A ruff around his neck, a bushy tail carried over his back, and a coat of bristling gray and white gave him an appearance different from that of the usual northern dog.

Oolik loved children and toys, and often was seen running with a rubber toy in his mouth, or lying on the porch with some toy between his forepaws. Mother and Helen were often called to the door by neighborhood children who came to complain that Oolik had taken their baseball or "Oolik took my doll out of my doll carriage." The children had to come for help because they wouldn't dare attempt to recover the toys by themselves. Oolik never damaged their toys, only carrying them about with him carefully, to the porch or to his kennel at the back of the house. When Mother or someone else stepped out to get the toy and return it to the children, Oolik would let out a roar like a lion, hoping not to lose his newest prize. But when his bluff was called, he gave up like a gentleman.

Oolik was a fighter but seldom the aggressor. All the other dogs respected him. He lived a pleasant and interesting life and made one long and difficult trip with me to the Yukon and back, 700 miles, sleeping out when the temperature was more than 60 degrees below zero.

Upon Oolik's death, the question of burial was discussed. Our Eskimo friend Dick, who shared many experiences with us, said "Oolik must not be buried on land. I will carry him far out on Bering Sea and place him on an ice floe. When the ice moves out in the spring, he will be carried north into the Arctic Ocean where his ancestors came from, and where he belongs." We were grateful to Dick for thinking of this appropriate ceremony and it was thus that we bade Oolik good-by.

Meanwhile, all of us were busy. Mother and Helen took care of household duties with the assistance of an Eskimo girl. Dad practiced his profession, keeping occupied straightening out miners' claims. I was employed as chief clerk in the office of the clerk of the District Court. Ralph worked in a bank and as secretary to one of the mine operators. Alfred was made the first circulation manager of the *Gold Digger,* one of the two daily newspapers in Nome, and subsequently became its manager.

In the summer of 1906 brother George joined us, completing the Lomen family circle in Nome. An athlete, splendid ballplayer, and good storyteller, he made friends easily. The newly elected City Council became deadlocked on appointments in the spring of 1909 and the mayor-elect asked George to accept the post of city clerk. The city clerk was also municipal judge and city assessor. Having had no experience with which to discharge those offices, George declined. After much persuasion he changed his mind.

A few days after he took office a Nome character was arrested for assault. Being unable to put up bond, he was jailed. George's experience with legal matters being nil this, as he put it, was "a nice kettle of fish." Certain members of the bar had been waiting for just some such opportunity to show up George's inexperience.

George went to Father for advice and was told, "Remember that you are the Court. If onlookers become overly noisy or obstreperous, you have the authority to clear the courtroom. The attorneys [seven had volunteered to defend this one impoverished prisoner!] will make their arguments. Listen to them calmly. If you are in doubt as to a proper ruling, simply say, 'Motion overruled; proceed.' "

The courtroom was jammed. The defense attorneys filed in, loaded down with lawbooks. The bailiff rapped, crying, "Court is now in session!" Several attorneys sprang to their

64

feet. Quickly George said that they would be heard one at a time.

Argument followed argument, the "Court" attending to every word with serious expression. Now and then George overruled a motion. Once a witty sally from one of the defense attorneys caused the audience to roar with laughter. "Any further demonstration," said George firmly, "and the courtroom will be cleared."

When the evidence was all in, the Court pronounced sentence, a fine of ten dollars. The case was appealed to the District Court, which upheld George's decision. The attorneys had their fun, the defendant had a fair trial, the town had been entertained. George had won his spurs as a competent municipal judge.

In 1908 we boys bought a photographic studio; a year later we purchased a drugstore. Harry, Ralph, Alfred, and I were all equal partners, with Ralph as manager. Harry ran the photo studio. A little later Alfred left his newspaper job and joined Ralph in the drugstore. I used part of my chief clerk's salary for personal needs and turned over the balance to our business. At the close of each year our books showed a credit balance to Harry and me and a debit balance to Ralph and Alfred. But on the new year, without transfer of any funds, we would wipe out all personal debits and credits and start off with a clean slate. In that way nobody made any money during the early years, but, as it turned out, we were developing a sound business. We continued the original plan for more than a quarter of a century, until 1934, when fire almost wholly destroyed Nome, including the business interests of the Lomen Brothers.

Our drugstore, located in the center of Nome, became a popular meeting place for both men and women. The store was attractive, with soda fountain, cigar counter, a book section, and the usual equipment of a modern pharmacy.

Ralph and Alfred were "live wires" and popular with their customers. Much of our trade was peculiar in that many of them were so much at home that they preferred to wait on themselves rather than be waited on. They would enter, walk back of the counters, select what they wanted, ring up their sale, make change, wrap their parcel, and leave, with, perhaps, simply a cheery word of greeting.

One late afternoon I dropped in at the store en route home from my office. While I leaned against a counter, an Eskimo entered. He walked back of the counter, opened the case containing cigars, took out a handful, turned, rang up the sale, took out his change, and marched out again without a word having been spoken by either the Eskimo or myself. That could well be called "good will."

In contrast was the Eskimo who moved about the store in apparent puzzlement. "Can I help you?" inquired a clerk. "You wait, me talking inside," the native replied. He wanted the clerk to know that he was thinking.

Our cigar counter was near the front of the store. As was the custom in Nome, many patrons "shook dice" in making their purchases. We used what were termed "bingles," round aluminum disks the size of a quarter stamped with our name and "Good for 12½ cents in trade." Change was made with the bingles and many "shook dice" and, if successful, took bingles to be used for future purchases. One day a customer came in and said to Alfred: "Say, Al, what about one shake of the dice for the bingles I have—double or nothing?" "All right," answered Alfred, without asking any questions. They each threw the dice and Alfred won. With that the customer commenced emptying his pockets until the top of the counter was covered with bingles, several hundred dollars' worth. It seems the customer had been collecting bingles for a year or more, and considered it a good joke to spring a surprise on Alfred, though not so great as it would have been had the

66

customer been successful. We had wondered what had happened to our stock of "bingles."

On another occasion I entered the store and found a considerable group of men at the cigar counter. Alfred gave me a nod and I went to the rear of the store with him.

"There is something wrong going on here," he said, "but Ralph and I have not been able to figure out what. We must have lost several hundred dollars at the cigar counter today. They all want to shake dice and most of them win."

It took several days and a suggestion from one of Nome's professional gamblers to solve the mystery. "Put calipers on your dice," he advised us. We did and found that our dice were no longer exact cubes. The dice, we later learned, had been taken out one at a time, heated, placed in a vise, and given a gentle pressure, then returned to the store. The result was that certain numbers, known only to the inner circle, would turn up more often than other numbers, making "long odds" in favor of the customer and against the house.

New dice were rolled out, the old discarded, and the fun was over. This was done as a good joke on the "Lomen boys," though it proved a costly one for us.

We all took part in civic affairs, followed prospecting and placer gold mining, and interested ourselves in community matters that we believed would prove beneficial to Nome and to Alaska as a whole. During these years there was a federal prohibition on the ownership of female reindeer by whites. However, this did not prevent us from investigating the industry, and we devoted considerable time to learning all we could about it.

The winter public entertainments, given by the clubs or societies, were gala affairs. There were no automobiles but there were dog teams, though most people walked, bundled in furs. There would be maids in the ladies' dressing room to assist with overshoes, mukluks, and fur garments. Then the ladies would reappear dressed in the most up-to-date fashions. The Lomens, or some of them, were usually represented at these affairs. Mother was a fine dancer. She had grace and a queenly walk. I never tired of watching her, on her partner's arm, cross the floor. Home lunches followed the parties.

Most of the fraternal societies had branches in Nome, several having fine buildings big enough for 1,000 spectators. The Arctic Brotherhood and "Eagles" had halls large enough for our indoor baseball and basketball tournaments, field events, and 25-, 50-, and 100-mile foot races (25 miles one night, 25 the next night, and 50 the third day, starting at noon).

Contests between the various clubs became intense. A small group of us organized a Y.M.C.A. We were twelve members, none of whom smoked or used hard liquor. We rented space from the "Eagles" and practiced basketball several nights a week. Finally we issued a challenge to the Arctic Brotherhood that boasted a membership of more than 500. Their first reaction was that they considered it an insult. "Challenge our second team," we were told. Finally, two members of the A. B. put up trophies, and the A. B.'s accepted the challenge of the "Y" for a series of three out of five games of basketball. Excitement built up, and when the "Y," of which I was president, and Ralph and Alfred members of the team, won the first three games of the season, the town was ready to explode. The A. B.'s immediately challenged us for another series. We accepted, and this time we lost the trophies. In subsequent series the trophies went back and forth between the "Y" and the A. B.'s.

Eventually Nome considered that our boys were equal to anything the United States could offer in the basketball field and decided to send a team to the States. A composite team was made up of the two competing teams, and they

68

sailed on the last steamer the fall of 1907. Ralph and Alfred were both members.

Our team entered training at the University of Washington for six weeks and then commenced their tour. They were called the Arctic Brotherhood team. All wore fur parkas and were a picturesque group. They played through the Pacific Coast states, then through Utah, Wyoming, and Colorado, and on to Chicago. They lost to the Kansas City Athletic Club, then champions of the United States, the last two points on fouls just as the score was tied 40 to 40. They defeated the Crescent Five of Chicago and ended up with a record as fine players and clean sportsmen. The following year *Spalding's Basketball Guide* carried the picture of the Nome team on its cover.

Soon after we set up the photographic business we decided to obtain a panoramic view of Nome from the Bering Sea. A hundred yards offshore there was an eighty-foot tower whose base rested on a 200-ton concrete block. A heavy cable ran to shore from near the top of the tower, for the handling of freight.

Taking an 8 x 10 camera and his loyal Eskimo assistant Dick, Alfred went out to the tower and climbed to a platform built some ten feet from the top. Looking things over from that angle, he decided that the heavy cable would detract from the picture; so, while Dick remained on the platform, he climbed to the very top. It provided space only sufficient to spread the three telescopic legs of the tripod. As Alfred was ducking his head under the focusing cloth, one of the legs gave way, causing the heavy camera to tilt. Aware of what had happened, Alfred crouched low, his eyes still covered by the black cloth. Grabbing one of the other tripod legs, he held onto the camera for dear life; eighty feet would make a long drop. But Dick, seeing the danger, rushed to his rescue, relieving him of the burden of the camera and saving him from an icy plunge.

One spring, when the ship *Victoria* worked her way through the ice for the glory of being the first ship to reach Nome after a long, hard winter, these same courageous partners again went on the trail of taking interesting photos. As the steamer eased her way into the roadstead, they rowed out in a small dory with the heavy camera. The dory bottom was a poor support for such a piece of equipment, so Alfred looked around for an ice cake suitable for planting the tripod. The only one near enough was a small cake some ten feet long by six feet wide. He hopped onto it and set up the camera, Dick remaining with the dory to be ready to haul him out of the water if the cake of ice should take a notion to turn over. The several hundred passengers aboard the *Victoria* were amazed to see a photographer taking their pictures while riding on a small piece of ice and they themselves began to take pictures of the picture-maker.

A born sailor, Alfred loved the water. Respecting the power of the sea, he felt no fear of it. At sixteen he had been set on trying for the Navy. He took the examinations for Annapolis and passed. Months went by and then he received a wire: "Report Annapolis ten days."

This was impossible; in midwinter reaching the States involved a 1,200-mile trip by dog team. A telegram of explanation was dispatched to the Superintendent of the Naval Academy. By return wire Alfred was told, "Await instructions." He settled down to do so. But no instructions ever came and Alfred did not become an officer of the United States Navy.

The arrival of the first steamer in the spring was always a gala occasion in Nome. In 1905 Alfred and Dick rowed out in a dory to meet the S.S. *Oregon*. They encountered considerable drift ice, moving rapidly with the wind and tide. Several dories lined up at the foot of the gangway that had been lowered to permit the more daring passengers to be rowed ashore at two dollars a head.

Suddenly several dories, sideswiped by a large ice floe drifting rapidly along, capsized. Forcing their dory near to those struggling in the water, Alfred leaned over and grabbed a man by his coat collar, dropping him with Dick's help into the bottom of the boat. They picked up several more and rowed their boatload ashore, not adding anything to the two-dollar price for rescue. The first man they had pulled into the dory told them his name was Tex Rickard, the very man who was destined to become a famous and colorful fight promoter.

During the height of the "Alaska Sweepstakes" dog races, an army officer, Lieutenant Fred Boschen, donated a beautiful silver cup for the winner in an annual event for amateur drivers. Alfred entered a team, as did thirteen other drivers. The race was to be run over a seven-mile course, teams to leave two minutes apart, the drivers drawing for position.

Alfred drew a high number. He drove Siberians, with a lead dog whose chief ambition on the trail was to overtake anything that moved. This lead dog's teammates were all fleet of foot, willing to follow any pace set.

Alfred's leader, urged on by Alfred's bellowing voice, overtook one team after another and won by a wide margin. Years later Alfred was to visit the cup donor at West Point. Then an instructor, Colonel Boschen later was to become a major general and made Chief of Finance of the United States Army.

It is obvious that the Lomen brothers were into just about everything, including prospecting and gold mining, sports events, photography and pharmaceuticals, to say nothing about rolling the dice for "bingles." But the interest to which we were to devote many years of our lives was still in the future.

8.

A NEW superintendent for the Bureau of Education for the Northwestern District of Alaska arrived in Nome during the summer of 1908. Walter C. Shields, direct from the Washington office of the Bureau, was a man of intelligence and education. His presence ushered in a new era for the Eskimo and the reindeer. His personality and a love of adventure inspired confidence in both Eskimo and whites.

It did not take him long to grasp that the main problem confronting his Bureau in northwestern Alaska was the reindeer industry. The best way of advancing conditions for the native people was going to be to develop this industry. He was inspired by the challenge.

The Nome section of Alaska was commonly considered "dog country." Eskimo and whites alike used dogs for transportation. Putting both argument and personal example to work, Walter Shields began showing the deer men that they had a draft animal which for their purposes was far superior to the sled dog. Traveling any distance by dog team required many dogs, where at most only one or two reindeer were needed. For dogs, food had to be carried, adding considerably to load weight. Reindeer, on the contrary, could always live off the country, foraging for their food even when it was buried under the snow.

Shields bolstered his argument by proving that no trip was too difficult for him. When a dog driver said certain passes through the mountains would be too difficult for reindeer to negotiate, Shields set about proving it could be done. He traveled by boat in summer but in winter by reindeer. He fired his native helpers with pride in their animals and enthusiasm for their work. It was my privilege to make five lengthy winter trips as his guest, and we became fast friends. His district, extending from Barrow at the top of the continent to the southerly reaches of Seward Peninsula, took in an area of more than 100,000 square miles.

Shields saw my interest in reindeer, and believed that if whites could play a part through the investment of capital, the reindeer industry would benefit. So in the fall of 1913 he explained to me that Alfred Nilima's contract with the Government was going to expire the following summer and, should Nilima see fit to sell his holdings to whites, there would be no government objection. Immediately I passed on this information to my father, and he addressed a letter to Nilima at Kotzebue. Some weeks later we had an option on his herd at $22.50 a head, "run of the herd," to be taken over September 1, at which time a payment of $5,000 was to be made, with the balance covered by two notes of equal amount for one and two years. Associated with us in this undertaking were Jafet Lindeberg, at that time president of the Pioneer Mining and Ditch Company, Nome's largest, most successful mining corporation, and Dr. J. H. Mustard.

We held a meeting for the purpose of incorporating. In choosing a corporate name, Mr. Lindeberg pointed out that as the United States had Armour & Company, Swift & Company, Cudahy & Company, Alaska could well have Lomen & Company. There seemed no sound reason against it and we gave that name to the corporation.

The time for meeting Nilima at Keewalik was drawing near. The place was a point 200 miles distant, on Kotzebue Sound. At the time there were no airplanes in Alaska, and no boats were available. Alfred was twenty-three years old, and it was decided that he should make the trip across country on foot, carrying the $5,000 earnest money in cash.

There was very little currency in the country. The common medium of exchange was gold and silver coin, but hard money was too heavy for Alfred to transport. With difficulty the sum was finally rounded up in bills of small denomination and put into a money belt.

It was decided after many conferences that Alfred should have a companion on the trip. "Little Johnnie" Rauna was selected, a five-foot Lapp, cross-eyed and bowlegged, who had come over with the reindeer expedition from Norway. For precautionary reasons, no mention was made to him of the money Alfred was to carry.

Leaving Nome August 22, the two traveled a short distance on a narrow-gauge railroad, striking out on foot from the end of the line for Candle and Keewalik. They ran into flurries of bad weather. Alfred found the money belt around his waist a great inconvenience, so he removed it and placed it in his pack. Streams were swollen and Little Johnnie volunteered often to carry Alfred's pack but, thanking him, Alfred went on carrying it himself.

They took along one light blanket for the two of them; except for a slicker apiece, it was their only protection against the weather. One night, tired out, they lay down on the wet tundra, each covered by his slicker and sharing the blanket. Suddenly Alfred became aware in his sleep that someone was leaning over him. The money! Forcing himself to remain motionless, he tried to make out what was going on. What was happening was that his little Lapp companion was giving up his own slicker and spreading it protectively over Alfred. At a later time I mentioned the incident to Little Johnnie, and he grinned and said, "Alfred thought I didn't know about the money but I did. The slicker—he needed it more than me."

Six days out of Nome they reached the rendezvous safely and on time. Nilima was fifteen miles across the bay, at

Keewalik. Alfred had the necessary papers but when he produced the $5,000 in currency Nilima exclaimed, "I don't want money!"

"Then what do you want?" said Alfred, surprised.

"I want a check." This was a stumper. Alfred did not have $5,000 in funds in the bank at Nome. Nevertheless, he improvised a blank check, made it out in Nilima's name for $5,000 and handed it over.

Transfer of the herd was to be made at Choris Peninsula, still farther north. It would be several weeks before Alfred was back in Nome; meanwhile, he didn't want to be burdened with the rejected $5,000. Several coastwise schooners were riding at anchor in the bay and a couple of them were heading for Nome. Alfred was not acquainted with any of the skippers but, after looking them over critically in a saloon where they were busy "bending the elbow," he finally selected one and spoke to him.

"Captain, I understand you're sailing shortly for Nome."

"That's right. Something I can do for you?"

"Well, yes. I have a package here that I would like to send to my brother Carl."

"What's in the package?"

"Five thousand dollars in currency. I have drawn a check on the bank in Nome for that amount and I want my brother to deposit this cash to make the check good."

"I'll be glad to see that it's delivered," the skipper agreed.

Some two weeks later a man walked into my office in Nome, tossed a package on my desk, and remarked casually, "Here's five thousand in currency your brother Alfred sent down from Keewalik with me. He wants you to deposit it right away as he has issued a check for that amount and must be certain that the check is good." No receipt was asked for. The man who brought the money was Captain Frank Whitlam, later in command of the Bureau of Indian Affairs motor vessel *North Star*.

When was the check presented for payment? Two years later!

Meanwhile, Alfred and Johnnie went on to Choris Peninsula with Nilima. At the camp they met other Lapps: Andrew Bahr, Peter and Isaac Hatta, and M. I. K. Nilluka. With the transfer of 1,200 reindeer, our dreams had come true: Lomen and Company were reindeer owners at last!

Nilima was leaving for Norway, his homeland, so it was necessary for Alfred to select someone among the Lapps who could take over management of the herd. He chose Andrew Bahr; as superintendent of Kotzebue Herd No. 2 he became the Lomen Company's first employee.

Father was president of Lomen and Company, I was secretary-treasurer. Neither of us received any salary. So far our sole paid employee was Andrew Bahr.

To call it the reindeer *industry* was to make it seem more substantial than it really was. At the time we entered it, unfenced public domain was roamed by herds of semiwild but docile reindeer. Herding was done on foot by Lapps and Eskimo. Herds were small, animals valuable. Except for a few corrals and range shelters there was little or no equipment. There were no abattoirs or cold-storage plants, no refrigerated ships, no "outside markets" for meat or hides. Local markets were good, however, and meat prices high.

With actual purchase of the deer, we acquired such grazing privileges as had been held by our predecessors in interest, no more and no less. During the short summer months the deer grazed on the tender grass, mushrooms, berries, willow buds, and sedges, but for the greater part of the year they were dependent on reindeer moss, with which the area is plentifully supplied.

Reindeer moss is a lichen of which there are many varieties. In color it is whitish or grayish and, although unpalatable, furnishes food, if necessary, for man. As an experiment, one summer when Lawrence Palmer of the United States Bureau of Biological Survey, Department of Agriculture, was in Nome, he and my sister Helen gathered some moss, dried it, rolled it into powder, and made biscuits. The grayish color made them look unappetizing but the pungent flavor was not disagreeable. One man I knew, who ran out of food in the hills, lived on nothing but boiled moss for two weeks.

Reindeer moss is plentiful in most parts of the Arctic and sub-Arctic, often covering the landscape so thickly as to resemble a field of snow. It has an unusually slow growth, not exceeding an eighth of an inch a year. This factor makes it very necessary for reindeer owners not to permit overgrazing by their herds, as the extent of the lichen coverage controls the number of reindeer the land can support.

The reindeer "experiment" in Alaska, as many chose to refer to it, gave evidence of becoming successful beyond the expectations of even the most optimistic. In the forty years following their original importation, the herds had thrived, multiplying almost a thousandfold. Originally, as I have said, "mother stock" numbered 1,280 animals. By the early 1930's— the peak period of the industry—the herds were to total approximately a million animals, not counting the tens of thousands that were used for food and clothing in the intervening years.

Lomen and Company soon ran into reindeer-business problems. They had to do with such things as necessary corrals for handling of the deer, abattoirs for butchering the meat and dressing it properly, cold-storage plants to preserve it before shipment, refrigerated ships to transport meat from Alaska to the United States, and development of a market for the sale of the products.

Until early in the nineteenth century refrigeration without the use of natural ice was practically unknown. Even then, not until 1845, with the innovation of the so-called "air machine," in which cooled compressed air was permitted to expand, was there much progress. The next advance was the use of ammonia vapor in place of air, but the equipment required restricted its use to large establishments.

Refrigeration was a prime requisite in the development of the reindeer industry in Alaska. From 1915 on the surplus male animals of the herds in this rapidly expanding industry were more than the local market could absorb. The only substantial market was the United States. To reach that market with a product that must compete with long-established meat and packing-house products called for many improvements. The reindeer must be scientifically butchered and bled, the carcass neatly dressed and wrapped, solidly frozen in ammonia cold-storage plants, and shipped to the United States on refrigerated vessels a distance of some 3,000 miles.

Reindeer herds were many, each with its own grazing unit, occupying much of the area of western Alaska from the Kuskokwim River to the south, to Point Barrow, the northernmost point of the North American continent, a distance of upward of 1,000 miles. The combined herds totaled approximately a million animals, of which 10 per cent should be available for marketing each year. The number could be expected to increase with full expansion of the industry, for it was estimated that the territory could permanently support some 4,000,000 reindeer.

Accordingly we constructed three ammonia plants for preserving our reindeer meat. They were both small and costly. Lumber and other construction materials, necessary machinery, fuel oil and other supplies, as well as the men to superintend the construction of the buildings, and engineers to install the machinery, had to be brought up from the States. The operation company, Lomen Reindeer Corporation, determined the initial cost of each plant to be $30,000, each with a capacity of 1,000 carcasses weighing 150 pounds each. The plants could not be filled and emptied more than twice each year. The cost and capacity elements of refrigeration were the greatest problem of the reindeer industry.

Reindeer meat animals are at their prime the first of October, and the butchering season extended from mid-September to the first of the year. Therefore, another great obstacle was ocean navigation between northwestern Alaska and the United States. Bering Sea ports closed November 1, while those north of Bering Strait closed several weeks earlier. Refrigeration plants not emptied in the fall of the year, prior to the close of navigation, were forced to hold the product until the return of the steamers the following June and July. This proved very costly, as fuel oil was the motive power for the plants, which were thus forced to operate for several months during the spring of the year.

With an ever increasing number of surplus animals in the rapidly growing herds, the first specter of doubt arose as to whether the Lomen Reindeer Corporation could maintain its position as the marketing agency for the Eskimo herds, as well as for the company-owned animals. How to finance the construction of a sufficient number of cold-storage plants throughout the reindeer country and to operate at an expense level that would permit the product to compete with other meats on the American market? Ralph and Alfred and I, the active officers of the corporation, held the opinion that the problem could be solved.

The two largest company herds ranged in the Kotzebue-Buckland area north of Bering Strait. Meat animals from these herds could be driven on the hoof across country to the company herds south of the Strait, making them accessible for fall transportation. Another possibility that could be developed for utilizing the capacity of the plants would be to prepare boned products, thus providing more space for the meat itself.

During the summer of 1919 Alfred investigated the possibilities of natural cold storage in the valley of the Buckland

River, boundary line between the company's Kotzebue and Buckland ranges. Under a large area of the valley lies what is considered a prehistoric glacier. Along the seashore and in places where the streams cut through, the ice melts in summer and allows the soil to slough away. Here and there is revealed a bank of several feet of clear, solid ice topped by a layer of soil two to three feet thick.

At one point the local Eskimo reindeer men had sunk a shaft twenty feet deep, at the bottom of which they kept their reindeer meat in summer. Alfred examined this natural refrigerator, found it cold at the bottom and sufficiently low in temperature to preserve meat through the summer months. If a large chamber of this type could be chiseled out in the subterranean ice bed and properly ventilated, it would prove far cheaper than any commercial ammonia cold-storage plant. The idea certainly seemed feasible. Whether it would be so on a scale required by the company could be determined only by actual experiment.

We knew frozen earth offered great possibilities for refrigeration. During the fall of 1904 a woman died and was buried in the old cemetery near the beach of Bering Sea, just west of Nome. Her husband survived her. Burial during mild weather in frozen ground is something of a problem. The gravediggers must remain, bailing the water from the grave, until the arrival of the casket. The service is hurried, the casket lowered, the grave refilled. It will refreeze within a few days. The burial of this woman was similar to all others in the area.

The years passed, the husband remaining a widower. In the fall of 1913 Nome was visited by the most severe storm of its history. Coming out of the southeast, the weather swung to the southwest, piling up the waters of Bering Sea onto the Nome coast, causing great damage to property. The nights were dark, and the storm raged with great violence for three days. Many buildings were destroyed and others flooded.

The widower lived close to Snake River, which flowed into

the sea at Nome. The land upon which his cabin was built was low, but since the structure—though surrounded by water and with waves lapping at the door—was substantially built, the widower felt it could withstand the storm, so he remained.

Close to midnight of the second day there came a thump against the door. A few moments later there was a second thump. Fearing that some driftwood might break in his cabin door, the widower crawled out of his bunk, waded across the room in a foot of water, opened the door, and found the body of his wife—buried nine years before—in a perfect state of preservation. The gigantic sea waves had washed out the graves in the cemetery and smashed the coffins, thus liberating the bodies, all looking as they had on the day of their interment.

Of course the poor fellow's hair literally stood on end, for he was sure it was the day of resurrection.

The summer of 1920 I visited the Buckland area armed with several tested thermometers. The meat shaft belonging to the Eskimo was first examined. It was 3 x 4 x 20 feet deep, with a ladder down one side. The shaft mouth was covered with a walrus hide. The open-air temperature the day of the examination registered 72 degrees Fahrenheit. Three feet below the surface it was less than 50 degrees, and on the bottom the thermometer showed 23 degrees above zero Fahrenheit.

This shaft was located at the mouth of the Buckland River at Igloo Point. A contract was let to excavate, and next winter a small room 25 x 7 feet high was chiseled out of the frozen earth, not far from the Eskimo shaft, with an entrance slanting in from the riverbank, which at this point was quite high. Temperatures proved satisfactory and meat stored in the room was in perfect condition the following summer.

Men usually prospect for gold and other minerals. The Lomen Reindeer Corporation organized a prospecting expedition to look for suitable conditions for natural cold storage.

These factors had to be considered: accessibility to safe anchorage for ships and an area suitable for large expansion as the business grew. In addition, the site had to be high enough above the sea level to avoid any danger of flood. Allowance also had to be made for the height of the refrigeration rooms, plus sufficient overburden of moss and muck to protect the rooms against thawing during the summer months.

Following weeks of prospecting, a location was selected at a point twenty-four miles west of Igloo Point, a place called Elephant Point. The new site was first visited by the English explorer, Captain Frederic William Beechey of the Royal Navy, in 1826, and so named by him because of the great number of mammoth bones scattered about which seemed to him to be elephant bones and tusks. Elephant Point is on the south shore of Eschscholtz Bay, Kotzebue Sound.

Each summer bones of the prehistoric mammoth, the ox and the horse, were washed out of the high, frozen banks of Elephant Point and, in the near vicinity, the remains of a mammoth, with flesh and hair still intact, were found, substantiating the preserving qualities of the frozen ground.

Realizing the great advantage natural cold storage would give the industry, we made plans for very extensive work on a plant as soon as the winter season opened. The Lomens could thank Mother Nature for her kindness for she not only supplied free fodder for the animals the year round, but now she was ready to furnish a refrigerating system that would run itself and require no fuel.

A crew of thirty men, many of them seasoned gold placer miners expert in this type of work, were engaged to carve out of the frozen hillside, with pick and shovel, six large storage holding rooms with a total capacity of 10,000 reindeer carcasses. The consistency of the material excavated was approximately 85 per cent ice (water) and 15 per cent solid matter (sand and gravel).

A long tunnel was driven into the frozen hillside with a

slight upgrade for drainage. A series of rooms were then chiseled out, consisting of a hallway with rooms on each side, the partitions being of frozen earth and ice six to eight feet in thickness. Several modern, insulated cold-storage doors were placed between the entrance to the tunnel and the rooms, and other doors set in the entrance to each room as well. Ventilation was secured by means of double pipes driven through the roof, one just penetrating the ceiling at one end and the other close to the floor at the opposite end of each room. With open-air temperatures ranging from 55 degrees below zero Fahrenheit to 80 degrees above, the temperature of these rooms varied from 10 degrees to 18 degrees above zero during the twelve calendar months, keeping the meat in perfect condition.

Two shafts were sunk from the surface, tapping the tunnel. One was at the extreme end of the tunnel, the other midway to the entrance. Small cabins were constructed over the shafts and, in addition, the shafts were covered by tight wooden lids. A shed was built to connect with the entrance of the tunnel. It was well insulated by packed reindeer moss inside and out.

When completed, the Elephant Point Natural Cold Storage Plant was the most unique in the world. It was the largest, with six rooms, 18 x 36 x 7 feet high, and would readily lend itself to almost unlimited expansion at a minimum cost of development.

A narrow-gauge railway track was laid from the beach to the far end of the tunnel. Small flatcars transported the meat from storage to the scows, or lighters, which were used to carry the cargoes from the beach to the anchorage of the ships that would take them to the States.

The first winter a small butchering of 2,000 animals was done to test out the plant. The second summer, water flowed over the roof of the plant, causing some trouble, but ditches were cut to divert the water and that corrected the difficulty.

Following the storage of meat, hoarfrost gathered on the

ceiling and walls of the rooms, giving out a brilliant light when one entered with a candle.

At first boards, or ship's dunnage, were placed on the floors of the rooms and meat stacked on the boards, but it was noted that dust gathered. Then snow was placed on the floor, and the boards over the snow, and that difficulty was overcome.

The second year 8,000 deer were butchered and stored in the rooms—the record butchering on one range in the history of the industry.

When a herd was rounded up and brought in for butchering, it was held about six to ten miles from Elephant Point, where there was fairly good feed. When butchering operations were ready to begin, some 2,000 deer were cut out from the main herd and driven to the corral. About a mile and a half away was the mouth of a long lane formed by fence posts and wire. It was wide at the mouth and narrowed as it neared the corral. At a strategic point, a half-mile from the corral, men were stationed with several hundred yards of five-foot-wide burlap. These men were crouched and hidden from the view of the deer.

When the herders had driven the deer beyond this point, the men stood up and fell in behind the deer, holding the burlap upright, using it as a sort of walking fence. As the lane approached the corral, it narrowed rapidly and the deer soon realized they were trapped. They invariably became frightened and attempted to break back in the direction from which they had come, but the men were experienced and patient as they moved slowly forward. Finally the deer saw the opening leading into the corral and dashed toward it. The men with the burlap closed in, cutting off retreat. As soon as the deer were in the corral, the men ran forward and closed the opening with a movable section of corral fence. This winter corral was built entirely of twelve-foot lumber panels that were taken down and piled to one side when the work was completed. If the panels had been left standing, drifting snow would soon fill the corral. The panels were again erected when another butchering herd was brought up.

After being driven into the corral, the butchering animals were separated from the others by being worked through a series of small corrals and then through a chute. Here the selection of good meat animals was made. The deer chosen were turned into a holding corral, and the rejected ones sent back to the open range.

Since we feared that unusual weather conditions might someday be encountered, the middle room on the east side of the plant was lined and piped, and a small ammonia refrigerating plant constructed just beyond the entrance to the tunnel. Should temperatures in the room rise to a dangerous point at any time, the artificial plant could easily lower them. It was never found necessary to operate the artificial plant.

Meat held in these rooms for three years was found to be in excellent condition. During the winter months the shafts and doors were opened and fresh air forced through the rooms.

Elephant Point was a winter butchering station and summer headquarters for the Kotzebue and Buckland herds. It was equipped with modern buildings for the preparation of the meat and hides of the reindeer for market. There was a large abattoir, holding and boning rooms, and bins for the salting and stacking of hides. Also the corral system already described, and adequate living quarters for a large crew.

Winter butchering was carried on during the cold weather with temperatures ranging from 30 to 50 degrees below zero. After dressing, the carcasses were placed in the open air until frozen solidly, then transferred to the natural cold-storage rooms. It was not possible to place warm meat within the cold-storage rooms without damage, due to raising of temperatures, which caused sloughing off of ceilings and walls.

The construction of the natural cold-storage plant, together with the buildings and equipment at Elephant Point, showed an initial cost of slightly more than $100,000, but upkeep was practically nil. Farther north conditions were found comparable to those at Elephant Point with, perhaps, lower temperatures but less favorable for shipping.

There were many Eskimo herds ranging north to Point Barrow and eastward. We envisaged large winter drives of reindeer meat animals, in excess of local requirements, south to our Kotzebue and Buckland herds, to be purchased for butchering and storage in our Elephant Point plant until ships could transport the meat to the States.

The drives would be comparable to the cattle drives of the old West. Arrangements would be made months in advance, all herdsmen being notified of the contemplated drive. The work would be performed by the Eskimo deer men, the farthest north herd to be ready first. They would cut out the surplus animals they desired to dispose of, driving them to a rendezvous with their nearest southerly neighbors, who would have separated their animals and have the surplus awaiting the drive. When the deer of the northern herd were turned over, its herders would be given a receipt and return to their homes. The drive would then be continued by the herders of the second group, who would drive south to their nearest neighbors, gradually moving the ever increasing herd on toward the "reindeer stockyards." This method would not require much time on the part of any single herd and would provide an outlet for all northern reindeer owners beyond the reach of water transportation. We saw it as solving one of the most difficult problems confronting the deer men since it made possible adequate refrigeration at practically no operating cost.

Having overcome many seemingly insuperable difficulties and shown definite progress, it was our unanimous opinion that the Lomen brothers and the reindeer industry in Alaska were headed for success.

9.

I HAD RIDDEN behind reindeer many times with my Lapp and Eskimo friends. I had also visited and studied numerous herds during my fifteen years in Alaska. That experience was valuable when Lomen and Company started buying reindeer.

We purchased 1,000 head in 1915 from the Swedish Mission at Golovin; 319 from the Norwegian Mission at Teller in 1916; 1,717 from Andrew Bahr, John Nilima, and M. I. K. Nilluka in 1917; 2,032 from Nils Klementzen and Ole Bahr at Egavik in 1918; 819 from Peter Bals et al. at Egavik in 1919; 1,606 from Peter and Isaac Hatta at the Buckland in 1921—which, with the 1,200 we bought originally from Nilima, made a total of 8,693, at prices ranging from $18 to $30 per head. In addition, we had succeeded to herds at Kotzebue, Teller, Golovin, Egavik, and Buckland.

In all these dealings we received the assistance of government employees responsible for the reindeer operations under their control. They took keen interest in seeing white owners enter the industry, realizing that only in this way could substantial outside markets be built up.

There was the factual basis on which to estimate the possibilities of making reindeer a major industry of Alaska. Reindeer required no shelter. Alaska abounding in forage, the reindeer could subsist the year round. When trained, the Eskimo made an excellent herder. The meat of the animal was superior, with a flavor between breast of mallard duck and lamb. The skins and hides made up into very fine-grained leather.

Mounting divergence in growth trends of human and animal populations made conceivable a gradual change in national diet in the United States. Between the years 1900 and 1920 the population of the United States increased nearly 40 per cent while, according to the Department of Agriculture, the production of cattle decreased correspondingly. In 1900 there were 89 horned cattle for every 100 people in the United States; by 1920 there were to be but 43. As of the present, suffice it to say that there is a constantly increasing difficulty in supplying the American population with meat and meat products and in maintaining a surplus for export trade. There is a prospect of a beef shortage for this nation within a very few years.

Coupled with the decrease in cattle compared to population is the decrease in grazing lands. The great prairies of the old West are broken up by farms and can no longer support the great beef herds that ranged over these lands a few decades past.

The reindeer, being a domesticated grazing animal, living on the fresh, clean Arctic prairies, is fastidious in its selection of food and is therefore clean and free of disease. Living as it does in the open, it is not subject to tuberculosis, which is a disease of housing in the stable.

During my research I ran into the following theory of a great dietitian, Dr. Rowland Gilmore:

The flesh of the reindeer contains a much larger mineral value than meat of domestic animals, for the reason that they roam over a larger territory and consequently eat food raised on different soils. They also drink from widely scattered lakes and so receive the washings from many different types of soils. The flesh of animals that feed on lichens contains every necessary food element.

At first this statement sounded so extravagant that I consulted authorities at the Department of Agriculture in Washington. Dr. Louise Stanley, chief of the Bureau of Home Economics, suggested that lichens, on which reindeer feed, contain a high percentage of iodine. Later Dr. Harvey W. Wiley wrote me:

The suggestion that the reindeer may have food elements peculiar to the principal diet on which they live is in harmony with the established facts of nutrition. It is possible that the reindeer meat may contain some of the special elements which are found in the lichens and the other foods that the reindeer eat. I should suspect that this would be the case. Suggestion is made that the reindeer meat may be particularly rich in iodine. This is a statement which would be true if further investigations showed that lichens contained a considerable quantity of iodine. The reindeer meat industry is a new one, so promising that it deserves careful study, and approval of all who look for a larger and more varied and wholesome nutriment for our people.

I recall that one of the New York meat packers who handled thousands of pounds of reindeer boned meat pointed out to me that the iodine content of the meat was so great as to discolor the hands of the men handling it. Dr. Torleif Torland, a physician friend who for many years had practiced medicine in northern Norway, told me that, in regions where reindeer meat was the principal food of the people, he never saw a case of goiter.

During its first three years our company operated purely as a livestock corporation, without salaried officers. Our Kotzebue herd ranged more than 200 miles northeast of Nome, too far distant to take advantage of even local markets. We adopted the policy from the beginning of not competing with the Eskimo deer men in local markets, on the assumption that our province was to develop a market in the United States sufficient to absorb the surplus of all Alaska herds after local needs had been taken care of.

With the acquisition of the Golovin herd in 1915, we decided to butcher some of the steers and ship meat to the

United States. A drive was made from Golovin to Nome, 125 miles by trail, and seventy-four carcasses were prepared for market. It required upward of a year, with a salesman engaged for several months, to dispose of these carcasses.

Gradually our organization was built up. Shipments in pounds were as follows: 1916, 10,650; 1917, 33,000; 1918, 99,000; 1919, 37,000; 1920, 257,000. By 1920 we had distributors in Seattle, Portland, the twin cities, Oklahoma City, Chicago, New York, and Boston.

Our pioneering enterprise was to be fraught with many and diverse difficulties. Establishing the status of reindeer meat and other products was slow work. The first reindeer meat sold in the state of New York went to a Brooklyn dealer. The carcasses were quickly confiscated by the State Conservation Commission, the meat destroyed, and the dealer fined $125 for an assumed violation of state game laws; the Commission held the reindeer to be a game animal, hence making its sale unlawful.

There were, however, compensations among our disappointing business experiences. Although life in the North might at times prove rugged, it seldom was monotonous. Because of its location on Bering Sea, Nome was a crossroads of the world. As such it was often visited by colorful people. The explorers were of particular interest to me, as a breed of men, and individually. Beginning with the time Father, acting as vice-consul of Norway, wired an invitation to Roald Amundsen to visit Nome on his way south in the summer of 1906, I met many of them, and they always added to the richness of my experience with the Alaska in which I was by that time so thoroughly involved.

During the winter of 1905–1906 we had heard, from Eagle on the upper Yukon, that Amundsen, having negotiated the Northwest Passage, had traveled 600 miles from Herschel Island to advise the King of Norway by telegraph of the success of his expedition. It was thrilling to us to know that after 300 years of effort on the part of many nations this Norwegian had conquered that long-hoped-for passage north of the North American continent, from the North Atlantic westward to Bering Sea. He was three years en route.

Following Dad's invitation, on August 31, 1906, the United States Coast Guard notified him by telephone that about six miles to the westward there was a small sloop that appeared to be becalmed and they believed that Amundsen was on board.

It proved to be Amundsen's small sloop, the *Gjoa*. I was one of fifteen men who went up the coast by launch to render assistance. As Father was chairman of the reception committee he came along, and Mother with him.

We drew alongside, cheering the brave little vessel and her gallant crew. Captain Amundsen reported all on board to be well. He expressed pleasure at seeing the lights of Nome and said he would be greatly obliged if we would give him a tow. A rope was thrown aboard and made fast and we proceeded back at full speed to an anchorage in the Nome roadstead, where the *Gjoa* dropped her hook.

Captain Amundsen and Lieutenant Gotfred Hansen, second in command, entered our launch, and we headed for shore where the whole town waited to welcome the distinguished visitors. In the dusk it looked as though thousands of people were lining the beach. A searchlight ashore picked us up and followed us in. To the amazement of ourselves and the delight of our visitors Nome's brass band broke out in the strains of the Norwegian national anthem. Although in later years Amundsen reached the South Pole by dog team, flew across the North Pole in a semi-dirigible, and negotiated the North-east Passage by vessel, the navigation of the Northwest Passage remained his proudest achievement.

Two years later, in 1908, another explorer came out of the North. Einar Mikkelsen, a Dane, arrived by dog team. His vessel, the *Duchess of Bedford,* had been crushed by ice to the eastward of Point Barrow. Following several days of festivities, a purse of $600 was subscribed by several of our citizens, and the guest went on his way.

The summer of 1912 commenced an interesting and lasting friendship for me. Dropping in at our photographic studio at Nome after leaving my work at the Federal Court House, I saw a stranger sitting on the edge of a table talking to an Eskimo. When he spoke to the Eskimo in his native language, I became curious. Just then a friend came in and said, "Carl, I want you to meet Mr. Stefansson. We have just arrived. We were shipmates from Point Barrow on the Coast Guard Cutter *Bear.* What are you doing this evening?"

"I have no engagements," I said. "Could you and Mr. Stefansson come to our home so the other members of our family may share in the pleasure of this visit?"

"Fine. We would like nothing better," responded my friend.

My memory had clicked. I recalled a Sunday-supplement story published several years before of a young man who had an appointment at the mouth of the Mackenzie River, on the Arctic coast of Canada, to meet Einar Mikkelsen of the *Duchess of Bedford* and become part of that expedition as their anthropologist. He arrived on the Arctic coast in a blue serge suit, no hat, and a rifle with a quantity of ammunition. Then came word that the ship was crushed in the ice.

With the *Duchess of Bedford* lost, Stefansson concluded that there was no need to return south. As he couldn't join Mikkelsen, he decided to do some work among the Canadian Arctic Eskimo.

For the next four years he lived with the Eskimo, adopted their way of life, learned to speak their language, to hunt with them, and to eat their food, which he helped provide. The evening I met him he was comparing the dialect of the Nome Eskimo with that of the people he had lived with so long.

Brother George had a clothing store in Nome at that time. Stefansson required a new outfit before returning to the States. The clerk who waited on him, having heard that the stranger had spent years in the North living among the Eskimo, became curious.

"Four years in the Arctic?" he inquired. "How could you stand it?"

"Where have you been for the past four years?" Stefansson asked.

"Right here in this store."

"How could you stand it?" retorted Stefansson.

Stefansson is a tall, powerfully built man, once Viking blond, his hair now turned iron-gray. His deeply lined face expresses intelligence and kindliness; his manner is always gracious and unassuming, which is one reason for his popularity. As an explorer he has never resembled the conventional hero, tricked out by public-relations counsel and glorified by press agents. In the sporting sense, he was never out for records.

When anyone attempts to label him as brave, Stefansson is apt to be annoyed. Once he was asked to deliver an address on courage at a university but announced that he would talk instead about the vastly more important quality of adaptability.

Be that as it may, few feats in the entire history of Arctic exploration are regarded as more courageous than that of Stefansson and his two companions, going out on the floating ice of the Arctic Ocean in 1914 with forty days' food supply to live for months by hunting. Up to that time virtually all polar experts had agreed that there was no life in the Polar Sea.

Stefansson refused to accept this theory. He said the arguments against life in the Polar Sea might all be very reasonable, but he did not think the fish, seals, polar bear, and foxes were yet conversant with them. He would, he said, just go

93

out there, anyway, and live for a spell by hunting, to prove for one thing that the Polar Sea had been maligned! What he was doing was staking his life on the conviction that he was correct. He and his companions emerged from this trip a year and a half later in excellent health, thus proving his contention.

Stefansson always exhibited lively concern over any attempt to colonize the Arctic regions. For that reason he displayed keen interest in our work with the reindeer. He constantly contended that the Arctic was the logical place for expansion, as indeed it has turned out to be. *The Friendly Arctic,* the record of his last expedition, is the greatest handbook on the Arctic ever written. It is used for reference by many nations, and considered by all as the ultimate word on polar travel.

Other well-known explorers who were to visit us in Nome at one time or another were Lincoln Ellsworth and Riser Larsen of the *Norge,* and the Danes Knud Rasmussen and Peter Freuchen. Rasmussen had made the sled trip across the top of the continent from Greenland to Nome with two Eskimo companions. A poet and a great man, Knud could converse with all Eskimo people of the North given an hour's time to distinguish the difference in the dialect. There being a few Eskimo on the Asiatic mainland, Knud was anxious to meet them. He made his way across Bering Strait in a small schooner but was given no freedom by the Russians. When the Soviet officials learned that Knud was a Dane, that Denmark was a kingdom, and that Denmark's queen was a sister of the former Czarina, they cried, *"Kaput!",* making a gesture strongly suggestive of slitting the throat. Rasmussen could take a hint and was thus forced to return to Alaska without fulfilling his mission.

Peter Freuchen was the storyteller *par excellence.* He came north as technical assistant to Metro-Goldwyn-Mayer in the filming of his book about the Greenland Eskimo. Standing six foot three, with a peg leg and a flowing red beard, Peter was a sight to behold. He told us stories by the hour of the people, the Eskimo of Greenland. One tale made a lasting impression on me. It had to do with a total misunderstanding between natives and a conniving sea captain who exchanged trade goods for their fox skins. They howled with mirth, believing that the great sailor did not know the value of fox skins. While he busied himself with cheating them, they laughed among themselves over the fact that he thought they were stupid. Their reason? It never occurred to these guileless people that anyone would wish to cheat them.

Because of my Alaska residence, it was my privilege to meet many explorers in New York and Washington, as well as in Alaska, and to get to know them well. General Greeley, Fridtjof Nansen, Matt Hensen, Admiral Richard E. Byrd, Larry Gould, Bernt Balchen, Anthony Fiala, and Donald MacMillan were among them. Each name conjures up memories of pleasant visits and great admiration for their achievements.

With the passing years new accomplishments added to the glory of our friends. In 1912 word came that Amundsen had planted the Norwegian flag at the South Pole. Father cabled, "Amundsen Hobard [in Tasmania] Skaal Lomen." Just four words, but they reached Amundsen, pleasing him mightily.

The tragic disappointment of the British Scott Expedition came just eighteen days after Amundsen planted the Norwegian flag. Scott arrived to find Amundsen's marker "right on the Pole." One can imagine the feelings of the Scott party, nearing the Pole and discovering ski tracks that could only mean that the Norwegians were ahead of them.

The year 1920 was to witness the accomplishment of the Northeast Passage, north of Eurasia, by Amundsen in the motor vessel *Maud*. Amundsen was not the first; a fellow countryman, Nordensjold, had that honor. However, Amundsen was the first to circumnavigate the globe at the Arctic Circle.

Came 1927 and the race for the North Pole. Richard Byrd and Floyd Bennett in a plane; Amundsen, Lincoln Ellsworth, and Nobile in a semi-dirigible airship, the *Norge*. Byrd and Bennett were to attempt the flight from Spitzbergen to the Pole and back. The *Norge* was to cross the Arctic to Nome, passing en route over the Pole. There was plenty of rivalry, yet each party received the good wishes of the other.

Byrd was off first and made a thrilling flight. The *Norge* was off three days later. My brother Ralph had been commissioned by Amundsen to engage a large crew of men and have them at the airport at Nome with ropes to hold the *Norge* fast when she arrived.

When the flash came over the radio: *"Norge* with Amundsen and party at Teller, Alaska," I was in Minneapolis, 4,000 miles from Nome. Immediately I sent a wire to Ralph at Nome, 100 miles from Teller, which was the first he knew of the *Norge*'s whereabouts. Ralph dispatched our schooner *Silver Wave* to Teller to bring down the crew of the *Norge*. Our station at Teller boasted an ancient wireless sending set that had been out of use for several years. But the radio operator of the *Norge* repaired it, so our company station had the distinction of broadcasting to the world the success of their flight.

In connection with these two flights there was an interesting company incident. We supplied Byrd with his fur garments: reindeer parkas, mukluks, fur pants, and mittens, together with a small hickory sled, in case he and Bennett were forced down on the ice.

When Amundsen and Ellsworth reached Nome, they were taken to the Eni Club where they were to stay. As they entered, Ellsworth took off a heavy pair of reindeer mittens

96

and threw them on a table. Ralph saw them and inquired in surprise:

"Where did you get Byrd's mittens?"

"Well, they're Byrd's mittens all right, but how did you know?"

"Oh, I had them made for Byrd last spring." Ralph laughed.

They had been made in Nome and, together with other furs, shipped to New York to Byrd. They had been taken to Spitzbergen, worn by Byrd on his flight to the Pole and back, and presented by him to Ellsworth who made use of them on his flight in the *Norge*. Twice to the North Pole, with two separate expeditions, in less than a week's time! The Lomens also had the distinction and pleasure of supplying reindeer fur clothing for Admiral Byrd's first two Antarctic expeditions, and for Ellsworth's historic flight across the Antarctic.

The proposed flight of the *Norge* was to create great interest. In the spring of 1927 two officials of the United States Geological Survey, Dr. Philip S. Smith and Gerald Fitzgerald, made an overland trip from Fairbanks, Alaska, to the Arctic coast, reaching their objective early in June. Meeting an Eskimo with a dog team, they stopped to shake hands and pass the time of day. What they were most anxious to learn was whether the *Norge* had made the intended flight.

"Did anything unusual happen around here lately?" he was asked.

At first the Eskimo was vague. Finally, after they had pressed him with several questions, he announced:

"Oh, yes, one day Jesus and the whale, they go right over!"

In the summer of 1930 I happened to be in a hotel barbershop in Washington, D. C. The barber's hot towel was over my face when I heard a surprising announcement issuing from the radio:

"Admiral Byrd at Little America is attempting to talk to Alfred Lomen on board a ship off Nome, Alaska."

I figured that very likely Nome had been selected as being

about the most distant place anyone could think of. Then I heard my brother talking, but was unable to distinguish the Admiral's words.

Explorers are indeed courageous men. While I never became one myself, I am happy that I was able to touch the hem of their glory.

10.

IN THE FALL of 1914 William Lopp and Walter Shields decided that a Reindeer Fair should be held during the winter on Seward Peninsula. Eskimo herdsmen had little opportunity to exchange ideas because the herds were too widely separated, and the plan of a Reindeer Fair aroused great interest. The affair had to be scheduled in winter because travel was by reindeer and sleds and races could not be held in summer months when there was no snow on the tundra. Herdsmen were also busy in July and August handling the reindeer, marking and castrating them, et cetera.

Delegates were to be selected from among the most competent deer men with each herd. A week spent in friendly rivalry, competitions, and visiting would give everybody an opportunity to observe various methods in action and to exchange techniques of handling the animals. It was hoped this would result in increased interest in the industry and spur the deer men on to greater efforts.

The Eskimo village of Igloo was chosen as it was central for reindeer herds of that area and there was good moss pasture in the vicinity and plenty of wood for the camp stoves. The Fair was set for the second week in January. All local reindeer superintendents, teachers, and reindeer men were notified. Arrangements were made for supplying food to the delegates. The local superintendent at Igloo was instructed to select a good site, stake out race trails, set up tents, cut wood, and have stoves in readiness.

Mr. Shields invited me to be his guest, accompanying his party. We left Nome January 7, 1915, via Sinrock and Mosquito Pass. The party included Mr. Shields; Miss Harriet Kenley, his sister-in-law, a nurse and teacher of sanitation; Walter H. Johnson, assistant superintendent of the Federal Bureau of Education for the Nome District; Tautuk, an Eskimo and chief herder of the Nome Government herd; Amuktoolik, his brother—all as delegates; and myself. We were driving eight deer hitched to eight sleds, and leading Tautuk's fleet racer, Dynamite. Tautuk, who had high hopes of winning some of the races with Dynamite, handled four deer and three sleds, tandem.

We traveled twenty-two miles up the coast to Sinrock, where we put up for the night with an old sourdough and keeper of the roadhouse, our longtime friend Sinrock Charlie. Charlie, an excellent cook, not only supplied us with good food but with equally appetizing conversation.

Following along the Sinrock River the next morning, we had good going on the snow-covered ice. As far as the eye could see the country was covered by a white blanket, scarcely broken even by the willows dotting the landscape. Once Shields halted the caravan and pointed to two big white Arctic hares up the mountainside some distance ahead. Taking their rifles, he and Amuktoolik approached to within a hundred yards of their quarry. At a given word they fired simultaneously, killing both animals. They would make excellent mulligan stew for dinner.

We reached the camp of three white prospectors by noon of that day. They were thrilled when they learned that there was a woman in our party, as their camp had never entertained one before. Nothing was too good for us. We must stay for grub, partake of their best delicacies. One of our hosts raised a trapdoor in the center of the cabin. We saw a small hole, insulated by moss and sod, and in it a box of apples.

There was also ptarmigan, cleaned and frozen. We were soon seated around their hospitable board.

We planned to spend the coming night in an unoccupied cabin on the American River some twelve miles away and, as it was a difficult place to find, we asked our miner friends to give us directions.

"Right after lunch," one of them said, "I'll hook up our dogs, run to the top of the hill just beyond here, and point the way out to you."

The weather was none too good, with the temperature down around 30 below zero and a light wind blowing. We hooked up our deer and resumed the trail. When we got to the top of the hill, we found that our friend Gus Jones had not stopped but was far ahead on the trail leading up the Sinrock. We caught up with him some ten miles farther on. He had stopped to make sure we were able to follow his trail, since it was already growing dusk.

"It's only a little farther," he yelled to me, and sped on.

Rounding a bend some two miles on, we saw sparks streaming from the smokestack of a small cabin that was practically buried in a huge snowdrift. Gus had reached the cabin, built a fire, and made everything very comfortable for us. We felt he had greatly inconvenienced himself and invited him to share the mulligan with us and spend the night.

"No," he said, "I'll be going right back; it's good exercise for my dogs. Even though it's dark, they'll see me through all right."

Waving good-by, with twelve miles to go, he took off into the pitch black. The way he looked at it, it was no inconvenience to him. He had made certain that a lady would have comfortable lodging for the night, a privilege not often enjoyed around there. From our viewpoint, he had done us a big favor, for without his expert guidance we most certainly would have slept out in some snowdrift.

The next morning was cold, still 30 degrees below. After

replacing the firewood we had used, and laying a fire for the next traveler—the rule of the trail—we fastened the door securely and headed off into a stiff north wind. By early afternoon we reached the summit of Mosquito Pass, having covered fifteen rugged miles. We stopped to let the deer feed, unhooking them from the front of the sleds and tying them to the sides so that they could easily paw down through the snow and feed on the moss beneath. We ate a hasty lunch consisting of canned sardines, hardtack, and coffee from our thermos bottles. After a twenty-minute rest we hooked up the deer and continued on our way.

The strong wind blowing through the Pass cut channels in the snow, making travel extremely difficult. As darkness approached, it became impossible to see the deep channels that were causing the sleds to upset frequently. Our faces were frostbitten several times. A sting on the cheek, nose, or chin gave warning, but a vigorous rub soon remedied it. Reaching level ground near the Cobblestone River, we made camp where there was an abundance of moss for the deer. Placing two empty sleds upright for poles, we threw our tent over them and soon had comfortable shelter. The wind had dropped, the sky was clear, and the stars seemingly very low in the heavens.

We ate supper in our mushing togs. Two primus stoves served for the preparation of our food and to warm the tent. We soon crawled into our reindeer-skin sleeping bags and called it a day, weary but content, as we had made some thirty miles.

Mosquito Pass had always been considered hazardous for dog teams but downright foolhardy for reindeer. However, we met with no real difficulty and our trip added new laurels to the reindeer's stamina under severe conditions.

The next morning Tautuk served coffee to us while we were still in our sleeping bags. The weather was colder so we all dressed well. I got out my reindeer fur pants and three parkas, one of squirrel with fur side in, one of reindeer with fur out, and a drill parka to wear over both. The other members of the party put on warmer clothing, too.

We broke camp long before daylight and cut across country for Igloo, reaching our destination in early afternoon, having traveled 100 miles. Shortly before arriving at Igloo, we stopped while Tautuk and Amuktoolik donned their finest garments to impress the people of the village.

We were the first of the visitors to get there. All of the people of the village were out to greet us and we were given a royal welcome.

Within a very few minutes a shout went up from the Igloo boys: "Here come some more deer!"

The new arrivals proved to be the government teacher at Deering, Mr. Replogle, and the Deering delegate with fifteen sleds and twenty-five deer. They were dressed in fur garments made especially for the Fair, each man driving two deer and leading one with a trailer sled, their sleds bedecked with colors as gay as any to be seen on a parade float in the States. In that snowy landscape they presented a spectacular appearance. They had come direct over the mountains from Deering, 136 miles away, and had been seven days on the trail.

Close upon the Deering delegation came the Shishmaref delegation from a still greater distance, represented by two delegates and five reindeer. They had met with stormy weather that delayed their departure and forced them to make long drives to arrive on time. They drove upward of fifty miles a day which, in the short days of January, meant many hours' traveling in the dark.

The next visitor proved to be the daughter of the missionary at Teller, Miss Dagny Brevig, who arrived by dog team with an Eskimo driver. Miss Brevig, a beautiful young woman of eighteen who had grown up at the Mission, spoke the Eskimo language fluently and was the most competent interpreter it has been my pleasure to listen to. She acted as one of the interpreters during the Fair. All the Eskimo understood English and most of them spoke it but, strangely enough, they preferred the use of interpreters because of the many dialects among the delegates. Two interpreters were needed at many of the meetings so all would understand.

In late afternoon the cheering outdoors announced the arrival of more deer and more delegates, the Teller delegation. The Rev. Mr. Brevig accompanied them. Now delegates were arriving from all points of the compass.

Mr. Hunnicutt, the government schoolteacher at Igloo, and his wife were on hand to greet all comers. They had saved their Christmas turkey to serve when Mr. Shields arrived and it was in the oven. Tautuk and his brother joined their new Eskimo friends for a supper of reindeer stew with a bowl of seal oil in which to dip their meat while eating. The rest of us, including the Brevigs, enjoyed the wonderful dinner Mrs. Hunnicutt prepared.

In the evening everyone went to the schoolhouse. The Rev. Mr. Brevig opened the meeting with a sacred service, followed by a song of welcome written by an Eskimo from Igloo and sung by an Eskimo quartet. The schoolroom was filled to capacity with well over a hundred people. Mr. Shields explained the purpose of the Fair, after which several Eskimo responded, expressing their thoughts on the benefits of such a gathering of reindeer men.

The Fair grounds were five miles from Igloo on the Pilgrim River. The day following our arrival the delegates and our party drove to the site where tents had been erected by the Igloo boys for our accommodation.

The weather ranged from 30 to 40 below zero all during the week of the Fair, but there were no complaints about the cold. Our first evening in camp we walked a mile to the Kruzamapa Hot Springs, sulphur springs so hot it is necessary to stir the water with a paddle before venturing into the tank. A frame building covered the pool. Following our swim we sat and sweated it out in the steam room, then stepped outside for a roll in the snow in lieu of a cold shower.

Now the serious business of the Fair began. The first item of interest was the butchering and dressing by three different methods used by the Eskimo deer men, and another method explained and demonstrated by a member of the United States Department of Agriculture, then on a visit to Alaska. The delegates had an opportunity of witnessing the various methods and determining the one which they wished to use themselves.

Some deer from one of the Igloo herds stationed a few miles from the Fair grounds were driven up, the deer lassoed and butchered and, as an innovation, Simon Mukpeadluk carved up one of the carcasses, using only his belt knife.

Many deer men agreed that they were amply repaid for their time and expense in coming to the Fair by the butchering demonstration alone.

Next on the program was a rifle-shooting contest, 50 and 100 yards, five shots for each man at a three-inch target. Since most of the Eskimo had been hunters from birth, some excellent scores were made.

Following the Eskimo shooting contest, the delegates requested that the white men—we were three, Walter Shields, Walter Johnson, and I—try their skill. Though I was not the most expert shot of our trio, my shots for this particular event added up to the best score, so I was awarded the "blue ribbon."

After the shooting events I became the recipient of a gift from an Eskimo friend of mine. It was a small wooden toy rifle. Wrapped about the gun was a letter that read as follows:

Long time ago I see you shootem deer. I think mebbe you not savvy shootem rifle much. Long time you very much my friend. I feel plenty bad inside when I see you not much savvy shoot. I think mebbe when Fair come I make you big present. Too bad I no can give you good eye so you shoot good. Mebbe some big doctor sometime fixum your eyes so you shoot good! I think mebbe

I help you little bit. I think mebbe your rifle too big for you. Mebbe too strong for you. So here I give you present. Now I want you do what I say—so mebbe by an by plenty long time you savvy shoot a little bit—not too much!

This little rifle you all time shoot. You shoot um plenty time every day. Mebbe this rifle peluk [gone] by an by you ketch um one all the same. After while you savvy this little gun you buy um .22 Special. You shoot um that gun all the time, long time, plenty time. By and by you savvy .22 Special you ketch um .30 U.S. —all same government gun. You use um plenty time mebbe little bit you savvy that gun. Then you steal um .22 High Power. Plenty cost that gun! Mebbe you got no money better you steal um! Then you have big gun—all same man gun. Other gun all same woman gun.

Some mans work long time no can savvy shoot—mebbe you all same that kind. You savvy Seals [Walter Shields, who was standing right at my elbow]? Plenty can shoot that fellow. Plenty savvy rifle. He good man! Plenty can cook! Plenty can eat! Him good mans!

It was with mixed feelings that I received this present, since Shields took it all in with a broad grin. But I accepted it in the spirit with which it was given and thanked the Eskimo graciously for it, knowing that it was Shields who was the author of the letter.

Next came a burden race—distance five miles with two deer —burden 250 pounds of sand. The clear, cold weather proved ideal for driving reindeer. There were seven entries; the winning time, 16 minutes, 21 seconds.

During the evenings we had some interesting conversations about Eskimo and deer. The Eskimo is something of a humorist. His trials and tribulations are many. Civilized men would become despondent living under like conditions, but the Eskimo meets them lightheartedly. He exhibits no concern whatsoever for the morrow.

One evening the Rev. Mr. Brevig told us of his experiences when first arriving at Port Clarence Bay in 1894. He brought with him a small organ that was a source of great wonderment to the Eskimo.

One old Eskimo, upon hearing it for the first time, surveyed it from all angles and then tentatively estimated its dimensions with his arms in order to "find out the number of white people in the box." Later he told the Rev. Mr. Brevig to open up the box so he could see "the people who made so much noise." He exhibited an intense curiosity about these people who lived in the box. Judging from the noise they made, there must be many of them, and yet the box was quite small. He thought they must be a different sort of white man than the ones he could see in the church. The Rev. Mr. Brevig finally opened the organ and the old native was stunned to find no people in it.

Several evenings we had indoor contests such as sled lashing and sled-harness and fur-clothing shows. The purpose of the Fair was to instill in the Eskimo the possibilities the deer held for him. The competitive spirit is very much alive in the Eskimo. They take great pride in their dress and trappings of all sorts.

The Lapps had taught the Eskimo the use of harness for reindeer, and for such an occasion as this the Eskimo had embellished them in their own way and they were truly works of art.

No finer garment has ever been known to the north country than the parka, made and used by the Eskimo for the whole family. Reindeer fawn skins taken in middle or late July are considered prime for most purposes. For dress occasions the women are particularly fond of spotted skins, similar in markings to those of a calico pony, as they are more spectacular and attract more attention. Using her arms, hands, and fingers as measuring rules, the Eskimo seamstress makes the parka a perfect fit. Loose fitting at the shoulders, the sleeves take form with a large armhole, providing ample room for arm action. The sleeves close in as they reach the forearm.

The garment is knee length and at that point attains a flare. Even the hood is patterned in an ingenious fashion to give extreme ease of action and comfort. By hoisting the parka over the head and reaching for the sleeves, it soon falls in place. On the hood a band or ruff of wolf skin frames the face. This long hair of wolf-skin trimming blows across the face in a wind, thus protecting it from icy blasts. A narrow strip of wolverine, a shorter oily hair, protrudes from under the wolf skin next to the face, preventing the forming of tiny hairy icicles that come on other fur from congealed moisture of the breath.

Eskimo women have various ways of adding their artful ideas to beautify the parka. Their genius is most noticeable in the strip of three- or four-inch trimming around the bottom of the skirt of the parka. These bands are of geometrical design, cut from tiny pieces of white and brown reindeer fur, usually triangular in shape and perfectly fitted together. Each sewer creates or selects her own design, and the women vie with each other to make the handsomest garments for the family. Wolf-skin mittens also display the Eskimo art. The complete wolf head covers the top of the hand. The mukluk, or knee-length boot, offers opportunity for more fancy work.

All sewing of the fur garments is done with thread made from the back sinew of the reindeer. It outlasts any other material known for the purpose.

The main outdoor events of the Fair included lassoing of deer, throwing a lasso for distance, burden races, one- and two-deer races of five and eleven miles, four-deer teams—five miles, single deer pulling heavy loads and, for the grand finale, a parade of all delegates and visitors, with reindeer and sleds. This was a very colorful spectacle with flags and streamers flying and everyone dressed in the finest of fur garments. Many well-dressed women in the States would have been envious of the wonderful furs worn by the Eskimo women at that first Reindeer Fair.

Some of the evening talks by the Eskimo delegates were of genuine interest. Okok of Deering, winner of the rifle contest, gave a talk on shooting, showing how a man should stand, position of gun, how flinching and jerking the trigger throw the gun off the target, and how to overcome these faults by a steady pull and by watching the target to know just where the bullet hits. He concluded by saying, "Perhaps someday you will have only one cartridge and you will see but one thing to shoot at. If you have no food you must make that shot count!"

Allokeok of Shishmaref suggested, "When you work with deer, make your work effective. If you wish a good living from your deer, you should think and plan how to care for them. If you don't, your herd will decrease."

Simon of Council, best sled maker in the entire North, said, "They want me to talk of sleds and because they do I will, but I am afraid they will not learn much from me. Today I saw many kinds of sleds, sleds that were big enough for two sleds; sleds that were strong and others that were weak. A strong sled will not break in a day even if you have a bad trail and a heavy load, but a weak sled will not finish the day so well. When you make a sled for yourself you make it good, but many of you when you make it for sale make it not so good. You should make a sled as well for others as for yourself, also snowshoes. Make it always well, for then you can sell it, and if you should happen to want to use it yourself it will last longer. You who know mukluks know this: cheap mukluks are poorly made and are no good. Always make things for others as you would for yourself, for it will always prove to be the best."

One of the most picturesque events of the Fair was the lassoing contest. The contest continued for thirty minutes each day for three days. There were fourteen entries. The man lassoing the greatest number of animals during the ninety minutes was the winner. Only bulls without horns and marked with a cloth about the neck were to be counted. When once roped the animal was released and could again be roped.

The herd of more than 800 reindeer was driven to a large, flat expanse and the spectators surrounded the herd to make a human corral. At a given signal the lassoers ran to the center of the herd and the excitement began. It was an interesting sight, packed with action on the part of the spectators as well as the contestants, since the audience had to keep moving back and forth to maintain the human wall surrounding the herd. The trained collie dogs kept circling the outskirts of the herd, ready to pick up any deer that strayed through the crowd. The bulls, after once being lassoed, became quite tricky, dodging back and forth, running close to the other deer, and doing everything possible to avoid being caught again. At the close of the ninety-minute period the winner had eleven deer to his credit, three ropers being tied for second place with nine deer each.

The contest that created the most merriment was driving a wild deer a half-mile and then returning. There were fourteen entries. The herd was held, by men and herd dogs, back of the starting line. At a given signal the contestant was to enter the herd and rope, throw, harness, hitch up, and drive a hornless, unbroken bull one-half mile up the river and return to the starting point, unhitch, unharness, and remove the halter unassisted. The contestant could have his sled brought up to the point where he had his deer, but the man bringing it must give no actual assistance with the deer. Deer could be driven, dragged, or hauled.

This contest was the acid test of a man's ability as a reindeer man. When a wild bull was lassoed, it fought to escape and the driver was forced to throw it. When the assistant brought up the sled, the maneuvering to harness the struggling animal was laughable and very exciting. No sooner was the harness fastened than the bull started to run and would throw the driver all about.

One of the smallest contestants lassoed the largest bull in the herd and found it impossible to drive the beast at all. He threw the bull alongside the sled, which he tipped on edge, and then rolled Mr. Bull right onto the sled, tied him down, so he could not roll off, and started up the river, pulling the sled himself. I laughed until the tears rolled down my cheeks. And the usually phlegmatic Eskimo were in stitches, too.

Other contestants dragged their deer a short distance at a time, held it down while they got their wind, and then proceeded. There was no difficulty with the return trip. It was only necessary to turn the deer around. He spied the herd and was off at breakneck speed to get back as quickly as possible. We saw some hair-raising rides.

Our trail mate and guide, Tautuk, had been giving this event real thought but had confided in no one. We noticed he had draped his fur parka over the handle bars of his sled and, in addition to a towline of some thirty feet in length, he carried a second line of the same length with him. When he had roped and harnessed his animal, the assistant brought the sled close enough for Tautuk to secure the end of the towline to the animal's harness and to snap the second line, which turned out to be a driving line, to the halter of the deer. Then Tautuk slid off the thrown bull and, holding the driving line close to the animal's head, continued to give out more rope. The bull would not approach Tautuk but tried its best to break away. The parka draped over the handle bars of the sled looked like a man so there was only one direction in which the bull could travel—straight down the course.

Tautuk trotted abreast of the deer some thirty feet away. The bull would not turn back because of the parka and could not get away from Tautuk because of the firm hold he had on the driving line. They made good time to the halfway point. Then Tautuk turned the deer and they came traveling back to the herd with hurricane speed. Tautuk was an easy victor in the race. Many instances of native shrewdness of this character were displayed at the Fair.

The sled-lashing contest was very interesting to most of us since the lashings must withstand the battering to which the sled is continually subjected. The contestant stood alongside his basketlike sled. On the ground was a tarpaulin or canvas cover, a stove, a grub box, war sack, and sleeping bag. At a given signal the canvas cover had to be draped inside the basket of the sled, the stove, grub box, war sack, and sleeping bag stowed on the canvas, the ends of the tarpaulin wrapped over the load, a rifle and snowshoes placed on top, and all lashed and secured so no snow could enter. The same load was used for each sled, and the only contestants considered in this exhibition were those whose loads withstood the rough and thorough tests of the judges, who rolled the sled over and over several times. If the load was then in good condition and snowproof, the man's time was taken. Winning time for this event was 2 minutes, 24 seconds.

The big sporting event of the Fair was the eleven-mile one-deer race. The best and fastest deer of each delegate had been held out of the other events and saved for this race. It was in this event that Tautuk expected to race his reindeer, Dynamite. By this time Tautuk's chest was covered with blue and red ribbons. His brother, Amuktoolik, had none. Tautuk very generously suggested that Amuktoolik drive Dynamite, which he did. The winning time was 41 minutes, 38 seconds. Dynamite ran fourth. It was a very close race, with all of the first four deer coming in well bunched, only three-and-a-half seconds apart. Had Tautuk been driving, he probably would have won, since Dynamite always seemed to put forth extra effort for him.

The big race closed the Fair. The weather changed and it commenced to storm. Everyone broke camp and we drove back to Igloo for the distribution of the prizes. The Fair was unanimously pronounced a great success and a meeting was held to discuss plans for the following year.

With the promise of an annual Fair, a spirit of friendly competition was aroused. It indicated, too, that haphazard methods in use by the Eskimo would gradually be replaced by standardized methods of improving the herds. The natives would return from the Fair to their villages. Those who had won prizes would be heroes and accordingly stimulated to greater effort to win more of them in the future. Those who had failed to win anything at all would, it was hoped, make a greater effort in the expectation of winning a prize at the next Fair.

Therefore, reindeer people all over northwestern Alaska looked forward to the 1916 Fair. The location was changed from the previous site to the "Hot Springs." The time was set for February, one month later than before. The later date promised longer periods of daylight, but the reindeer would be far less picturesque, as most of the males would have shed their antlers. This deeply disappointed the photographers.

Invitations to the second Fair were extended to Alfred, Dr. D. S. Newman, in charge of medical work among the Eskimo of the Nome District, and me. Tautuk again accompanied us, and assisting him were Marcus, Henry, and Charlie, all Nome delegates and all experienced Eskimo travelers and deer men.

Alfred and I drove our own reindeer as some of our company employees had recently arrived from the Kotzebue Sound country with reindeer and turned the sled deer over to us.

We took a different route than the year before, up the Flambeau River, across the divide to Salmon Lake, and on through Golden Gate Pass to the Kruzamapa Hot Springs. Our party traveled with nine deer and nine sleds. Two deer and two sleds were under Tautuk's guidance. We were eight men, four whites, and four Eskimo. The ninth sled was used for transporting camp equipment. Each member of the party was an independent unit with changes of clothing, sleeping bags, and thermos bottles, as well as the customary compass, waterproof match case, belt knife, and rifle.

Between the handle bars of the sled was attached a canvas bag called a sled bag, with a snap flap to protect the contents from the snow. In this bag we carried extra socks, gloves, and mittens for emergency use, and small articles that might be useful during the day, such as pipe, tobacco, or cigarettes, matches, and shelled nuts for emergency rations.

In our pockets we carried extra pairs of gloves or mittens to be kept warm by the heat of our bodies. When the ones we wore became too damp for comfort, from handling the harness of the reindeer or other causes, we changed, donning the warm gloves from the pocket and depositing the damp ones in the sled bag.

In one of the rear corners of the sled we always carried a thermos bottle filled with soup, coffee, or tea. This was contained in a cylindrical bag made of winter reindeer skin with the fur inside, protecting the bottle from breakage. Everyone wore Eskimo footgear, fur for cold dry weather, sealskin boots for damp weather.

The morning of the third day on the trail a storm was raging when we awakened. The wind was so strong one leaned into it at a thirty-degree angle to keep balance. We were well equipped and, after a consultation, decided to travel. We had no rivers to cross so there was no danger of overflows. If the storm became too bad, we could always make camp. Often before, and now once again, I had great admiration for the Eskimo who, without hesitation and without landmarks to guide them, brought us safely through the blinding blizzard.

Toward noon of that day Walter Shields, Marcus, and I

were leading the caravan. I happened to glance back and discovered the rest of our party could not be seen. I quickly ran forward and suggested to Walter that we stop and wait for the others to catch up. He agreed. As I held the rear position I watched the back trail, although I could see but a few feet into the storm. After several moments I looked ahead again and found that Shields and Marcus had disappeared from view.

I determined to remain where I was, feeling certain that the reindeer would trail the deer ahead. I watched for some minutes when suddenly a dark shadow moved toward me. A reindeer passed me a few feet distant, then a sled, followed by another deer and another sled until six deer and six sleds passed by. They were all tied together, so I attached my driving line to the handle bars of the last sled and then sat on my sled wondering where Shields and Marcus might be.

A little later I felt a tug on my sled and discovered that the two missing members of the party had attached themselves to my sled. Tautuk and the others had not seen me as they passed, nor had I seen Shields and Marcus as they stood waiting for the long line, formed by our deer and sleds, to pass. There was less visibility that day than I had ever seen on the trail before. The delay of Tautuk and the others was due to the fact that Tautuk had suggested they fasten their deer and sleds together to avoid being separated.

We reached the Fair on schedule, but many of the delegates were delayed because of the severity of the weather. We were pleased to be on the grounds to meet the others as they arrived, for it was always a thrilling sight, with flags and banners flying, beautiful fur clothing, and men and deer covered with hoarfrost but happy. There was much laughter and handshaking as we greeted old friends.

For the second Fair, Mr. Shields had secured a small circus tent in which the delegates ate and slept. Here also were held the evening meetings and all articles made for the Fair were displayed.

Some sixty different events took place and several remarkable records were established, notably the running of ten miles by single deer and driver in 37 minutes, 8 seconds, and the pulling of a sled loaded with 2,242 pounds of sand by one deer for a distance of fifty yards. All records of distance, weights, and time were carefully and accurately taken.

This Fair proved an even greater success than the first one. Everything was better handled and the natives worked much harder. The various events served to develop a new and earnest incentive in the Eskimo deer men.

In addition to the fair at the Hot Springs, fairs were held that year at Noorvik, Shaktoolik, and at Akiak, thus covering the whole of western Alaska.

Mr. Shields made a farseeing observation at the conclusion of the Fair of 1916:

"In engaging in the reindeer industry there are two things to be studied—the reindeer and the Eskimo who has to be employed to take care of them. The Bureau of Education can claim no qualification for scientific study of reindeer, but the employees of the Bureau do claim to be especially qualified to handle the Eskimo. That is our work. We must never forget that to the Bureau of Education the reindeer industry is just one means of development of the Eskimo. To the white owner, the Eskimo is just one means for the proper development of the reindeer industry. That is important to remember."

11.

WITH THE approach of the 1917 Reindeer Fair, Walter Shields was on one of his far northerly trips. He wrote to me, requesting that Mrs. Shields and the Shields twins, Sally and Tom, aged four, accompany our party to the Fair, saying he would meet us en route.

Our party was a large one. Tautuk was our guide once more. Besides Mrs. Shields and the children there were Miss Anpher, secretary to the United States marshal; Dan Crowley, our field superintendent; William Marx, our Teller herd manager; Tautuk's wife Mary, with their infant child; brother Harry and I.

It was pure pleasure to me to be on the trail with sled deer. For one thing, you have greater comfort than with a dog team. Your outfit is not limited, because you can always hitch on another sled and deer if necessary; thus each person has his own sled, and plenty of room. He can ride or run, as he wishes. His sled is packed to make riding convenient. Good deer, well trained and with good sleds and harnesses, can be better controlled than an equally good dog team. Naturally this will be disputed by every dog-team driver. But I still maintain, from my experience, that good deer, driven by lines, make easier handling than voice-driven dogs.

To my mind an important part of the preferability of reindeer over dogs for winter travel is the safety factor. The menace of winter travel with dogs is in the possibility of sudden storms, causing delays in which food for the dogs may run out. A prime condition of animal transport is food, and reindeer will find their own, even if they have to dig it out from under the snow.

We traveled the Nome–Pilgrim River trail. Progress was slow because the snow was deep. Brother Harry had had infantile paralysis when four years old, leaving him lame and somewhat handicapped, but still a patient and willing traveler.

Leaving Nome, we tied most of the sleds together as some in the party were inexperienced in driving reindeer. On the first downgrade the reindeer tied to the handle bars of Harry's sled shied, capsized his sled, spilling him into a snowbank, then stepped on his face in passing, giving him a bloody nose. Harry jumped to his feet, laughing and taking it as just part of the game.

The third day out Walter Shields and his assistant, Simon Mukpeadluk, joined us at Nugget Road House.

The next day, approaching the dreaded Golden Gate Pass, we met one of Alaska's fine dog teams, Victor Anderson with his team of nineteen Siberians. Reindeer and dogs stopped some distance apart. Shields, Tautuk, and I walked over for trail information from Victor.

"I just came through the pass with a fair wind and drifting snow and found it difficult," he said. "With women and children in your party, my advice is not to attempt it with the wind against you. You will have to buck it all through the pass."

Our party held a conference. We were warmly dressed and decided to go on. The deer and sleds were tied tandem fashion, and the ladies were instructed to sit in their sleds with backs to the wind. Harry, not to be outdone by the other men of the party, rode the sled runners with the result that when we negotiated the pass and reached Hot Springs, we discovered that Harry's face from chin to ear, was badly frozen. Before going into the roadhouse we rubbed his face

118

with snow and applied the warmth of our hands to thaw him out. To Harry it was another thrill of the trail.

Our first evening at the Fair Walter Shields dashed off a poem that he presented with a flourish to Harry.

The toughest musher in the bunch,
The greatest punisher of lunch.
The one who faced the stiff north breeze,
And laughed though chin and cheek would freeze.

The one who dared the Golden Gate
To make him break his Hot Springs date.
Who smashed his nose and shed his gore,
Then mushed and ate and mushed some more.

Who put each roadhouse on the bum,
The "Nugget," too—that's going some.
He drove his deer like twenty Lapps,
Which means one Eskimo—perhaps!

Then here's to Harry, good old scout!
Who dragged his deer when they played out.
And here's to Harry, game old sport!
For facing storms is sure his forte.

Three cheers for Harry—tough old whale;
The King of all the Reindeer Trail.

The Reindeer Fair in 1917 is one that will always linger in my memory. The Eskimo delegates arrived with their sled deer from all points of the compass in finer and more colorful costumes than ever before. Even the harness of their reindeer was ablaze with color. Beautifully carved pieces of walrus ivory were made into buckles and clasps to connect various parts of the harness. Pompons of bright-colored yarns the size of tennis balls—reds, yellows, and greens predominant—were fastened at various points, and the five-inch-wide strip of harness across the back of the deer was a work of art. It was at a time when the herders of each village were regarded as the leading men of the community and looked up to by all other Eskimo. Consequently, they must dress the part. The style and quality of their clothing indicated their social standing in the community.

The fairs adopted a flag of their own, a red reindeer on a white field, with a blue border. It was about ten feet square, the pride and joy of the herders, and shared honors with the American flag.

A very impressive event connected with the Fair was the salute to the flag each evening. One of the teachers would play "America" on a small field organ. From the back of the tent in which the evening ceremonies were held two of the most prominent herders would march, each with a 30-30 rifle. Next came an old Eskimo man carrying an American flag. He was followed by two younger men with rifles. They lined up in front of the gathering and sang, "America." During the entire ceremony the audience stood and held their right hands at salute. It was a real thrill to see older Eskimo, men and women of the village, struggle to their feet and hold that salute. I noticed some of the older folks, who did not thoroughly understand the salute, holding their hands over their eyes, and I saw their lips move as though in prayer. There are no people who love and revere their government more than the Eskimo.

During this Fair we had two bright, clear nights when the moon was full, and the Eskimo indulged their passion for playing football. Their "football" was a sealskin ball stuffed with reindeer hair. They tumbled out of their tents, running after the ball and falling over one another in great delight. In this game they kick the ball rather than attempting to carry it. When the snow is soft, it is difficult to run and propel the ball along, but soon it becomes hard-packed, then the slippery surface provides all the more fun. Eskimo merriment at such times is spontaneous and makes one glad that a people perpetually faced with an existence as grim as theirs can find such ready escape in play.

The most laugh-provoking event was always the wild-bull race. It invariably was a mad struggle to find out who would be tossed to the ground, the man or the reindeer, when the herder "bulldogged" the deer and attempted to throw him to the ground so that he might harness him. In spite of the fact that more accidents occurred in this event than in any other, it never lacked for contestants, since all the Eskimo considered themselves "plenty good" at bulldogging the deer. The deer horns are sharp and the animals become frantic in the attempt to escape what they consider punishment. The deer's feet are their most wicked weapons, since they are extremely sharp. Always the bulldogger must strive to keep the animal close to him to prevent the deer from rearing and using his forefeet. It was a tough battle of endurance between the bulldogger and the deer.

The Ipanee (old-timer) fire-making contests were exciting. Old Seecup Seraluk, in his wolverine wig, vigorously whirling his fire drill, the sweat streaming from his wrinkled face, got the most applause. Some thought his success was due in part to the red flannel shirt he wore, but anyhow he made a fire in 1 minute 32 seconds. Best time for the young men was 35 seconds.

Men on the trail do not eat snow as reindeer do, as there is danger of chilling the stomach, so a snow-melting contest was held, to see who could get the most water quickly under difficult conditions. Each man was allowed only one match, the idea being to whittle his own kindling and melt a tin cupful of snow. Titkak of Noatak won in 9 minutes and 37 seconds.

The delegates took turns at cooking for the crowd and the

most frequent question asked was, "What nation will cook tonight?" One "nation" woke the camp one morning at five o'clock for breakfast. To get even for this another "nation" "dished up" the enormous bean cakes, which are standard ration for the herders, though everyone expected something better on such a festive occasion. These bean cakes are made far differently than they would be in the States. A huge kettle filled with white navy beans is hung over a steady fire. They are simmered for hours. When the beans are tender, sliced reindeer meat and back fat from the deer are thrown in and cooked until it becomes a gelatinous mass. This mixture is poured into deep pie tins and allowed to freeze. The cakes are then tossed into a carrying sack and can be carried around all winter, if necessary. When it comes time to eat them, the procedure is very simple. A cake is placed in a large frying pan and heated piping hot. Scalding coffee or tea, plus a portion of bean-cake ration, makes a substantial meal for a man on the trail.

A song written for this Fair by one of the Eskimo delegates was greatly enjoyed by all and destined to be sung many times.

Tumee Seeko Aseruk
(The trail on the ice is bad)

Sled deer song number one by Kobuk

Long time sled deer plenty savvy me
All the time I travel, much I see,
But one trail makes me much iregee,
Drive me over rock or niggerhead,
Anywhere at all that I can tread,
But that shing seeko much I dread—
Tumee seeko aseruk!

Once I climbed, oh my! a big divide,
Plenty steep so white man could not ride;
Then I look down on the other side,
All the river ice was slick and glare,
Overflows of emuuk too were there;
Then we sled deer, oh! we plenty scare—
    Tumee seeko aseruk!

Konyeet scare of ice, stop in the brush,
Sled stuck tuk in overflow and slush,
Men they pull and holler "oof" and "mush"
Quick all savvy peluk, soon get mad,
White man nothing speak, but much think bad,
Eskimo talk innuit—no glad—
    Tumee seeko aseruk!

Sled him skid, and reindeer slip and slide,
Go two steps, then legs they spread out wide,
Fall and maybe broke something inside,
Mukluks slip and men all same as dance,
Then—oh my! sit down on deerskin pants,
Yet they want the deer to take a chance—
    Tumee seeko aseruk!

Look to me men by and by should know,
(Not Nulamuit, but the Eskimo)
That on ice it no good to go,
Long time sled deer, plenty ipanee,
All the time I savvy what I see,
Man, him peluk brains, it looks to me—
    Tumee seeko aseruk!

(Iregee, afraid; seeko, ice; emuuk, water; Konyeet, reindeer; peluk, gone; innuit, Eskimo; Nulamuit, white man; ipanee, old.)

In 1918 the young men of Alaska, including brothers Ralph and Alfred, were inducted into the army. Stationed for some weeks at Fort Davis, a few miles east of Nome, the local contingent was ordered to sail on the last steamer of the year, to report at Camp Lewis near Tacoma, Washington. I had been appointed Federal Food Administrator under Herbert Hoover for northern Alaska and was a passenger on the same boat. Two days from Nome sickness broke out among the passengers and soon developed into an epidemic. Upon arrival in Seattle, November 5, our ship was met by seventeen ambulances. Ralph was in charge of the enlisted men and had just enough well men to carry the sick ashore. Thirty-five of the passengers and ship's crew died. We then learned that the disease was the dreaded "Spanish influenza," now popularly known as "the flu."

Our ship, on its northbound trip to Nome, had carried the disease. The day following our arrival in Seattle we received the terrible news that influenza had broken out in Nome, and that among the first to succumb was Walter Shields.

Within twenty days' time, 21 whites and 187 Eskimo died. The epidemic spread up and down the coast, causing the death of many whites and more than 700 Eskimo. Some of the smaller villages were completely wiped out. The epidemic proved a severe blow to the reindeer industry, as scores of the best and ablest of the Eskimo reindeer men died.

Through the estates of the Eskimo reindeer men who died, the title to the animals was spread to their many heirs, most of whom were minors. Adjoining our Teller herd was an Eskimo herd known as the California herd. All adult owners and herders had perished, and the herd was now uncared for. Many of the orphaned children were taken into the Lutheran Mission near Teller. The Mission called upon us for help, and on our recommendation the California herd was mixed with our Teller herd. The former was a small herd, the deer so marked that there could be no loss of animals to the owners. The new owners of the California herd became known as "The Orphans."

The losses from influenza were appalling. Most of the real leaders among the Eskimo reindeer men succumbed. With Walter Shields' death the reindeer service lost not alone his great ability but all of his enthusiasm and imagination, qualities so necessary in the development of any new industry.

The reindeer fairs were never revived.

12.

OUR COUNTRY'S treatment of the American Indian has been most unsavory, as history proves. Over the years the general opinion grew that the whites look on any primitive people as common prey to be exploited.

But in Alaska, following the establishment of civil government and the advent of permanent American traders, the white man soon realized that his ultimate success depended in great measure upon the well-being and development of the native people residing within his trading area. It become enlightened self-interest, "good business," for the trader to assist his natives in their everyday concerns such as hunting, fishing, and purchasing. With the passing of time it became clear that the most successful traders were those who had around them the most progressive natives. Thus the practice grew of helping the natives to help themselves.

When the whites entered the reindeer industry in 1914, the attention of most residents of western Alaska was fixed on gold placer mining. The reindeer industry was of little or no interest to them.

But then herds increased in numbers, plants were constructed, ranges equipped. The white owners employed Lapps and Eskimo, together with a few white superintendents or foremen. And it was the Eskimo who were the herders and watched over the deer.

The Lapps knew the reindeer and appreciated its great worth. The Eskimo soon learned that the animal was a great asset to him, as it furnished meat for food, warm skins for clothing and bedding, and supplied a means of transportation. The white owner had to look beyond local needs and requirements. His real interest was to create a commercial industry; to raise the animals on the tundra of the North and to ship the hides and meat to the markets of the United States. It was a work of fascinating elements: a most interesting and docile animal to work with, a native people of high caliber who required aid with their problems and who were co-operative by nature.

Almost virgin pasturage of millions of acres constituted fine grazing lands of which no other domesticated animal could take advantage, because of the rigors of the country. The members of our family felt that here was an unparalleled opportunity that could come to few: to build a new industry; to develop a new food product in so far as the American people were concerned; to assist a primitive people in becoming self-supporting. When it became necessary to look to the States for funds with which to carry on, our argument that a native people would be assisted was always the one that carried the most weight.

There were Eskimo-owned deer in all herds, and some of our animals ranged in Eskimo herds as strays. During the early years the animals were handled in circular corrals; when they had to be handled, all animals, including fawns, were roped. It was rough on the animals and many were crippled. Owners and ropers tried to mark a fawn with the same mark carried by its mother, but in the confusion of the corral this system was difficult and soon became impossible with the greatly increased numbers driven into the corral, approximating 4,000 deer at a time. A fair apportionment of fawn and unmarked adult deer had to be made, so the percentage system of marking was established. A record was kept of all deer and their ownership. The new crop of fawns was marked and distributed according to the number of female deer belonging to the several owners. When a herd had been handled, a complete record was made and an "over and short" list prepared that showed all owners who had received more or less than the increase to which they were entitled; corrections were made at the next handling. This bookkeeping was rather puzzling to the Eskimo owners, but eventually was adopted throughout the reindeer country.

At a meeting in Nome the Eskimo representatives were asked which marking method they preferred.

"According to mother," they said, "but can't do it because herds are too big."

Reindeer are marked by cutting notches in the ear, and all owners had their individual marks to identify the animals. It is preferable to apply the mark when the animal is young, as the ears then are thin, and marking causes them little inconvenience.

The matter of the homing instinct of reindeer was disputed by many reindeer men. Even W. T. Lopp, among the most experienced of the early department officials, said he had never known of a Siberian, Lapp, or Eskimo deer man who believed reindeer returned to the place of their birth.

During the early years of our company we secured 20,000 buttons, numbered consecutively; these were placed in the ears of the animals. Some 15,000 were used and entries made in a large volume which we called *The Button Record*.

When deer were handled for any special purpose, the numbers of the buttons were listed and sent in to the home office, where the record was kept. Two large drives of males, two years apart, were made from our northern herds south to the Golovin and Teller herds, a distance of more than 200 miles. Seven hundred animals—500 bulls, 200 steers—were brought down on the first drive. A record of all 700 was entered. Two years later the second drive from the same northern herd took place. And our organization was surprised to learn that a great many of the deer of the second drive, who had been transferred to the Golovin or Teller herd two years before, had drifted away during that time and returned to their home pasture!

Because of our enlarged work and several herds, with equipment far superior to any in use in other herds, we were intensely interested in constantly learning all we could about the reindeer. When walking, the reindeer produces a peculiar crackling sound, caused by the working of sinews just above the fetlock. This sound, as well as an oily substance that exudes from a gland between the toes, forms a dual system of sound and scent signals. The Lapps claim that the reindeer "oils his horns" with the exudation of the gland and can "shape the antlers." It is, indeed, often seen to rub its horns with one of its hind legs. This is, however, probably due to an itching sensation caused by the growth of the tines.

The hair of the reindeer has been developed by nature in such a way as to protect the animals from freezing in the most inclement weather. However, sudden and extreme cold after a rain or thaw is a severe test and is sometimes disastrous, especially to the young animals. Such weather conditions often cause starvation of large numbers because an icy coating and crust cover the ground and the animals cannot dig through to the moss.

Owing to the apparent necessity for a change of food, and perhaps also to avoid the fly pest, reindeer seek new pastures in summer, preferably the seashore, but in high altitudes as well. They also seek sheltered fawning places. In feeding, they travel long distances, nibbling as they go. Thus their natural range becomes very extensive.

It is interesting to watch a reindeer herd feeding. The front of the herd appears to be stationary, the rear always on the move. The animals head in the same direction. When an animal finds itself at the rear, it stops feeding and travels through the herd until it reaches the front. It feeds there until it is again at the rear of the herd and then repeats the process.

The reindeer is the most docile of animals. During the summer season, when the herds are corraled for marking, with several thousand deer in the corral, young children four or five years of age may play safely in the middle of the corral with the herd milling about them. That could not be done safely with any other domesticated animal. When confined in the wings or chutes of the corral, the animals will raise their horns to avoid striking the herder or handler. Of course, when they stampede it is a different matter, as then they are compressed into a compact mass and will trample over anything in their path.

The herders lead or follow the reindeer on the open range. One of Lapland's immortals was Johan Turi, author and sage. Writing of the reindeer, he said:

The reindeer were created before man, and man was created simply to look after them and follow them wherever they go, and support himself by them. In his own estimation, man is much wiser than the reindeer; but in spite of that he must trudge along behind the reindeer wherever they go. It is quite reasonable that the reindeer ought to do what man thinks; but man has not the sense to do it in just the way the reindeer thinks. Man assumes he is looking after the reindeer, whereas the reindeer probably thinks he is looking after men.

Once our field superintendent, Dan Crowley, happened to be covering the Teller range during the fawning season. He came upon a very young fawn that seemed lost from its mother. A quarter of a mile away he could see a number of deer, so he tried to "shoo" the fawn in their direction. The little thing would run a short distance, then circle back to the spot where it was found. Realizing that the little one could not be driven, Dan walked to the adult deer and drove them back to the fawn.

When they were still some distance from the youngster, a female deer separated herself from the rest of the herd and ran to the fawn. For a moment she nuzzled it, then struck it a severe blow, knocking it flat on the snow. Dan ran toward the mother, angrily calling her a brute. But the fawn picked itself up, and fawn and mother trotted peacefully back to the rest of the herd.

What had happened was that the mother had left her youngster in a sheltered place to rest and it was supposed to stay there until she returned for it. The mother carefully trains the youngster to remain still while she is gone, in order to avoid the danger of an attack by some predatory animal. Unwittingly Dan had caused the fawn to be punished, by forcing it to move when Mama wanted it to stay quiet.

The early system of circular corrals, driving in the entire herd and roping all animals to be handled, was slow and often resulted in great damage to the deer. With several ropers in the corral there would be great excitement, the herd would mill nervously, and confusion was increased by workers on foot vying with one another as to who could rope the greatest number of animals. For some reason they seemed to find it great sport to throw the animals as heavily as possible. At the close of the day's work the corral would be opened and the herd released, only to be driven back the following morning as animals that had already gone through the ordeal could not be cut out.

One evening following such a day I sat on the corral fence and watched the herd let out. The deer had been held from their food for many hours and made a frantic rush to get away. Adult and fawn cripples brought up the rear, many limping, and a number with broken horns. It seemed unfair that the same animals should be forced back into the corral the next day. It was, I reflected, a crude, cruel, costly, and inefficient procedure and an improvement certainly was needed.

I gave the idea much thought, and the following winter my brothers and I drew up plans for a new corral system. The following spring we shipped in lumber and engaged a carpenter to carry out our idea. We retained the circular feature of the old corral, but in the big corral we built a series of pens along the side, graduated in size, each separated by sliding doors, the smallest one leading to a long chute thirty or more feet in length. The tally keepers, bulldoggers, and markers took their places at the end of the chute farthest from the corral.

We wanted a site for the corral, if possible, on a peninsula that could be fenced off and form a pasture of sufficient area to accommodate the entire herd. The corral was constructed at the outer edge of the pasture and the chute led to the open range. Three or four thousand reindeer were driven into the corral—a number sufficient for one day's work. After waiting for the herd to quiet down, a number of men entered the corral, using a long strip of burlap as a moving fence, and cut off a hundred or more animals, driving them into the first small pocket. From that pocket a few animals were moved along to the adjoining pocket, and finally into the chute. As an animal that already bore an earmark came through the chute, its ownership and sex were called by the Eskimo chief herder and recorded by white and Eskimo tally keepers. The animal was then permitted to return to the open range to feed.

The fawns were taken by the men stationed at the side of the chute, who grasped them by the horns and passed them on to the markers. Mothers and their young were often separated for some time and there were great bleating and grunting until they met again.

Our first attempt at improvement of the corral system was made at our Golovin and Buckland herds. Brother Alfred went to the Buckland, I to Golovin. Upon my arrival I arranged for a competent man to be stationed at each sliding gate. The first small corral was filled and the deer carefully moved along. The chute was constructed three feet wide at the bottom, thirty to forty feet long, with sides flared out at the top to permit the passage of the wide antlers. On the first try we discovered that the chute was so wide it enabled the animals to turn around and go back when they saw the men stationed at the end of the chute. We stopped all work immediately, moved one side of the chute in, and made another try at it. We kept on experimenting until the width of the chute at the bottom was but six inches, and the problem was solved. This revolutionized the system of handling a herd of reindeer during the marking season.

When the Lapp and Eskimo herdsmen saw the results they yelled out, "Now we can throw away our lassos!"

More improvements were made until we were able to handle 1,000 animals an hour, including marking and castrating. Bulls are castrated to make them steers. This produces a more palatable meat. Our method of handling the herds was an eye opener to Western cattlemen, many of whom later watched the procedure. Brother Alfred went me one better at the Buckland and had two chutes constructed. There was always a flow of deer at the end of one of the chutes; the marking crew simply moved from one chute to the other. The chute system was adopted for all herds in Alaska.

The method of marking reindeer by notching the ears had been used for generations, both in Siberia and in northern Europe. Now we wondered if branding would be preferable. We decided to experiment on a few deer. We selected a brand—the "broken circle"—had branding irons made, and agreed to apply the brand to the flank of the animals. Again Alfred took the northern herds, Kotzebue and Buckland, while I traveled south to Golovin and Egavik.

Upon reaching Golovin, I realized we had not agreed upon which flank to brand. I went right ahead with the plans, certain that Alfred would select the same flank as I, for reindeer always mill clockwise and the left flank is the one exposed. We therefore applied the iron to the left flank of the few animals branded.

Branding reindeer is not a simple matter. The hair of the animal is thick and the skin is thin. The person applying the brand must use great care not to burn the animals. We first applied water to the hair to wet it down and control the brand. If the iron was held too long, it would cause a deep burn and suffering to the animal. We applied the brand to several hundred animals and also earmarked them to make certain the ownership mark would remain. Upon our return to Nome several weeks later Alfred and I compared notes.

"By the way, Al, which flank did you brand?" I asked.

"Right, of course."

"Why do you say, 'Right, of course'?"

"Because the herds mill counterclockwise and it is the right flank that is exposed."

"There must be a mistake here," I protested. "I have handled herds for some years and have yet to see a herd turn counterclockwise."

"You must be mixed up, Carl," he disagreed. "I have never seen a herd mill clockwise and I have handled them quite a while, too."

During my trip afield I had taken a lot of pictures of both herds being handled, many of which were snapped within the corrals and showed the deer milling. I brought out a dozen or more photos and Alfred looked them over.

"Do you know," he said, puzzled, "I have never seen a herd mill like those pictures show."

We had made a curious discovery. All herds mill. An individual herd never varied in the direction it milled. Our herds were only a few hundred miles apart, yet they milled in opposite directions. Had they been located north and south of the equator we would have credited the rotation of the earth. We considered the location of the corrals in reference to the sea—in reference to rivers—but why one herd always turns one way and the other herd mills the opposite way is still a mystery to us.

We did, however, appreciate the value of the discovery and the importance of it in relation to the proper construction of the corrals. A herd owner contemplating the construction of a new corral must first ascertain the direction in which his herd mills, as a herd will more easily drift into the separating pens when they are constructed on the proper side of the corral, in accordance with the way the animals mill, thus greatly lessening the work of the men handling them.

After we had acquired several herds, in 1918, we tried to improve the living conditions of both Lapp and Eskimo. The year following the purchase of the Buckland herd, Alfred made a trip to the north by dog team, to the winter quarters of the herd. The weather was extremely cold, 50 degrees below zero, and he was surprised to discover that the winter camp consisted of only a few canvas tents.

"Why don't you build some log cabins here?" he inquired of the natives. "They would certainly be more comfortable."

"We don't know how long we'll be here."

"How long has this location been your winter camp?"

"Oh"—a pause—"about eighteen years."

Arrangements were shortly made for logs to be cut on the upper Buckland River where there were good stands of spruce timber, for both cabins and corrals. Under the joint efforts of Lapp, Eskimo, and whites, sufficient logs were cut during the winter months. They were floated downstream following the spring breakup of the river, and a new Buckland village constructed at a more advantageous location, with the Eskimo occupying one bank and the Lapps and whites the other.

I often wondered which had the stranger habits, the Lapps or the Eskimo.

13.

OUR CORPORATION was small, the stock issue closely held. Our income was modest, partly because of continuing lack of sufficient ocean refrigeration to carry our product to American markets.

When we needed funds, a block of stock was issued and distributed at par to our stockholders on a pro-rata basis. Our construction campaign was ambitious, in part instigated and backed up by the more prosperous among our stockholders.

"We will guarantee payment," they urged.

Sometimes we were affected by external events. One Saturday afternoon in midsummer 1921 word came to Nome that a bank in Tacoma, Washington, had failed. This was to have a great effect on our business.

The president of our Nome bank came to see Dad, who was attorney for the bank.

"Our correspondent bank in Tacoma has closed its doors!" he exclaimed. "The news has already reached several of our depositors; the result is that a large part of our cash was withdrawn this morning. It's fortunate this is Saturday and we closed at noon. The nearest bank, at Fairbanks, is 600 miles away. The trip up the Yukon and return would take two weeks so they're of no help in this situation. If we open the bank Monday, we won't last two hours. To protect all depositors there's nothing I can see to do but close the bank."

"Let me sleep on it," Dad said gravely. "I'll see you in the morning. In the meantime, make no move."

Sunday morning word was sent round to all depositors and business interests who could be reached of a meeting to be held that evening at Eagles Hall. Half of Nome turned out. Father opened the meeting and made a comprehensive statement.

"Our bank is solvent," he assured them. "There is no way of getting additional funds here in time to help out because the nearest bank is at Fairbanks, hundreds of miles off. If depositors insist on withdrawing their funds, the bank will be forced to close its doors. But if the people of Nome will simply carry on as usual, the bank will be in a position within a short time to meet all demands, and there will be no losses."

Father concluded his statement by proving that he was not asking anyone to do what he wouldn't do himself.

"If you agree to carry on," he said, "the Lomen family will pay into the assets of the bank, in the event of a closure, the sum of $5,000."

Others quickly came forward with like guarantees until $100,000 was subscribed.

Monday morning the main street of Nome was alive with the interested and the curious. The curtain on the front door of the bank was raised promptly at ten o'clock, and a cheer went up. People went into the bank all that day, their money and passbooks in plain sight, to make deposits. At closing time the bank's cash condition had been improved by many thousands of dollars, and Nome went on without any bank failure.

Nevertheless, with the closing of the Tacoma bank and of another in Seattle we personally lost the financial backing of our most valuable stockholder, Jafet Lindeberg. He had not only backed our enterprise, but had been one of those who urged us to develop important improvements. But since he was heavily hit by the bank failure, he was no longer able to help us carry the responsibility of developing the industry. Our company fell heavily into debt and it was urgent that we find additional financing.

Father made a hurried trip to New York. He was recalled, however, to accept appointment by President Harding as judge of the Federal District Court at Nome. Our officers then decided that I should go to New York to hunt for new capital. Reindeer capital in New York! What an assignment!

Though difficult, it proved to be an interesting adventure, extending over a period of several years. During the most trying months my expenses were paid by my younger brothers out of the proceeds of our small private business, the drugstore and photographic studio.

I learned that different types of people reacted in different ways to the word "reindeer." To the average American in the metropolitan centers it conjured up Santa and his prancing steeds. To cattle and sheep men it brought the specter of competition. To the social worker it suggested a new field of welfare: the need for supplying food, clothing, and advice to the native people of Alaska. To the northern whites with capital, reindeer suggested commercial enterprise. To the government bureaus it meant enlarged appropriations. One way and another, although the reindeer industry is old in history, I found out how little was really known about it in our own country.

The first person I arranged to meet in New York was a man very much in the public eye at that time, my old friend the great explorer Vilhjalmur Stefansson. He was naturally very much interested in our efforts to develop the reindeer industry, being himself the Arctic's greatest publicist. He had written articles about reindeer and musk oxen and, moreover, always was a willing and valuable friend of any sincere effort to prove the suitability of the far North to certain branches of industry.

Through Stefansson I met a broker in Wall Street. I was looking for $200,000, and he listened to my story.

"No," he said, surprisingly enough, "if it were $2,000,000 that you wanted, we would be interested. But $200,000 is too small for our house. Don't give up, though. I know another broker who is just the man for this deal. I will invite him to lunch with us tomorrow at the Bankers' Club and will introduce you."

The next day I met Edmund Seymour of 45 Wall Street, who was definitely interested and took me to meet his attorney, Leonard D. Baldwin, of the law firm of Griggs, Baldwin & Baldwin.

Mr. Seymour entered into an agreement to arrange for a $200,000 bond issue. Bonds were printed, salesmen engaged, literature prepared. We were all set for our big campaign when Mr. Seymour's brother passed away suddenly. Mr. Seymour was appointed executor and administrator of the estate, and as that took up all his time I continued to "bleed to death" in the reception room of his Wall Street office.

When eight months had passed, I asked him for a release from the contract we had entered into. He realized that his brother's estate would still monopolize much of his time, and he generously complied.

Now I found myself in a financial maze that apparently led nowhere. I made many contacts, had innumerable experiences; no group was too large, none too small for me to tackle. Personally or through friends, I looked high and low for aid, including such corporate groups as the Rockefellers, Fords, Whitneys, even Stinnes in Germany, besides many others.

Whereas many men in New York professed to be able to "deliver the goods" in raising capital, I learned that most of them were false alarms when it came to actual performance. Some of my experiences were weird. I recall one that is fairly typical.

One evening a man called me at my club, saying that he

wished to meet me, and we set a time. Through him I was introduced to a wealthy man who was much in the public press, because of divorces, breach-of-promise suits, and other family difficulties. But I was in no position to refuse help from almost any source.

The wealthy friend gave a large stag dinner one evening at a famous New York club and I was invited. I found myself sitting next to an official high in Standard Oil of New Jersey. In the course of the dinner he turned to me, saying, "You see the gentleman seated on our host's right? Well, he doesn't know it, but he will be named the corespondent in our host's next divorce suit!"

I was flabbergasted. "You mean the guest of honor at this dinner will actually be named corespondent?" I thought he must be joking.

"Oh," said my informant flippantly, "that's a mere trifle to our host!"

Later on I learned that the individual who had looked me up at my club had served a term in Dannemora prison, having been a cook, and killed a fellow cook with a butcher knife. His millionaire friends typed him as a character and included him in all their parties. I shortly found it convenient to sever all connections with these two interesting and colorful acquaintances.

I discovered that New York was headquarters for a gold-dredging company, operating in the area near Nome. The Alaska manager of the company was well known to me. I also knew there was great wealth among the company stockholders, although the gold-dredging operation was none too successful. However, I began to cultivate some of them. They relished the opportunity of joining up with a live concern and we entered into a contract to consolidate our interests. The dredging company would purchase $50,000 of our preferred stock at par and common stock for the sale of their assets. The money paid for our preferred stock being insufficient to meet our obligations, the offer of a loan was made to me by the attorney for the dredging company and its largest stockholder: $50,000 for one year, in return for $10,000 plus $10,000 of my personal common stock, which I anticipated would be repaid by our company.

Usury or no usury, the need was urgent and a deal had to be made. I turned over the stock, the $10,000 deducted from the $50,000; a note for one year was given for $50,000, and I was able to proceed to Nome with $90,000—and one year's time to find a way of repaying the loan!

The year passed successfully for our company, although we were in no position to take up the $50,000 note. We were in fact at a very dangerous point indeed, for I sensed that the holder of the note was not the type of man to allow many days of grace. I was sure that he would ask for his money on the dot.

In the quiet of Nome, where thinking somehow always seemed much clearer than amid the clamor of New York, I reviewed all contacts I had made in the metropolis with leading men of finance. I finally decided that the one who, above all the others, combined vision, experience, wealth, and courage, was Mr. Leonard D. Baldwin. If I could arrange a meeting between Mr. Baldwin and Mr. Burroughs, the man who had loaned us the $50,000, something advantageous to our company was bound to result.

Back in New York again, I spoke to each of the other, and they both expressed a desire to meet. Mr. Baldwin took the initiative, suggesting that I extend an invitation in his name to Mr. Burroughs to be his guest at lunch at the Grosvenor Hotel the following Friday at one o'clock.

Mr. Burroughs accepted. I told him I would call for him at his office at twelve-thirty and accompany him to the Grosvenor. I spent Friday morning at the office of a friend, checking my watch from time to time. But I arrived late at

Burroughs' office for the appointment. My watch—which had always kept perfect time—was one hour slow!

The secretary informed me that, having waited for me for half an hour, he had gone to lunch downstairs. As I headed for the door, she called, "Here, take his topcoat; if you find him, it will save his coming back before your meeting."

I saw Mr. Burroughs at a table in the restaurant. Storm clouds were plain to see as I approached him. My apologies and explanations were sincere enough, but the expression on my face must have conveyed my realization that no businessman would be in any hurry to entrust a large sum of money to someone who couldn't keep an important appointment on time. How could he know that all my life I had been a stickler for promptness?

"Mr. Burroughs," I said contritely, "I don't know what happened to my watch to make it drop an hour out of my life. But Mr. Baldwin will be waiting."

"Very sorry, Lomen," he replied. "I have another appointment. I waited half an hour for you."

"Well, I brought your topcoat," I said. "I'll carry it back to your office."

"Leave it; I'll take it back myself."

I thought to myself, *Oh, what's the use.* I could visualize the destruction of years of effort on the part of my brothers and myself. I turned away from the table.

"Lomen!" Mr. Burroughs called after me. "Say to Mr. Baldwin that if he can make it, I will be pleased to have him lunch here with me tomorrow."

I thanked him and was off. Hopping into a taxi, I made fast time to the Grosvenor. Entering, I noticed that there was a smile on Mr. Baldwin's face. He had a man with him at the table. I made my apologies, explained the incident of the watch to Mr. Baldwin, and conveyed Mr. Burroughs' invitation.

"I'll accept," he said promptly. "I'll bring my brother Arthur along, too."

We met the next day at lunch. With the coffee Arthur Baldwin asked Mr. Burroughs what he knew "about this reindeer business."

"It has possibilities," Mr. Burroughs replied. "Lomen wants to sell the remainder of his preferred-stock issue, $318,000. If he would change that to a five-year loan I would take half."

"Well," said Arthur Baldwin thoughtfully, "I can't see why you should do more than my brother and I. We will take the other half."

I wanted to shout for joy. Instead, I contained myself and said, quite calmly, "Gentlemen, that's fine. Will you give me a memo covering your pledges?"

"No memo is needed," said Mr. Burroughs. "We have already told you what we will do."

We separated and I rushed off to send a wire to Nome to ease my family and other associates there.

The pledges were paid over, the Burroughs note was redeemed, and the first boat north in June carried me back to Nome.

On July 27, 1920, it happened that Dr. E. W. Nelson, chief of the Bureau of Biological Survey, Department of Agriculture, arrived at Nome on the S. S. *Victoria*. He had wired that he was in a party of four and he was anxious to see us but had to leave again with the ship.

During the previous winter in Washington I had helped in securing a congressional appropriation for the Biological Survey to establish an experimental station in Alaska for the scientific study of reindeer. Of course I was anxious to have as much time as possible with Dr. Nelson now.

Angry waves were pounding the beach, seemingly daring anyone to ride them. For safety the *Victoria* was anchored seven miles off shore. I secured a small cabin launch and three experienced surf men to go out with me. Our first attempt to leave the mouth of the river was unsuccessful. We tried again, in very rough going. The *Victoria* spotted us, Captain Fred Warner steamed a little farther in, and finally we were able to pull up alongside. We yelled to the skipper that we had come for Dr. Nelson and his party and one or two other passengers. We asked him also if he could lend us several life preservers.

We got our passengers down over the side on a rope ladder. The trip back to shore was hazardous, and when we entered the river we found that hundreds of people had collected to see if we could make it.

In Dad's office we settled down to a discussion of reindeer matters but were interrupted by an unexpected and dramatic telephone call to the effect that Roald Amundsen had arrived in Nome. Having completed the Northeast Passage, he had left his ship, the *Maud*, in the lee of Sledge Island and come to Nome in a coastwise boat.

Amundsen joined us all for dinner that evening at our home. Mother, always cordial and gracious, had with little advance notice prepared a fine reindeer roast that brought compliments from all our guests.

Amundsen told many tales of his three years' trip and, among other things, described a bird that he had not been able to classify.

"Ross's gull!" said Dr. Nelson positively.

Amundsen described another bird unfamiliar to him. Dr. Nelson identified it at once. Amundsen looked flabbergasted until, laughing, I identified Dr. Nelson as chief of the Biological Survey.

"And here *I* was telling about birds!" Amundsen muttered in wry apology.

Besides being a leading biologist and ornithologist, Dr. Nelson had a close kinship with exploration. As a young man he had lived four years at St. Michael, on a small island 110 miles southeast of Nome, and in 1881 had joined the revenue cutter *Corwin*'s search for the ill-fated DeLong expedition.

Alaskans found it difficult to understand the divided activity emanating from Washington concerning reindeer and the lack of co-operation between federal agencies. Federal control of the Eskimo reindeer industry resided with the United States Department of the Interior, to which Congress was annually making appropriations for its development. But the experimental station established to assist the industry was in the hands of the Department of Agriculture's Biological Survey.

In January 1921 I happened to be visiting with one of the scientific members of the Biological Survey, in Washington.

"Of course you know, Mr. Lomen," he casually remarked, "that it is unlawful to sell reindeer meat in the District of Columbia?"

I shot out of my chair in startled dismay.

"What!" I exclaimed. "Even though two federal departments are furthering development of the reindeer industry, and Congress has appropriated funds for its support, you mean to say we would be breaking the law if we sold the meat here? Why, as a matter of fact, at this very minute reindeer meat is in transit to this city from Seattle!"

"Well," said my informant dryly, "if the meat is located, it will simply be confiscated and destroyed. Eventually, of course, we will try to have the law corrected."

Eventually was altogether too remote to suit me. I could see that what I needed in place of a scientific man was a man of action.

I hurried to Mr. George Lawyer, Chief Game Warden of the United States, and told him the story.

"You must be mistaken," he said in surprise. "That can't possibly be the law!"

146

"We'd better look it up," I said.

"Well," said Mr. Lawyer, after we had done so, "it's the law all right. But it certainly never was intended to stop reindeer shipments. Come along with me to the district corporation counsel; we'll get his interpretation of this law."

We did, and at my request Mr. Lawyer presented the matter at issue, pointing out that it was never contemplated to include "reindeer" in the local law. To this the counsel agreed and said to us: "Let the meat come on. We'll instruct our men to pay no attention to it."

A few days later the corporation counsel handed down an opinion: "The Alaska reindeer is a domesticated animal, that has been his status in Scandinavian countries for centuries, hence it is not subject to game laws."

Naturally, I was much relieved.

The firm of A. Silz of New York, largest game house in the United States, had become very much interested in this new product, reindeer meat. Experiments showed its superiority as a canned product; its soup stock, or broth content, was twice that of beef; and arrangements were entered into for the production of canned meat.

The status of reindeer as a domesticated animal had by now been established in the state of New York. Another state law required "game" meats to be tagged by the Conservation Commission of the state (six metal tags to each carcass at a cost of five cents a tag). The Commission requested that we agree to the "tagging" of the reindeer to make it possible for their deputies to "follow" the caribou and wild-deer sales in the state. Wishing to be helpful, we agreed. Unknown to us, the Game Commission had the state law amended to include reindeer among the animals required to be tagged, and that brought us up against still another law that prohibited the use of any meat tagged for canning. This was too much for the firm of A. Silz and they discontinued their efforts to produce a new canned product—to our great regret.

The eastern market of the United States, because of the dense population, was naturally the one to develop. To reach that market we had an ocean and rail haul of upward of 6,000 miles at a cost of six cents per pound. Reindeer was a product that was practically unknown and would require both publicity and advertising to excite sufficient curiosity in the minds of prospective customers to cause them to buy it. A small amount of reindeer meat was being imported from Norway. As we put forth efforts to develop an eastern market, naturally shipments from abroad would increase. Alaska could not compete, as production costs were less in Europe and lower freight rates existed between Europe and the United States. Our only protection would be a duty on reindeer and venison shipments from abroad.

I appeared before the Ways and Means Committee of the House of Representatives in 1921 and was successful in securing a duty of four cents per pound. This was later increased to six cents per pound in 1929.

I took my pattern from the *Self-Made Merchant* of the meat-packing industry, so aptly described by George Horace Lorimer: "Eat pork, talk pork, sleep pork!" I simply substituted reindeer.

My opportunities were great, the industry was growing, and I had no fear of the future. But we must have publicity. The reindeer was a romantic animal, the industry new, and Alaska a fascinating territory. The press and magazines were generous with their space. Soon the newspapers tagged me with the sobriquet of "Reindeer King." I did not object, since it meant more publicity for the reindeer industry.

More and more of my time was spent in the States—both in our Seattle office and in Washington, D. C., where the necessary legislation had to be secured to sustain the industry. I looked forward with anticipation to getting back to Alaska, as life was never dull when in the field supervising reindeer operations. It was at the same time a great relief to get away from Washington with all its uncertainties, slowness, and diversified problems. I enjoyed the big open spaces. It was a thrill to see a herd of reindeer and a pleasure to visit with my Eskimo friends after months of absence.

Besides my part in the technical details of our business I thought I could advance the reindeer industry by carrying on a running publicity campaign for reindeer meat. For instance, when the New York *World* mentioned reinder meat disparagingly, I seized on it as an opportunity to educate potential customers by calling the newspaper story to the attention both of the federal departments interested in the industry, and influential men in New York and elsewhere. Soon the following editorial appeared:

OH, REINDEER, GENTLE, KIND AND TENDER

Some weeks ago, in a relaxed and misguided moment, we printed an editorial, the writer of which permitted himself some humorously disparaging remarks about reindeer meat. Since then we have suffered. Reindeer corporations have denounced us. The Bureau of Education, Alaska Division, of the Department of the Interior, has taken us sternly to task. We have been bombarded with Congressional reports, statistics, testimony of dieticians and food experts, including Oscar of the Waldorf—all extolling the excellence and importance of reindeer meat.

We have been abused by pretty much everybody concerned except the reindeer, and we begin to fear these simple creatures may not understand we are doing them a service. We live in bodily terror lest presently a huge pair of antlers crash through the door and a mighty beast with fiery eyes and smoking nostrils pulverize us under resentful hoofs.

Then, too, Christmas is coming. Santa Claus is still an old-fashioned, old-world gentleman. We bet it will be years before he buys an automobile. It would be a dismal thing indeed if his famous team refused to pull up alongside our chimney. Safety first. We have decided the best part of valor is to back down abjectly on this reindeer business, wash the slate, hope that by-gones may be bygones, and become even as little children—ready to listen and learn.

One day in 1924 Heywood Broun said in his column:

A few days ago I complained of the unromantic nature of menus on dining cars. That reproach may not fairly be leveled against the St. Louisan, of the Pennsylvania System. On the bill of fare yesterday they had reindeer chops, which ought to be exotic enough for any man. I ate the chops, but with a certain diffidence. Never before had I thought of reindeer in any connection save that of the night before Christmas. I could hardly have been more embarrassed if I had been invited to dine on Santa Claus sauté. I wept a little but still I did eat the chops.

I could not resist replying and wrote this letter to Mr. Broun:

DEAR MR. BROUN:

I read with considerable interest your paragraph in last Saturday's *World,* expressing surprise at discovering that the St. Louisan of the Pennsylvania System was serving reindeer chops in their diner, and that you had never before thought of reindeer in any connection save that of the night before Christmas. I also can confess to surprise that one of New York's foremost newspaper-men should "weep a little" at the thought of eating a reindeer chop, because of the part that that noble animal, the reindeer, plays in the festivities of the Yuletide.

My dear Mr. Broun, you were, unknowingly, assisting dear old Santa when you ate that chop. The situation is this: Hit by the high cost of living, Santa Claus—whose herds in Alaska have increased to more than 325,000 animals—is now placing some of his choicest animals on the market, to secure funds to buy gifts for his sack, and also to supply the good people of these United States with an additional and welcome food product.

Santa selects the speediest animals in the herd each year for his sled, and markets the balance of his surplus male animals. Some of the more progressive corporations of this country—such as our leading railroads, the larger hotels in New York and other leading cities—have been in conference with Santa, and after ascertaining that the meat itself is superior to most domestic meats, and to assist the great friend of our childhood days, now offer this great treat to the people of the United States.

The writer speaks with authority, as he happens to be in charge of this branch of Santa's establishment. New Yorkers are provincial, but good scouts for all that! With best wishes, and the hope that you enjoyed the chops, I am,

Very truly yours,
CARL J. LOMEN

In the midwinter of 1926 I thought it would be a great boon to the sale of reindeer meat if the subject could be dramatized somehow. I submitted a proposal to my two friends, Leonard and Arthur Baldwin. Shortly Jimmie Walker, then mayor of City of New York, declared April 5–10 as "New York Reindeer Week." Headquarters were set up in the Hotel McAlpin and the hotel's publicity man, Harry C. Klemfuss, spearheaded a great publicity drive. Arthur Baldwin, then president of the National Publishers Association, was chairman.

Committees were appointed, with many nationally known men and women serving, among them Senator Thomas J. Walsh of Montana, Dr. Royal S. Copeland of New York, Vilhjalmur Stefansson, Roald Amundsen, Lieutenant Commander Richard E. Byrd; John B. Burnham, president of the American Game Protective Association; food experts, Alfred W. McCann and Ida Bailey Allen; authors Elizabeth Sears, James Oliver Curwood, and Constance Lindsay Skinner; Gilbert M. Grosvenor, editor of the *National Geographic Magazine;* John J. Tigert, Federal Commissioner of Education; Dan Sutherland, Alaska's delegate in Congress; Archibald B. Roosevelt, banker; Dr. George Bird Grinnell, dean of American sportsmen; Thomas Riggs, Jr., former govenor of Alaska, and many more impressive names. We received much excellent publicity, furnishing speakers to address a number of luncheon clubs and to talk on the radio.

One morning I picked up a New York newspaper and my eye caught the word *reindeer* in a well-known column.

So this is Reindeer Week! And to be patriotic one should eat reindeer meat. I felt patriotic yesterday so I walked down to the corner meat market and asked of the Dutchman behind the block,
"Have you any reindeer?"
"Vat iss dat?"
"Have you any reindeer?" I repeated.
"I don't know, sveetheart, I vill call up der wedder bureau an' find out."

Before the close of this campaign thousands of people in the metropolitan area were acquainted with the fact that reindeer meat was carried in the New York markets and that, besides being something new in the way of meat for home consumption, it was high in nutritive value. Although its retail price was then twice that of beef, sales of reindeer meat rose swiftly.

In February 1927, after we had closed a highly successful "Christmas Reindeer" season, my brother Ralph, Dan Crowley, our field superintendent, and I were all in New York. We had realized for some time that such an industry as ours required larger capital for its proper development. Our planning had been logical and sound but sufficient cash financing had been difficult to obtain. Now we needed $1,000,000.

In the evenings Ralph and I worked on a prospectus, he taking one aspect of the work, I another: reindeer, trading, mining, etc. Each morning we took our written material to Leonard Baldwin for his examination. Our best judgment was for a preferred stock issue of $1,000,000, bearing 8 per cent interest together with a bonus of common stock.

One day Mr. Baldwin suddenly tossed a bombshell at us.

"You can't get by with $1,000,000," he pointed out, "and

you can't pay 8 per cent interest. What you've got to have is $1,200,000, and you must not pay more than 6 per cent."

"Who," I asked skeptically, "would be interested in investing money in reindeer in Alaska at 6 per cent?"

"I don't know yet," Mr. Baldwin admitted. "But you still can't pay 8 per cent."

Day after day we plugged along. We were invited to spend a weekend at the Baldwin home in East Orange, New Jersey. After dinner Arthur Baldwin suggested a conference.

"Come on, boys, let's go upstairs and talk."

By now both Baldwins were thoroughly familiar with our operations, our business principles, and our financial condition.

"Is this plan you have outlined," Arthur Baldwin asked, "fair to your stockholders?"

"The Lomen family is the most heavily interested of our stockholders," I replied, "and we would feel happy to see it carried through."

"Is the plan fair to the purchasers of the new issue?" he persisted.

"Entirely so," Ralph assured him. "Our one regret is that the Lomen family isn't in a financial position to purchase all of it."

"Well, boys," Arthur Baldwin smiled, "Leonard and I have talked it over and we've decided to take the entire issue ourselves."

Dan Crowley excitedly leaped out of his chair, landing on the rug.

"What was that you said?" he yelled.

Ralph and I could hardly believe our ears, either.

Admonishing us not to stay up talking all night, our hosts went to their rooms.

Ralph, Dan, and I got no sleep that night. We sat up, talking and planning—for plan we could—with an immediately available cash fund of $1,200,000!

14.

BY 1924 various problems of the reindeer business compelled me to spend my winters in New York and Washington. When things were particularly troublesome, I got into the habit of consulting with Stefansson. One day in the spring of that year I happened to be visiting him and his former secretary, D. M. LeBourdais, in Stefansson's rooms at the Harvard Club in New York.

"Carl," Stefansson inquired out of a clear blue sky, "how would you like to take Wrangel Island off my hands?"

I knew quite a bit about the island, since my brothers and I had had a lot to do with the people involved in several of its tragic chapters.

"Well now, that's a rather surprising question," I replied.

Certainly such a thought had never entered my mind. Stefansson's own interest in the island went back to 1913, when he learned that the survivors of his flagship the *Karluk* had reached Wrangel; later they were rescued.

"Why have you decided to give it up?" I asked.

"It's simply that I can't afford the luxury any longer," he explained. "Besides, I won't have time to look after it. I'm booked for a lecture tour in Australia. Anyhow, if I did continue to keep the colony up there, you'd have to keep an eye on it for me."

"If an expedition develops," LeBourdais spoke up, "count me in as the press correspondent."

Wrangel, maverick land of the Arctic, is a wasteland of

mystery and tragedy. It's just about as cold a bit of landscape as there is on the face of the earth. Situated 100 miles north of the Siberian coast, more than 400 miles northwest of Bering Strait, it is well on the way to the North Pole. Its climate is unbearable, yet it does have a few good points: it abounds in white fox; the surrounding waters are alive with fish, seal, walrus, and polar bear; and its 3,400 square miles can support many reindeer.

I turned over in my mind Stefansson's offer and what I knew of the island.

Discovered in 1849 by the Britisher, Captain Kellett, R.N., of H.M.S. *Harold,* the island had been claimed in turn by the United States, Great Britain, Canada, and Russia. Kellett's landing place was a small island 350 miles due west of Point Barrow, Alaska; he took possession in the name of Queen Victoria. To the westward he sighted a larger mass of mountainous terrain; the island on which he landed became known as Harold Island, the land to the westward as Kellett Land.

Twenty years later an American skipper, Thomas Long, sailed past the coast of Kellett Land. As it was unmarked on the chart, he naturally believed he had discovered new territory. Recalling that in 1824 the Russian, Baron Wrangel, had sought land in that vicinity, he named it Wrangel Land.

During 1879 James Gordon Bennett, owner of the New York *Herald,* sent out an expedition in the *Jeannette* under the command of Lieutenant DeLong, U.S.N., to attempt to reach the North Pole. DeLong cruised beyond Wrangel Land and proved that it was an island. He continued northward until his ship was crushed in the ice off the Lena Delta; some members of the crew succeeded in reaching shore and safety; many, however, including DeLong, perished on the Siberian coast.

Meanwhile, anxiety regarding the DeLong expedition mounted in the United States. Government vessels and other craft cruising the Arctic were requested to keep a lookout for evidence of them. It was a United States Reserve vessel, the U.S.S. *Corwin*, Captain Calvin Hooper, searching for the *Jeannette*, that reached Wrangel and made the first recorded landing on the island, August 12, 1881. Captain Hooper took possession of the island in the name of the United States and, after a few hours ashore, sailed away. Oddly, a few days later the United States Navy ship *Rodgers*, commanded by Lieutenant (later Rear Admiral) Berry, also searching for the *Jeannette*, reached Wrangel Island and remained nineteen days. Again the island was taken possession of in the name of the United States and the Stars and Stripes raised. Lieutenant Berry explored and circumnavigated the island.

Baron Wrangel, sent out by Catherine the Great of Russia in 1822 to explore the north coast of Siberia, had thought there was land to the north of Siberia because of the flight of birds north of the mainland; but he found none. The first time any Russian ever landed on the island was in 1911, when two Russian icebreakers, the *Taymir* and *Vaigatch*, doing hydrographic work in North Siberian waters, spent a few days on Wrangel Island and erected a beacon on the southwestern point.

Stefansson had become interested when the *Karluk*, flagship of the Canadian Arctic Expedition, commanded by Captain Bob Bartlett, reached Point Barrow en route to the Canadian Arctic, during the early summer of 1913. The ship's meat supply was running short, and Stefansson, commander of the expedition, suggested that Bartlett go ashore on the north coast of Alaska and hunt caribou. A few days later an easterly storm broke, developing shortly into a full-scale blizzard. The ice commenced to move and, with it, the *Karluk*. The storm raged for days, with winds upward of seventy miles per hour. The ship was now caught solidly in the pack ice, drifting with the wind and tides.

Weeks passed. Captain Bartlett made camp on the ice—a shelter built of boxes and packing cases—and stocked it with food and other supplies that might be needed. On January 10 the pressure finally became too great for the ship, crushing her timbers. Captain Bartlett, knowing that this was the end for his gallant ship, ordered all crew members out onto the ice.

He had a feeling that he wanted to be alone with his old ship during her last hours, so he sent all his men to their temporary quarters on the ice. Then he went down alone into the cabin and sat and thought about what the *Karluk* had been through. There was a phonograph in the cabin and more than 100 records. With the cracking of the timbers and the rushing of waters around him, he played tune after tune. And as he finished playing each record he threw it into the stove.

About an hour later the ship began to settle in earnest. Pretty soon the lower decks were awash. Putting a record of Chopin's "Funeral March" on the victrola, he started it up. When water came trickling along the upper deck and splashing into the hatch, he ran up and stood on deck. Slowly the *Karluk* dipped into a header. When her rail was level with the ice, Captain Bartlett stepped off. As the stricken ship went down by the head into thirty-eight fathoms of water, the victrola could be heard playing the strains of the "Funeral March."

Four of the men asked Captain Bartlett's permission to strike out on their own, in an attempt to reach Alaska: A. Forbes MacKay, James Murray, H. Bouchat, and S. S. Morris. The remainder of the party reached Wrangel Island after twenty-two days of hardship, traveling over some of the worst ice any of them had ever seen. High-pressure ridges and ice debris were everywhere, compelling them to travel two miles up and down for every mile they traveled forward. Time and again they wrecked their sledges and bruised their bodies on this man-killing trip. The temperature ranged between 45 and 55 degrees below zero, with a howling wind buffeting them at every step. However, as it was move or die, they kept on traveling. When they finally reached Wrangel Island some of the men were in very bad shape.

There was plenty of driftwood around the shores of the island, and an abundance of seals, so Bob Bartlett took seven dogs, one sledge, and the Eskimo Katiklovick, and started off to Siberia for help. It took them seventeen days to reach land, through a driving snowstorm all the way. Bartlett was practically blind from the snow, and both he and the Eskimo were physically exhausted. However, both men were possessed of such dogged courage that they immediately set out down the Siberian coast and eventually reached East Cape. From there they went by water to Nome.

The cutter *Bear* headed for Wrangel Island early in September 1914, but on the way met the trading schooner *King and Winge,* bringing the survivors of the *Karluk.* Four men had died during the winter, but the remainder were in fair shape.

In August 1920 the *Silver Wave,* financed by Stefansson, landed on Wrangel Island with a party of four men and an Eskimo seamstress. They were to trap there on shares, and laid claim to the island in the name of Great Britain. They were Alan Crawford, Lorne Knight, Frederick Maurer, Milton Galle, and Ada Blackjack, the Eskimo woman hired in Nome to keep them supplied with fur clothing.

The British flag was run up as soon as their supplies were landed, and they settled down to trapping white fox, so plentiful on the island.

The relief ship that was supposed to land their supplies the following year could not make it through the ice; in consequence, scurvy threatened. Crawford, Maurer, and Galle set out across the ice to Siberia for help, leaving Ada Blackjack to care for Lorne Knight, who was very ill.

In August 1923 Harold Noice pushed the nose of his gas schooner *Donaldson* against the icy shores of Rodgers Harbor on Wrangel Island and was greeted by Ada, who came running and leaping down to the water's edge to welcome them, tears streaming down her face. Lorne Knight had died six months before and his body still lay in his sleeping bag. Ada had cared for him to the very last, shooting seals and catching fish for their food. After his death she had thought herself abandoned by all the world.

One way and another we Lomens had been involved with these events. We assisted in outfitting the expedition in the *Silver Wave;* acting for Stefansson, we engaged Captain Joe Bernard to carry supplies to Wrangel, although on account of the heavy ice conditions he failed to reach the island after a thirty-day effort. When Noice was commissioned by Stefansson to make the trip to Wrangel, we outfitted him; Noice left Charles Wells, a Pennsylvanian, and twelve Eskimo on the island, to continue hunting and trapping operations.

I considered Wrangel Island of the same strategic importance to the Arctic as Malta is to the Mediterranean. As aviation grew it would be bound to be considered of value by many nations. With these thoughts running through my mind, I asked Stefansson what he wanted for his interest.

"Well, there are thirteen persons on the island now—one white man and twelve Eskimo. They've been there since last year, trapping on the share basis, and they're equipped for two years more. You'd have to send a ship to visit them this summer, but your share of the fur catch would more than repay you."

"I'm not especially concerned with the financial aspects of the case," I answered. "What does appeal to me is the thought that I might be able to add a valuable island to the territory of the United States."

"Quite right," Stefansson agreed. "Aviation will revolutionize the far North. I think myself Wrangel Island is likely to become of great strategic value."

"If we take over the island, could I claim for the United States the benefit of your three years of occupancy?"

"It might be worth trying."

"Your proposal appeals to me," I concluded. "I'll let you know more very soon."

A few days later I accepted Stefansson's proposal.

I returned to Washington to ascertain the attitude of our Government relative to Wrangel Island and secured an appointment with the Hon. Charles Evans Hughes, then Secretary of State. Much to my surprise, the Secretary swiftly recited the history of the island, inquired as to our plans, and then remarked:

"This is the first concrete American move that has been made. Personally, I say go and hold it. The only claim the Russians could advance would be one of contiguity, and that would not hold in international law."

To me, that was sufficient authority for us to consider that we had the backing and approval of the Government in our effort to bring the island under the American flag.

This was to be a "Lomen Brothers" venture, and we invited to join us the two brothers who had already played such a generous part in our ventures, Leonard and Arthur Baldwin.

The following spring LeBourdais joined our party in Seattle; northward bound, too, he was commissioned by the North American Newspaper Alliance to cover the Wrangel Island story.

In Nome I discussed with my brothers the prospect of sending a ship to the island. A few days later a three-masted schooner slid in at Nome from the south. It was the *Herman,* a whaler that had been sailing the Arctic for years. When her skipper, Louis Lane, came ashore, we learned he was bound for Wrangel Island.

Louis Lane was an old friend and one of the great ice skippers of the North. He told us he intended to hunt walrus north of the Siberian coast and, in the fall, to kill bowhead whale in the vicinity of Wrangel Island.

We soon came to terms, and he agreed to go to Wrangel Island, raise the Stars and Stripes, and take possession in the name of the United States. He was also to bring away whatever furs the party might have on hand and, if they wished, to return our colony to the Alaska coast. LeBourdais shipped with Captain Lane.

The *Herman,* an old whaler of 325 tons with a 250 horsepower diesel, was slow. With a fair wind she was good for six knots. Captain Lane had ill luck on this northward cruise. The crankshaft broke in the diesel and they were compelled to put back to Nome under sail for repairs. It was the seventh of September when the *Herman* turned her nose northward again. In the words of Captain Lane:

We ran into a heavy bank of fog on the third day out, fog so thick that one could hardly see the bow from the wheelhouse. It meant keeping a constant bow lookout to watch for ice floes. The temperature dropped below freezing with the result that by morning our rigging was a shimmering mass of ice, turning the vessel into a lovely sight, very much as if our running gear had been dipped into cake frosting.

By evening the fog lifted. We were at the edge of a tremendous ice field. Picking a promising lead, while conning the vessel from the crow's nest, I pushed the *Herman* into it and for the next few hours we made our way through the lead, which was a couple of miles wide most of the time. Far in the distance, we picked out Harold Island and off to the northwest of it could be made out the hazy outline of Wrangel Island. Finally we reached the end of the lead we had been following and I ordered out the ice anchor to await further developments. They were not long in coming.

All hell suddenly broke loose. From the pack came a whining noise, like the singing you hear along telephone wires on a windy night in the country. This signified ice pressure and with it came a gale from the south. From the pack rose a noise like the shrieking of steamer whistles, the thunder of heavy artillery, and the roaring of a hurricane all blended together, as down the open lead

161

behind us, driven by winds of hurricane force, came immense pieces of floe ice. Sliding on end, rolling over and over, they churned and battered each other and crashed against the thick edges of the ice pack, into which we were wedged, with such horrible screechings and groanings that it looked as if doomsday were upon us.

Occasionally a berg jammed in the lead, blocking the current. When that happened, the terrific pressure from behind sheared it off level with the ice pack and slid it forward toward us. In this manner the pressure ridges kept building up higher and higher, creeping ever closer to us.

I gave orders to be ready to abandon ship. Supplies were hastily gathered on deck and we stood by to see what would happen. When the ice juggernaut was scarcely a hundred yards from our stern, the pressure eased off, then ceased completely, leaving our tortured ears and jumpy nerves to return to normal as best they could.

Ten days we were wedged in that spot, wondering if we could ever get out. Shortly after midnight on the tenth day, I was awakened by the pounding of feet across the deck. Jumping into my clothes, I hurried out and was amazed to find open water stretching from our bow as far ahead as one could see. The pack had opened once more.

The split in the ice was as straight and clean as though laid out by an engineer's transit. It was getting wider all the time so we hastily got under way as the wind commenced blowing from astern again and the oncoming ice struck us and commenced pushing us right down that wide-open lead. I ordered the engine shut down for fear a stray ice cake might get afoul of the propeller, and we waited to see what would happen next. We were rammed through that canal between solid banks of ice. Floe icebergs as big as houses bobbed up and down alongside, like whales. The *Herman* was pushed down the open lead, rammed and hammered from all angles.

This hair-raising trip lasted for a full two hours. Then suddenly we were pushed out into a large open bay in the ice where the current lost its speed and left us drifting aimlessly about. Once again we started the engine and now we headed down an enormous lead that led directly toward Harold Island. The ice cleared away from its western side and we were able to gain shelter there, free of howling wind and lashing waves. The island is only six miles in length and we anchored near the southern end.

Next day we made an attempt to get through to Wrangel Island. The lookout in the crow's nest shouted down that he had spotted the remains of a camp on the north end of Harold Island as we started to cruise past. I had a boat lowered away and three of us, including LeBourdais, went ashore to investigate. First thing we spotted was a sled standing on end with the runners banked high with stones to keep it upright.

A weird sight awaited us. We found a large drift log lying at right angles to the sled and behind it was what was left of a tent and bed. The tent had fallen down over the bed. As we removed the rotted canvas we found human bones to which adhered fragments of reindeer sleeping bags. From the bones we estimated that there must have been four men.

Queerest of all, it was a fully equipped camp. In addition to the sled, ammunition, packs, shovels, snowshoes, skis, knives and binoculars, many other things were scattered about. There were two rifles, so badly rusted the bolts would not open. There were no diaries, but from the various articles we identified the remains as the party of four men from Stefansson's ship *Karluk* which had sunk in 1914 about sixty miles northwest of Wrangel Island. . . .

Finally we managed to back into a promising lead and headed south once again, since there seemed to be an impenetrable ice field between us and Wrangel Island.

When the *Herman* reached Nome, very disheartening news awaited them.

"Did you see the Russians?" I asked Captain Lane as he landed on the beach.

"Russians?" he demanded. "What Russians?"

"Captain Aarnout Castel was in here a few days ago," I replied, "and he left word that the Soviet icebreaker *Red October* had taken all the colonists off Wrangel Island, together with their furs, and transported them to Siberia!"

"No!" he exclaimed.

"Did you see any signs of their ship?"

"Certainly didn't!" Captain Lane replied. "How did Castel

know about it? This year Wrangel Island is locked in by ice all the way around."

"Castel just returned from a trading trip along the Siberian coast—it seemed to be common knowledge there."

"Probably took them off by force then," growled Captain Lane.

"On the contrary, I heard that they went willingly. Yet it doesn't seem logical that the Eskimo in the party would sail right by the Diomede Islands and not request to be put ashore there."

"Sounds just like the Reds!" Captain Lane said with a glare. "They're plenty highhanded these days; wouldn't be a bit surprised to see them sail right into Nome and make off with whatever they happened to want at the moment!"

During the gold-rush days Senator Key Pittman, chairman of the Foreign Relations Committee, had practiced law in Nome. I often called on him at his office when I was in the Capital. Now I wanted his help for our Wrangel Island colony. I tried to impress him with the strategic importance of the island to the United States.

"Senator," I pointed out, "should it become necessary for you to proceed to Manila, Philippine Islands, by the shortest and quickest route by plane from Washington, D. C., you would fly right over Wrangel Island."

"Say that again," requested the Senator.

I repeated my startling statement.

"Show that to me on the globe."

I took a string, placing one end on Washington and the other at Manila, and he saw for himself that the string touched Wrangel Island, situated 110 miles north of the north coast of Siberia.

"Well, what do you know!" he exclaimed.

Immediately in the Senator's eyes Wrangel Island took on greater importance.

When the rumor was verified that the Russian warship *Red October* had reached Wrangel Island, confiscated our supplies, and removed our people, Wells and twelve Eskimo, I hastened to Washington to consult with the State Department. The press reported that Wells and party had been taken south, through Bering Strait, just a few miles from the homes of the Eskimo, to Vladivostok, Siberia, some 2,000 miles distant.

The State Department was very solicitous but apparently powerless to take action for the reason that at the moment we had no diplomatic relations with the U.S.S.R. The Department pointed out that if our people had been sailors, it could take action. I replied that the party was made up of American citizens and the newspapers had reported that Wells was ill.

"He may be dead in a week!" I declared.

My statement stemmed from awareness that Wells would be the only one of the party who would know what had actually taken place and where they were; hence the Russians would not care to see him return to the United States. As I had anticipated, within the week Wells was reported dead, and the Eskimo were forced into North China by the Soviets.

Unable to secure help from the State Department, I approached Colonel Bicknell of the American Red Cross. That conference resulted in $1,600 being paid to the State Department by the Red Cross, for the purpose of returning the Eskimo to the United States. In the absence of diplomatic relations, action was taken through the British. With the assistance of the British Vice-Consul at Harbin, China, the unfortunate Eskimo, minus two children who had died, were shipped to Seattle, Washington, from which port they were returned to their Alaska homes.

LeBourdais broke the story about Stefansson disposing of his interest in Wrangel Island to us, and our intention to send a new expedition up there. His report pointed out that "Vilhjalmur Stefansson has been active for several years in trying to hold Wrangel Island as British territory," but had finally disposed of his interest to us.

A flurry of controversy blew up. The Toronto *Star* took the position that British sovereignty of the island was not affected by Stefansson's action, inasmuch as the British claim rested on the fact of the occupation by Allan Crawford. Though an American citizen could, of course, hold private property rights in a British island, the sovereignty claim arising from the occupation held good for five years.

From Washington came a statement that the United States had no plans for attempting to establish sovereignty in the Arctic, and would have none until the Navy Department explored the polar region the following summer with the Navy dirigible *Shenandoah*.

The only information we could obtain following the kidnaping of the colony was contained in press reports about two months later from Russian sources. A Russian expedition had been ordered to take Wrangel Island, it was said, and to arrest all inhabitants. The vessel involved was the *Red October*, as we had heard. Bound through the ice from Petropavlovsk, Kamchatka Peninsula, for Wrangel Island, it had taken the inhabitants prisoner, seized all supplies, and established Russian ownership of the island in the name of the Soviet Government.

October 17 the New York *Times* carried a dispatch, datelined Nome, confirming that the colony had been carried off by the Russian armed transport *Red October*, after raising the Russian flag.

Six days later it was reported in the Utica, New York, *Press*, in a dispatch from Petropavlovsk, that the *Red October* had arrived there "with Charles Wells of Uniontown, Pennsylvania, a survivor of Stefansson's expedition to Wrangel, and with twelve Eskimo members of the expedition, who were American citizens. Wells and his companions attempted to flee when they caught sight of the Red flag over the island, fearing they would be cast into prison or executed. Their alarm was dispelled, however, when the Soviet officials assured them they intended no harm."

The reason given for carrying Wells and his companions away was that they "were operating on Russian territory without a license, and without other necessary authorizations." It was said that Wells undoubtedly believed, when told they must leave with the *Red October,* that he and the other colonists would be given transportation to Nome or Seattle. Instead, they were landed at Vladivostok. All were destitute because their fur catch had been confiscated.

Wells appealed to the Government at Washington. Eventually some financial aid was sent to him. But it came too late, for he died in Vladivostok on January 9, 1925, a victim of hardship and pneumonia, far from his native land.

Pursuant to our agreement with Stefansson, we felt that we had a perfect right to proceed to and take possession of Wrangel Island, especially since the new Labor Government of Great Britain repudiated the claims of the preceding Conservative Government, thereby forfeiting British claims to the island.

We engaged the services of Mrs. Mabel Walker Willebrandt, a former Assistant Attorney General of the United States. Mrs. Willebrandt and I consulted not only with the Secretary of State but with the General Counsel of the State Department, the chairman of the Senate Foreign Relations Committee, and other senators. We were assured by the General Counsel that we had a valid claim for damages against the Soviets and requested to file same with the State Department.

Later, when the Department seemed to lose interest, I suggested that we withdraw our claim.

"Oh, no," they said. "You have a valid claim and we want you to maintain it."

We felt that at least we had provided our Government with a strong case. If the day ever comes when representatives of the American and Soviet governments sit down at the counsel table for the settlement of claims, the matter of American sovereignty over Wrangel Island should prove of importance.

15.

WE HAD organized the Enterprise Steamship Company in 1923, acquiring by purchase two small schooners, *Nokatak* and *Silver Wave*. During the next year the *Silver Wave* was frozen in the ice near Kotzebue and carried to sea by the ice pack. The schooner was lost, but the crew managed to get to shore and after a month reached Nome. Several years later we had reports that the vessel had landed on the Siberian coast, but we ourselves never saw her again.

The following year we purchased a newly built motor vessel that we also named *Silver Wave;* a sixty-footer, strongly built, twin-screw, a splendid carrier. This vessel was for coastwise service in Alaska waters, particularly between our several stations.

Our cold-storage plants were widely separated to accommodate our several herds. The steamship company operating in the Bering Sea did not consider it advisable to send their ships to the ports where our cold-storage plants were located, but suggested that we transfer the contents of the plants to some port which they did serve. This was not economically feasible for us, however. Our plants were stationary, located at strategic points to serve the herds. Moreover, the frozen meat could not be moved except at great expense, and with danger of spoilage because it would be without refrigeration while in transit. And anyway, the steamship company ships had insufficient refrigeration to meet our needs.

In an effort to resolve our problem, Leonard and Arthur

Baldwin and I met in New York with the managing director of the steamship company.

When we explained our needs he said, "We will enlarge the refrigeration facilities on the ships and meet your requirements—but you'll pay well for it!"

Specifically, they agreed to enlarge the cold-storage space *if* we would contract to use and pay for each trip of the ships into our waters—whether we used the space or not—at the rate of forty-two dollars per ton!

As we left the conference, Arthur Baldwin placed his hand on my shoulder and said, "No wonder you can't get along in this business. Young man, you are up against it."

I had suspected that for some time. I returned to Seattle and a few days later received a telegram from New York:

MEET ME PALACE HOTEL, SAN FRANCISCO, MONDAY MORNING AT NINE O'CLOCK. ARTHUR J. BALDWIN.

Monday morning found me at the appointed place. Punctually at nine Mr. Baldwin walked in. Within a week's time we had purchased a ship and contracted with a shipbuilding company to insulate the entire forward hold of the vessel with five inches of slab cork, and to install a refrigerating plant sufficient to hold temperatures at zero. This was completed in a month, and we now had the largest and most efficient carrier of frozen foods in the Alaska service.

It was weeks later that I learned what prompted Mr. Baldwin's wire to me. A few days after the New York conference with the head of the steamship company, Mr. Baldwin, en route to the Bankers' Club to lunch with some business friends, entered a crowded elevator. On the far side of the car was this same steamship executive. Seeing Mr. Baldwin, he called to him across the heads of the others, "Baldwin, I understand that you are backing this reindeer business in

Alaska. I just want to tell you that you are going to lose your money."

"All in a lifetime," answered Mr. Baldwin philosophically. Nevertheless, the incident greatly provoked him and got up his "Irish." Immediately after lunch he called on some friends who were operators of a large transatlantic steamship company to inquire about a ship suitable for our purposes. That step led to the telegram to me.

We now owned our own vessel, making it possible to service our plants in Alaska direct. We were common carriers and, to make the operation of the vessel profitable, it was necessary to secure freight other than that originating with our own company. Paradoxically, that placed us in the category of a competitor, adding to our difficulties.

"Business" is a nervous institution when the specter of competition arises—as we soon found out. The steamship company, with which we had not seen eye to eye, then joined forces with our opposition. But we carried on.

Along the San Francisco water front any transfer of ownership of a motor vessel of 2,000 tons' registry and upward was always an item of interest. We discovered that this was the case with our acquisition of the M. S. *Sierra*. Most, if not all, of the marine insurance companies sent representatives to call on me. I shortly learned that premiums in all companies were the same; that an accident the *Sierra* had met with prior to our ownership penalized the vessel with an increased insurance premium; I could secure not to exceed $70,000 insurance and the premium would be 18 per cent. Since we had just paid out more than that sum to install the refrigeration plant, I was in a quandary. Could we afford to pay such a premium and still operate at a profit? I wired my associates in New York, explaining the situation. They immediately replied: "Decision rests with you." When the wire was delivered there were three insurance men with me. I read the message, turned to my visitors, and said: "I know what I am going to do. We

171

will carry our own insurance. Thank you, gentlemen, and good day."

Brother Ralph was President of our Arctic Transport Company. We required additional transportation, and two years after acquiring the *Sierra*, he learned of a ship in San Francisco Bay that could be purchased at a very reasonable price. It was the proper tonnage and 240 feet in length. There was one great drawback. The ship had been anchored for several years and a dry-docking job would be necessary to ascertain the condition of the hull. The cost of dry-docking would be borne by the purchaser. Should we take a chance? Others were interested but did not care to take the gamble.

Ralph gave orders to have the ship placed in dry dock. She was thoroughly examined and found to be in perfect condition. The ship could then have been sold for double the price, but shortly thereafter, following her reconditioning, she sailed for the Bering Sea ports, flying the flag of our company, and under her new name, *Arthur J. Baldwin*.

We operated without hull insurance for many years, but we did have two or three rather frightening experiences. On one northbound trip the *Sierra* put in at Akatan to discharge some freight for the whaling station located there. As there was another ship tied up at the dock, the *Sierra* tied up to the other ship. Someone had been pumping out the bilge of a gasoline boat, dumping quantities of gasoline into the bay.

Suddenly both ships were surrounded by a wall of fire with flames rising to the mastheads. The *Sierra* carried a heavy cargo of gasoline and dynamite. A retired colonel, a combat officer of World War I, was a passenger on the *Sierra* as a guest of our company. He was standing at the bow of the ship when the flames shot skyward. He ran aft but found himself cut off completely. The heat was so great that the pitch was bubbling between the deck flooring. The ship's mate was below but reached the deck in a hurry and, climbing into the rigging, directed the fire fighting. The gasoline covering the water soon burned itself out and, aside from the flames charring the sides of the wooden vessel, caused no real damage; but it was a close call.

The Arctic Transport Company grew apace as our business expanded. The *Sierra, Donaldson, Baldwin,* and *Silver Wave* were our main ships. As tugs for the lighterage service, we had the *Genevieve, Dayton, Wave,* and *Sawtooth.* In addition, we had many scows for transporting goods from the ships lying anchored off Nome in to the beach. We lightered goods ashore both for the Alaska Steamship Company and ourselves.

We also purchased a refrigerated barge, the *Trinder,* 150 feet in length, 34 feet beam, with refrigeration space of 8 feet 10 inches above the deck. It was completely housed, with three coolers, a sharp freezer, and a storeroom. Piping was on all walls and ceiling. We moved her between Kotzebue and Eschscholtz Bay, wherever butchering was convenient, loaded her down, and held the meat aboard for transfer to the *Sierra* with its cold-storage facilities for transportation to Seattle.

Our Elephant Point plant was for holding only; we could freeze no meat there except during winter. Using the *Trinder* in the north, we could butcher during the summer to take care of additional orders that had not been filled by animals butchered during the winter. We also used the *Trinder* to lighter frozen deer from Elephant Point, eight miles to ship side, fully protecting the meat from rain or fog, which, on open barges, often caused considerable damage.

While butchering, we left the *Trinder* anchored with her bow on the beach, packing the newly butchered animals aboard and into the sharp freezer. She was the logical answer to what to do about widely scattered herds. Obviously, it would be too expensive to build a freezing plant in each area where deer were to be butchered. We had much discussion over this before acquiring her, however, as she could easily be sunk in the pack ice that floats for so many months of the year in the areas where we intended to use her. It was a calculated risk but one that paid off.

Since there were no stores in the area where we operated, we opened trading posts for the convenience of our employees. The Buckland Store was an anomaly, simply locating wherever the storekeeper happened to be—in winter at Nunacheck, the winter headquarters, at Elephant Point, at Igloo Point, and on the *Trinder* when that was operating.

About this time we developed a large market for fawn hides. Most people would suppose it was unsound business to kill the fawns. But the Eskimo deer men and their families required proper garments for winter wear, and the fawn skins furnished the finest and warmest material for parkas, fur pants, and mittens—and the Arctic traveler needed them, too.

We discovered there was a tremendous market in the States for boned meat. Much of this went into sausage and, immediately on being landed in Seattle, was thus converted. This type of meat cost us nothing in the States for cold-storage charges, which ate up a great deal of profit on whole carcasses. Also, it was quick cash, since we were paid for it immediately.

Boning was cheaper in the Arctic than in Seattle as the Eskimo were all expert and marvelously fast with a knife. We found, too, that the money spent in the States stayed in the States, whereas the money paid to our employees in Alaska remained in the country.

Our company was attempting to adapt an old industry to new methods and it continually called for new lines of thought. It was a business that required plenty of imagination and we constantly tried out new and scientific methods of operation.

Midway between Unimak Pass and Nome lies the island of Nunivak, seventy-six miles long and forty-six miles at its widest point. We investigated the possibilities of establishing a reindeer herd there as the climate was favorable and the island had a very fine growth of lichen forage. Approximately 200 Eskimo lived on Nunivak, a kindly people, though among the most primitive of the natives. Having survived through uncounted generations upon an island on which not a single tree grows, and with few contacts either with other Eskimo or whites, they had not developed equally with similar Alaskan Eskimo groups. Their habitations were denlike, earth-covered huts studded with chunks of driftwood. Small villages of a few huts each were built in the sand-dune formations near the mouths of the streams where fishing was best.

These people lived on the beaches and traveled along the shores in their skin boats. Their fuel, driftwood, was always scarce, eked out with dried sphagnum moss, pressed and dipped in seal oil. Being fisheaters, they caught halibut, codfish, herring, trout, and salmon; in season, they hunted seal and walrus; they also hunted the red and white fox.

The sea held mystery and charm for these primitive people. In fact, it might well be said that they were sea worshipers, as they revered the mighty sea for giving them everything needful for their welfare.

Nunivak proved to be the most ideal range in Alaska for reindeer. There were no wolves or other predators on the island; consequently it became a valuable laboratory for some of our experiments.

In 1920 we chartered the steamer *Ketchikan* to transport 200 reindeer from Golovin to Nunivak Island. When the steamer arrived at Nunivak during late September, it was blowing and snowing so hard the crew of the vessel could not even see the shore line. The moss they had taken along to feed the deer was almost gone, so the skipper of the vessel slung each animal over the side with the cargo boom and dropped it into the water to swim ashore. The poor animals were so frightened in that turmoil of wind and water that they tried to climb right back up the steel sides of the vessel. Since there was nothing the men on the steamer could do to help the bewildered deer, they upped anchor and left them to mill around in the water. Only ninety-eight reindeer managed to reach the beach. They were the nucleus of what later became our best herd.

We kept very accurate records over a period of many years to prove our point that these hardy animals were capable of doubling in number every three years. But still it was difficult for Government agents, and for others lacking practical experience, to accept what they called "staggering" figures of increase. A check on the wild-deer population of the United States would have proven most convincing had the skeptics troubled to investigate.

Consider the three states of Michigan, Wisconsin, and Minnesota. With a combined area of less than 200,000 square miles—one third the area of Alaska, comparable to the grazing area of Alaska suitable for reindeer, and with a population of 11,000,000 people—these three states each year supply more than 200,000 deer to the hunters, to mention only the deer killed and reported. The mystery is how a sufficient number survive—deer, not hunters—to maintain the deer population for future sportsmen.

The woodland caribou of Alaska is much larger than the domesticated reindeer. We had many discussions with the federal agencies in Washington as to ways and means of building up the size of the reindeer and improving and protecting the stock. One thought was to try to cross our animals with the caribou. Other experiments included separation of males and females at certain times of the year; elimination of all surplus bulls by castration; dehorning; movement of herds from grub-infested ground; selection of the best method of castration; use of small cowbells on certain reindeer in the herd to frighten predators; determining which method was preferable, earmarking or branding; developing a superior corral; and proving to the Eskimo deer men, by example and observation, why one method was superior to another.

With the acquisition of Nunivak Island, crossbreeding of the reindeer with the caribou could be tested. The Nunivak herd was increasing. In 1924 we signed a contract with the Bureau of Biological Survey, and they agreed to place ten woodland caribou bulls on Nunivak Island, we to castrate all of the adult reindeer bulls. We agreed to give to the Government in return fifty crossbred bulls each year for a period of twenty years. These crossbred animals were to be transported to the mainland of Alaska by the Bureau and placed in the Eskimo reindeer herds.

Ten woodland caribou bulls were secured near Kokrines on the Yukon River and successfully landed on Nunivak Island during the summer of 1925. The experiment proved a great success in that the crossbred animals were larger, the crossbred fawns being heavier at birth than the full blood of either species.

To formulate plans for a summer's handling of our several herds, the most northerly and southerly of which were some 600 miles apart—with meager communication and transportation facilities—required months. The spring of 1927 we were most anxious that W. B. Miller of the Biological Survey be present during the handling of our herd on Nunivak Island, 300 miles south of Nome. Miller was in Fairbanks, Alaska, 600 miles east of Nome. Our motor vessel *Silver Wave* was berthed in Seattle. She would sail early in May for Nome via Seward and Nunivak Island and would carry north the Eskimo herders who had spent the winter in the States as helpers to Santa Claus and the Christmas reindeer, a story I'll tell a bit later. These herders were to assist in the handling of the herd on Nunivak. We notified Miller of our plans, knowing that he would want to check on the caribou placed on Nunivak by his Bureau. Miller left Fairbanks on the Alaska Railroad and boarded the *Silver Wave* at Seward. Miller held his Master's Degree in botany and was one of the most able and expert in the study of the reindeer industry of all Government men, contributing greatly to the success of the cross-breeding experiment on Nunivak Island.

Miller reported to us later in the summer:

Seventy-five miles north of False Pass the ship got into ice and fully half the time until we reached Nunivak we were unable to move on account of ice. Numerous herds of walrus were sighted. We found the ice jammed solid on Cape Manning (easternmost point on Nunivak). Finally we battered our way into a lead in the ice pack and soon found the only place we might be able to approach the island at all was at Cape Etolin. There we finally made a landing. I was pleasantly surprised, once we got ashore, to find almost the entire population of Nunivak waiting to greet us. The only open water around the island was there and they had congregated for the spring hunting.

The M.S. *Silver Wave* headed for Nome again that same day but became jammed in the ice, where she drifted around, plainly visible to us for about a week, before she was able to head for Nome.

Due to ice conditions, we were forced to stay at Cape Etolin for some time. We finally reached Mekorryok village, where the roundup corrals were located. The sea around Nunivak at this time was jammed full of soft and dangerous ice. One of the natives drowned a couple of days after we landed.

Finally, on June 7, we commenced the reindeer roundup. I found the winter had been a bad one on Nunivak. At fawning time, in April, a severe blizzard had sprung up with very cold weather. The herders picked up many of the new-born fawns and warmed them under their parkas until they started to move around. In every case, so they informed me, the mother remained close at hand and immediately accepted the youngster as soon as it was released from the parka. The loss would have been extremely high if this hadn't been done.

Strangely enough, Miller found that the ten caribou bulls, planted on Nunivak the year before to increase the size of the crossbred reindeer, herded by themselves. The only time they mixed with the reindeer was during the breeding season.

In the herd the caribou males are leaders [Miller reported], being much larger, stronger, more agile and aggressive than even the finest reindeer males. The horns of caribou males were at this time much more developed than the horns of reindeer, which is indicative of hardiness, better condition, and virility. They appear indifferent to the male reindeer. It is certain that reindeer males cannot compete during the rutting period. I am satisfied that practically all offspring this year were caribou crosses, as evidenced by their tendency toward having Roman noses, larger and coarser ears, hump at shoulders more pronounced, bigger hind feet, longer tails, larger frame, and general features and conformation more resembling that of caribou. The crosses are more easily recognized among yearling animals. Paul Ivanoff, whose experience dates back many years, says he can see a marked difference and great improvement in the Nunivak herd since the caribou have been introduced.

In former times on Nunivak, when the fish failed to run at the proper season of the year, many of the natives starved and the ones who did not were forced to live on the bark of the ground willow and various roots. It was a wonderful day for them when reindeer were introduced to the island. They showed their gratitude by killing off all but twenty of their sled dogs, and even kept them chained up so they would not molest the deer.

Knud Rasmussen, the Danish explorer, once told me that Paul Ivanoff, our manager on Nunivak, was the most intelligent Eskimo he knew. Paul certainly was an outstanding man. He understood the rudiments of business, was a fair bookkeeper, was a trapper, and knew fur; he was an expert in reindeer raising; an excellent mechanic; a teacher; he sang well, and played both the piano and organ. When he first went to Nunivak, he had very little work to do, so we secured textbooks from the Bureau of Education and sent them to him. For two years he conducted, without remuneration, a school for the Eskimo there. He taught them how to make baskets, which they exchanged for supplies at our trading post.

We sent walrus tusks for them to carve. In order to help these people better themselves, we bought all of the souvenir material from them as fast as they made it, although there was very little demand for either baskets or carved ivory in Alaska in those days. At one time we thought we would have to stop buying from them because of such a tremendous oversupply, but finally a market for their handiwork was found.

In January of 1920 I received an invitation from Dr. Stefansson to attend a dinner he was giving at the Harvard Club in New York. There were about twenty guests, and the purpose of the affair was to plan ways and means of raising funds to help save the musk ox, or *Ovibos,* from extermination, as there were only a few left in the world. Many years ago musk oxen had ranged in Alaska but, as in other parts of the Arctic regions, had been killed off. There were small herds of the animals, valuable for food and wool, still ranging on eastern Greenland, Ellesmere Land, and other islands in the Canadian Arctic. It was Stefansson's thought that, if the danger of extinction that threatened this animal was brought to the attention of the general public, some plan could be evolved to save them. One guest present expressed his willingness to contribute $25,000. Others considered this to be a government project, rather than a private one.

Stefansson later visited Dr. Edward W. Nelson, chief of the Bureau of Biological Survey, who became most enthusiastic, giving the matter his full support. It was slow work and the years dragged by. Finally the idea was submitted to Senator Peter Norbeck, of South Dakota, who made it his personal business to secure an appropriation from Congress.

The money was made available and an agreement was entered into with a Norwegian whaler who claimed he could capture some young stock on the east coast of Greenland, take them to Norway, and ship them from there to the United States.

A small herd of thirty animals was landed in New York, transported across the United States, then by steamer and rail to College, Alaska, the location of Alaska's University.

The College, or Fairbanks, country of Alaska is wooded and not the best type of country for musk oxen. I was consulted by the Biological Survey and recommended that the animals be shipped to Nunivak Island as we were very much interested in seeing that the project of propagating this animal prove successful. During the summer of 1936 the musk oxen were placed on Nunivak Island—twenty-seven head—under the care of Paul Ivanoff.

The musk ox is a tough animal and can usually protect itself against wolves. Musk oxen range as a herd and when attacked form a phalanx with the females and calves in the center, the bulls facing the predators with heads lowered. The wolf, from long experience, realizes it is best to search for weaker prey.

A full-grown animal weighs from 500 to 600 pounds, has short legs, and a coat of coarse wool overlaid with matted guard hair that grows to more than a foot in length. It has a bony head with heavy curling horns, and feeds on the toughest vegetation that grows.

With the knowledge that the food of the reindeer and musk oxen was so different, we felt the introduction of the latter animal would not deplete the forage on the island to the detriment of the reindeer herd, but would provide the island with a new and valuable asset. In 1953 the herd was to number close to 100 head, the only herd of musk oxen under the control of the United States.

16.

STEADILY we grew to know and like the Eskimo. We learned to understand them as a fine and honorable people, and how to accept their limitations. It had been our policy from the beginning not only to work with, but for, the Eskimo, as well as for ourselves. We found them to be individuals of a positive nature, with an approach to speech both strong and literal. Experience taught us to be careful in giving instructions to those in our employ; to be indefinite could prove both costly and embarrassing.

For example, you might ask an Eskimo, "Is that your dog?" and he would say "No."

"No?"

"Yes," meaning, "Yes, the answer is no."

One summer when I arrived at Igloo Point, at the mouth of the Buckland River, I was much puzzled by the behavior of Eskimo boys just back from the summer's roundup. I overheard such expressions as "fire in the bushes . . . whistling in the hills . . ." and I could see that they had been frightened.

"Did something unusual happen on the roundup?" I asked one of them.

"Oh, yes. We see four men: two large men, two small men."

"Did you speak to them?"

"Oh, no. Maybe they are bad men."

"What do you mean by 'bad men'?"

"Maybe Indians."

"Did you have your rifles?"

"Oh, yes."

"What did you do?"

"We hide."

"What would Indians be doing in the Buckland country?"

"Maybe stealing reindeer fawn skins."

"Where would the Indians come from?"

"Maybe Yukon River."

"How far is the Yukon River from here?"

"Maybe three hundred miles."

"How many green fawn skins could an Indian carry?"

"Don't know. Maybe not too many."

This was dangerous business. I reminded the boys that Indians would not risk coming into the Buckland country to steal fawn skins which they would have to pack back to the Yukon country on their backs. If the Eskimo weren't careful, someday they might kill an innocent person, perhaps a fine old prospector traveling through the country hunting for gold.

On my return to Nome I wrote a trader friend on the Yukon, requesting him to warn the Indians in his locality to send word ahead when they planned on entering Eskimo country.

I learned of similar misunderstandings. A few years before an Eskimo hunter of Shaktoolik happened to be in the country back of the village when he noticed a man in the distance, a stranger. The Shaktoolik man had his rifle and hid behind some brush to wait. The stranger was an Indian. The Eskimo shot him, buried him, and when he returned to his village, told no one. Many days passed. One day three dog teams, driven by Indians, came along from Yukon country. They said they were looking for a friend who had failed to return home from a trip to the coast. No one in the village could tell them anything. After they had traveled up and down the coast without finding any trace of their friend, the Indians returned home. And then, two years later, the Eskimo who had shot the Indian lay dying. On his deathbed he confided to his family that, since the stranger was an Indian, the Eskimo had been afraid he might harm some of the villagers, and had therefore killed him as the simplest way of preventing any trouble.

One of the Buckland boys told me that one summer he and another Eskimo had almost killed my brother Alfred at Elephant Point.

The boys said they saw two men coming down the coast on foot and they looked to be strangers. Someone said, "Let's kill them!" The Eskimo had their rifles and took position behind some brush. When the strangers were quite close, one of the boys recognized Alfred and warned the others. It seems that Alfred and his Lapp companion, Mike Nilluka, had been washed ashore up the coast and were on their way back to Keewalik on foot, forty miles distant. The Buckland boys stayed out of sight while Alfred and Mike passed by, unaware of their narrow brush with death.

One winter Alfred was on the Buckland. The weather was severe, with temperatures around fifty below. There were some 30,000 reindeer to handle. Alfred had expected to be in Nome for Thanksgiving at home but now Christmas was approaching. The Eskimo, too, wanted to spend the holidays in their own villages. But if the boys were to leave now, the herd would become scattered. Alfred tried suggesting to them that Christmas was for women and children but that they were men. What really placated them, though, was realizing that Alfred himself was reconciled to being away from home on Christmas for the sake of the herd. They, therefore, were willing to emulate the white man and make the same sacrifice.

An amusing example of Eskimo literalness came out at this time. One of the boys announced that he wanted to go to Candle, a day and a half distant by dog team. He promised to come right back. As Alfred had had no mail in weeks, he was glad for someone to make the trip and consented, even though he could not really spare any of the men. At the last moment he said to the boy, "By the way, go to the post office when you get to Candle and see if there is any mail for me."

"Sure," promised the Eskimo.

Days passed. One evening Alfred heard a dog team drive up. It was dark and very cold but, pulling on his parka, Alfred hurried out to see if it was his boy. It was. After greetings and a handshake, he said, "Any mail for me?"

"Oh, yes, plenty," said the boy.

"Well, where is it?"

"Oh, in the Candle post office," the Eskimo casually replied.

Too late Alfred remembered that he had told the boy to "see" if there was mail for him, omitting to say also "and bring it to me."

Then there was my Eskimo friend, "Doc." Doc had killed a white man years before and served a short sentence in a federal prison. One day while visiting him I asked the question: "Why did you kill that white man, Doc?"

He was taken by surprise, asking, "What do you know about that?"

I explained I had heard the story only in a general way and I wanted to know more.

Doc circled around for a few minutes and then faced me.

"I didn't mean to kick over the coffeepot!"

I made no comment, knowing that now I would hear the story.

"One summer, long time ago, I was helping a white man take a boat up the Kobuk River. We would camp every night. The white man had a jug of whisky with him. One day he broke the jug but saved some of the whisky. This he put in the coffeepot. Every night when we make camp the white man would carry the coffeepot ashore and I would carry everything

185

else ashore. One night I was unloading the boat. I picked up the tent. It was not folded—just thrown in. I picked it up and threw it over my shoulder. One piece hung over my head and I could not see, but that was all right. I waded ashore and kicked over the coffeepot. The white man he see this and he get very mad.

" 'I'll kill you for that!' he said.

"Oh, my! I feel very bad and go away. I meet an Eskimo boy and I tell him: 'That white man he say he kill me!' 'Why don't you kill him?' asked the boy. By and by I meet an Eskimo man and tell him. 'Why don't you kill him?' asked the man.

"The next morning the white man walked down to the boat and I hit him right here [pointing between his shoulder blades] with 30-30."

It was a clear case of self-defense, in so far as Doc was concerned.

I was inclined to agree with him. The white man had intended no harm to the Eskimo. "I'll kill you!" was simply an expression of disgust. But it was accepted by Doc as a threat literally meant.

An Eskimo man came into my office in Nome one day and handed me a note without comment. It read:

I want to owe you $27.75. I want you to get my package from the post office. It is the clothes I want. I will try pay you back again because I haven't any other clothes to wear. I got to have them. I try to get from Bureau of Education. He said no and only give me hell! What kind of government is he?

The Eskimo had ordered clothes from one of the mail-order houses and had received notice from the post office that his package had arrived. He had no money but could not understand why the government would not give him the money when he wanted it. If he'd had the money and the Government had asked for it, he would have given it willingly. Such is the deadly logic of the Eskimo.

On another occasion the chief herder at Golovin sent me a note that read as follows: "I want some little packages but be sure the picture is on the package. If it have no picture I can't send it."

I puzzled over this for some time, then finally sent down a quantity of stamped envelopes, which was precisely what he needed.

At the winter headquarters of the Buckland herd brother Alfred and his dog-team driver, Pete Olsen, a husky Norwegian, had listened to tales of the power of the local medicine man. It was winter and very cold. The Buckland herd was being handled for marking and killing, and the crew numbered twenty-odd Eskimo. Living quarters consisted of one small log cabin. Cooking on a small wood stove for such a crew was no simple matter. Appetites were voracious, however, and no complaints were heard.

One matter that concerned the two white men was the influence over these people of the medicine man. One old Eskimo had told them how this medicine man could take a blue bead, talk to it, and then throw it into the night and say: "Now you will find the blue bead in one of the mukluks or mittens!"

A search would invariably produce the blue bead in the spot he had told them it would be.

"Plenty power!" the credulous Eskimo would say, shaking their heads.

Alfred suggested to Pete one morning, while they had the cabin to themselves, that they frame the medicine man by showing the Eskimo that others had the same power.

Searching in his pockets, Alfred found two ten-cent pieces. He took a shotgun shell and removed the powder. With a small file that was in the cabin he made an X on one of the coins and deposited it in one of the mittens hanging by a cord from the wall. A small box was placed on the floor directly under the mittens, where the aged Eskimo generally sat. Alfred then placed the powder in a piece of paper, folded it carefully, and put it in his pocket.

That evening, as soon as the dinner dishes had been put away and the group had seated themselves around the walls on sleeping bags and other bedding, with the old man below the mittens, Alfred turned to Pete and once more told the story of the medicine man and his blue bead.

"You know, Alfred, I have some power myself," Pete said assuredly. "I could do that if I had a blue bead."

"That's easy to say because there are no blue beads in camp!"

"I really don't have to have a bead."

Feeling in his pocket and taking out the ten-cent piece, Alfred inquired if the coin would do.

"Sure! That's just the thing!" Pete replied.

"Just a minute, Pete! I'll mark this coin so we can recognize it later. Is there a file around here?"

A file was produced and an X marked on the coin. This brought forth a laugh from the Eskimo as they thought it would ruin Pete's trick.

"Put any mark you want on it. That will make no difference," Pete stated with a confident air.

Pete took the ten-cent piece, placed it in a piece of paper, and then went from Eskimo to Eskimo to have them feel of the paper so they would know the coin was inside. When Pete reached Alfred and held out the paper, Alfred palmed the paper with the coin and handed Pete the paper containing the powder.

Pete then armed himself with a dishpan, and walked around the room singing Norwegian songs, pounding on the pan the while. Continuing with his hocus-pocus, he approached the small stove in which a hot fire was burning and, without a letup of his incantations, lifted the lid of the stove, tossed in the paper he carried, hurriedly replaced the lid, threw both arms into the air, and cried, "Shoosh!"

An explosion occurred a split second later, with hot coals following the stove lid out into the room.

Pete said, "Now you will find the coin in one of the mittens or mukluks!"

Eyes wide, the Eskimo all jumped to their feet and commenced making a hurried search. The old man who had been seated beneath the mittens naturally inspected them first. He soon found the coin and examined it, finding the X marked on its face.

Turning to Pete, he said, "Yes, you have plenty power but you get your power from Dunnuk [the devil]!"

The Eskimo were very thoughtful, saying nothing, as they crawled into their sleeping bags for the night. In fact, so disturbed did the Eskimo seem that Alfred and Pete decided to explain that they had simply played a trick, even to the point of showing them how it had been done. They added that their own "medicine men" had played the same kind of tricks on them for years. This made everybody feel better.

At this same reindeer marking one of the Eskimo boys came to Alfred and informed him that several years before he had killed one of the Lomen deer and now he wanted to make restitution. Alfred asked for more details.

"Three years ago," the native explained, "one other boy and I were far from home and we ran out of grub. We see some reindeer and they have the Lomen mark. We each afraid of the other so we each kill one deer. The other boy, he kill one and I kill one. Now I want to make restitution and give you two deer for the one I killed."

Alfred was pleased, and to prove the correctness of the old saw that "honesty is the best policy," he told the Eskimo that because he had come and told him of the killing of the deer, he had squared accounts and that he would not ask him to return either one or two deer to the Lomens.

The Eskimo boy did not look at all pleased, so Alfred asked him what was really on his mind.

"One of my Eskimo friends tell me that seven years ago he see one of my female deer in your Kotzebue herd. I think I should have increase."

"How much increase do you think you should have?"

"Maybe fifteen reindeer."

"Our records do not show that one of your deer was in our herd. Maybe it was there before the marking, and went back to your herd and took some of our deer with it. If it was in our herd at marking time, the Eskimo herders and handlers would have seen it."

"I guess so."

"You don't have to make restitution to us and we don't have to give you increase."

"All right!"

The Eskimo had intended to soften Alfred up to make it difficult for him to refuse the request on the larger deal. The Eskimo are far from being fools. But so was Alfred.

The Lapps, too, were always prepared to look out for their own interests. When we were getting ready for the great drive of deer to Canada, we discussed many phases of the trip with Andrew Bahr and his Lapp lieutenants. Every one of these men was an experienced reindeer man. In the States we had obtained the finest trained sheep dogs we could get from one of the great sheepmen of the western states. The Lapp, Ivar West, requested that he be permitted to take his own reindeer dog on the drive with him, so we gladly consented.

Ivar remained with the drive a year and a half, returning when the herd had traveled less than half the way. Final settlement of his wages was made at our office in Nome, where he received more money than he ever had had at one time before. Alfred, who paid him off, expected to see Ivar wearing a big smile but instead he was sullen.

"What is it, Ivar?" Alfred inquired. "Anything wrong?"

"I think I should have some rent for my dog."

"How much rent would you consider fair"

"Maybe fifty cents a day."

"How long was the dog on the drive?"

"Eighteen months."

"Does your dog eat?"

"Oh, yes!"

"Whose food did your dog eat during the year and a half?"

"Your food."

"Well, Ivar, we will not charge any rent for the food your dog ate, and you will not charge any rent for the dog."

"All right!" And Ivar went away perfectly happy and content.

Although these Eskimo and Lapps were not highly educated people, they were most exact logicians, nevertheless.

17.

THERE WERE several reasons why a Christmas campaign to bring the reindeer to the attention of the American public could prove beneficial to the industry. First was the animal itself, of which so little was known. As shown in the storybooks, Santa's reindeer were make-believe animals resembling but slightly the real ones. Santa would popularize the reindeer, which would then become less and less mythical, for it would be seen by millions of people. The children, when they realized that Santa depended upon sales of reindeer meat to secure funds for toy materials, would boost the commercial industry.

While visiting in 1925 with the advertising manager of a large New York department store during the Christmas shopping season, I casually asked whether his store used a Santa Claus.

"Why, of course!" he assured me.

"What would be your reaction as an advertising man to a Santa Claus with a team of live reindeer?"

He jumped at the idea but I changed the subject, as we were not in a position to follow through at that moment. However, I filed his favorable reaction in my memory for future reference.

The following winter my brother Ralph and I were lunching one day with a friend at the Bankers' Club in New York. Two advertising men were also at our table. Conversation roamed over a variety of subjects. At one point Ralph remarked, "In connection with the volume of merchandising during the holiday season, and Santa Claus on every street corner and in every store, can you visualize what it might mean if Santa had a team of live reindeer with him? If, in smaller cities and towns, a civic affair were made of Santa and his Christmas reindeer?"

One of the advertising men raised his hands in mock surrender.

"I'm sold!" he exclaimed.

"That's the first new Christmas idea," said the other, "since they took a fat man, hung chin whiskers on him, and called him Santa Claus!"

Our host was an attorney. Within a few days he drew up a contract between the advertising men and ourselves. We were to select the reindeer out of our herds, train them, and make shipment to Seattle. They were to prepare the advertising, and complete deliveries from Seattle to the various cities where the subscribers to the plan had their places of business.

We remained in New York for several weeks, assisting in the preparation of literature. A research department was set up and the subjects of Christmas, Santa Claus, and reindeer were studied as never before.

Six reindeer would compose a team, instead of the mythical eight, since they could be more easily handled. Santa would also have the help of an Eskimo driver. A forty-day program was built up with radio talks by Santa to the children each evening, together with advertising material for the press.

Upon our return to the North in the spring we engaged Lapp and Eskimo trainers, constructed large special pens for the reindeer, shipped in from the States foodstuffs consisting of cracked corn, wheat, rolled oats, and alfalfa tips to be used in weaning the animals from their natural foods.

Very soon a large camp was established at Golovin, where 100 reindeer were taken from the herd for training. Special attention was given to young animals with well-shaped antlers.

During the early days of feeding, lichens mixed with rolled oats was given the animals. They would shake the moss in order to free it of the rolled oats, but not always successfully. Gradually they paid less and less attention, until they would finally eat the rolled oats alone. The men worked with the animals each day, until they became very tame and docile.

Reports from the States assured us that the plan was being favorably and enthusiastically received and a minimum of seventy-five reindeer would be needed to fill the orders. Subscribers included department stores and newspapers in Brooklyn, Boston, Philadelphia, Detroit, St. Louis, Kansas City, Los Angeles, San Francisco, and Portland, Oregon.

The campaign was to open in October. A young girl would address a letter to the editor of the local paper.

"Dear Mr. Editor: I am worried. My playmates tell me that there is no Santa Claus. You know everything. Is there a Santa Claus?"

A facsimile of the letter appeared on the front page of the paper, followed with comments by the editor, who wrote that he had always believed in Santa Claus, although he had never seen him. What did the other children think? Was there a Santa Claus? Thousands of letters poured into the paper. The staff photographer visited the children's playgrounds, taking photographs. The interest rose to a high pitch and the editor finally decided to do something about it—a foregone conclusion, to be sure.

The paper then appealed to a correspondent in Alaska who might have some special information. He was contacted and advised his paper that he, too, had always believed in Santa and understood he lived far north of Nome, but he felt certain he could find him.

With this assurance from their representative, the editor took fast action. The correspondent was instructed by telegraph to engage the finest and swiftest dog team in all of Alaska, together with a competent Eskimo driver, and go out and find Santa. When he met him he was to extend, on behalf of the children of the city, an invitation to visit them; to come early so all could meet him, and remain with them as the guest of their city.

Daily wires were exchanged, all of which were actual telegrams, and these were published on the front pages of the paper. The correspondent, with his dog team and Eskimo driver, left Nome for the far North. Then came a break. No wire was received. The editor attempted to visualize what the difficulty was. Stories were written about dog-team driving, the Eskimo people, and the reindeer. Then an explanatory wire arrived. The correspondent and driver had been storm-bound at an Eskimo camp; one of the Eskimo at the camp knew Santa, knew where he lived, and would guide them to Santa's home the following day.

The next wire: "Santa found!" His home was at Icy Cape, and the correspondent's proudest moment was when he shook Santa by the hand. The invitation sent out by the children had been delivered.

Santa answered. He was very busy, for he expected to have the largest and finest assortment of toys that year he had ever carried south, but he felt he could not leave so early.

The following day came a second wire from Santa. He had reconsidered. He would accept the children's invitation, pick up his team of reindeer, and drive them to Nome, taking the steamer from there to Seattle. This change of plans would permit him to treat his reindeer to an ocean trip by steamer, and also give him the opportunity to complete his work on board ship.

Santa's next wire was dated at Nome. He had gone to Kringle Valley to get his deer. They were in splendid condition and he had brought them on to Nome and would embark for Seattle the following morning.

With Santa's departure from Nome, Mrs. Santa wired:

"Santa sailed this morning with his reindeer and a large variety of toys. I expect him back late Christmas Eve."

From the ship came daily radiograms. A severe storm was encountered. Santa was swept overboard but rescued by the sailors. One of Santa's team had rubbed up against a newly painted sleigh rail and was smeared with red paint. Blitzen had swallowed a mama doll, mistaking it for Arctic moss, and caused much merriment among the sailors as he kept saying, "Mama, Mama," while prancing about the deck.

Upon Santa's arrival in Seattle, the newspaper of the subscriber city kept in constant communication with him, and the city was all excitement when it was announced that Santa was due the following morning. He would drive through the streets of the city with his reindeer to the city park, which had been set aside for him as headquarters during his visit, and where the city had constructed a fine log stable with comfortable box stalls for the deer, an igloo for Santa's driver, and very comfortable quarters for Santa himself.

Our first shipment of reindeer arrived in Seattle early in October: seventy-six reindeer with sixteen Eskimo and Lapp drivers, all in charge of brother Alfred. It was so important that the arrival of this strange, romantic group be kept secret that detectives were planted on the dock to keep people away while reindeer and drivers were transferred from ship to express cars for shipment to various cities. The deer for Portland, San Francisco, and Los Angeles were trucked to a farm near Portland while they became acclimated.

Portland, Oregon, was the first city to make this interesting experiment in reindeer psychology. No one knew how the animals would react to city sounds, auto horns, and thousands of people. The Oregon *Journal* was our subscriber paper there. Clients in other cities watched results with great interest. Other subscribers included the San Francisco *Chronicle*, Los Angeles *Times*, Kansas City *Star*, Cleveland *News*, and Boston *American;* the Fair, Chicago; Strawbridge and Clothier, Philadelphia; Newcomb-Endicott, Detroit; and Rike-Kumler of Dayton, Ohio. We sold the plan for $15,000 to each participant in the Christmas campaign.

Following delivery of the deer to the farm outside of Portland, I received a telephone call at Seattle from the *Journal:* "We have just returned from the farm. The reindeer are so wild we can do nothing with them. You must come down and advise us what to do."

I was in Portland the following morning but would make no comment until I saw our boys and the deer. We drove to the farm where the deer were staked out, thirty to forty feet apart. Several were being exercised by the boys. I spoke to the chief herder, a Lapp, and asked him to show me the more gentle animals.

"That one is all right," he said, pointing, "and that one and that one."

I went over to the deer, untied one, and trotted about the pasture with it. I repeated it with the two others and then walked over to the *Journal* executives.

"I don't find the animals so wild," I said to them. "You must realize they were taken from an open range, spent many days aboard a ship, and then were trucked down here from Seattle. Naturally they are bewildered and excited. They will gentle down within a few days."

They all admitted substantial improvement since the day before, and I assured them the animals would show still greater progress by the following day.

We returned to Portland and held a long conference.

"Mr. Lomen," I was told, "we can do one of two things. We have advertised that Santa was arriving next Saturday morning and that his line of march would be along certain streets to the park that will be his headquarters while the guest of the city of Portland. We can have him go directly to the park and then say to the children that Santa surprised us by arriving during the night, or stick to our program and have him parade through the city."

I advised them to carry out their original plan. I suggested that Santa, as the city's honored guest, was entitled to an honor guard; that the guard should be composed of six men, one for each deer; the drivers and the honor guard would go to the farm on Thursday, take the Portland team, and lead them along the highway some seven or eight miles toward Portland, arranging in advance for a place for men and animals to spend the night. The next morning, a Friday, the reindeer would be hitched to a sleigh built about an auto chassis, the runners elevated a couple of inches so the wheels would carry the load, and then led to the outskirts of Portland, where they would bed down for the second night. On Saturday morning Santa, his driver, and the honor guard, all dressed in parkas, would come right on and proceed with the reindeer along the advertised line of march.

I returned to Seattle. Friday evening I received a phone call from the *Journal*. A voice, heavy with excitement, said, "The reindeer left the farm yesterday morning, covering seven or eight miles. They behaved well. This morning they were attached to the sleigh and traveled to the Portland city limits. Tomorrow morning they make their entry into Portland with Santa, and you must be here!"

All was excitement at the *Journal* office when I arrived the following morning. We were soon in cars headed for the suburbs to meet Portland's distinguished visitors. There was furor all about—boys and girls running and parents hurrying, all going in the same direction. We turned a corner and there, a block ahead, was a crowd of people with Santa, his driver, and team of reindeer, together with the guard of honor, in the midst of an immense gathering! Santa was ahead of schedule and had stopped. I noticed immediately that the animals were chewing their cuds, a sure sign they were not nervous. Santa was standing on the sleigh trying his utmost to fondle and praise all the little children who were passed up to him by loving parents. The honor guard was stationed at the heads of the reindeer to protect the children from any possibility of their being struck by the antlers, though the reindeer would not intentionally injure the youngsters.

Santa, his reindeer, and the retinue moved on, the crowd following and constantly growing larger. When the *Journal* offices were reached, a group of lovely young girls, dressed all in white, rushed out with large bouquets of flowers which they presented to Santa. Then on to the park with its festive decorations and its attractive stable and igloo. Here, waiting to welcome Santa, were the city and county officials and thousands of Portland's citizens. It was a memorable occasion and an immensely satisfying one to me because of the thousands of "happiness hours" it created for young and old alike, and, too, the realization that our subscriber was more than satisfied in our combined campaign to make Christmas a genuinely civic affair.

Following a luncheon for Santa Claus, who was by that time almost exhausted, we returned to the *Journal* office, where the managing editor sent telegrams to all other subscribers stating that his paper was thrilled with the tremendous success of Santa's entry into Portland, and that they all felt well repaid for their efforts.

Frantic calls came from our eastern subscribers. Reindeer and Eskimo drivers had arrived, but more "expert" advice was demanded. Alfred hurried east but could make only one city at a time, so there were delays.

It was found that the natives and deer were calm and undisturbed but that the people placed in charge of the local exhibitions were greatly worried for fear of failure. Professional actors were engaged in most cities to play the part of Santa, and animal trainers were hired to take care of the reindeer. It was soon discovered that the latter move was unnecessary.

Philadelphia produced an unusual situation. A large department store was the subscriber, and when Alfred called on its executives he was told that a competitor was also showing Santa's reindeer, and that was a violation of our contract, as we had stipulated that our subscriber would be the only one with reindeer in his particular city. Alfred asked that he be taken to see these other deer, only to discover that the animals were young elk, not reindeer.

"You know it, but how many others will know these animals are not reindeer? Could you have some expert other than yourself come to Philadelphia to state that those animals are not reindeer?"

Alfred first suggested the chief of the Biological Survey in Washington, D. C., but, on second thought, asked that a telephone call be put through to the Waldorf-Astoria Hotel in New York to ascertain whether Captain Roald Amundsen, well-known explorer and discoverer of the South Pole, was registered. He was, and happened to be in.

Alfred took the phone and said, "Captain Amundsen, this is Alfred Lomen. I am in Philadelphia and I am in trouble. I there any chance of your coming down here to help us out?"

"An excellent chance," replied Amundsen. "I am scheduled for a lecture in Washington tomorrow night. I will take an early train and stop over for a few hours with you in Philadelphia."

All was excitement the next morning as Amundsen was met by the officials of the store, newsmen, and photographers. The reindeer were seen and approved, and then the competing department store was visited.

"Those are not reindeer," was Amundsen's verdict; "they are elk!"

Word spread around, and the following day the elk were removed from the other store.

There were variations in the programs at several cities. Brooklyn, for instance, was notified by Santa that he was extremely busy and was sending his reindeer team and driver on ahead; that he would fly with Clarence Chamberlain, who had recently flown the Atlantic, and would join his team at the city's Prospect Park.

The reindeer and Eskimo driver had arrived and were awaiting Santa at the park, as also were thirty mounted police trying to calm some 100,000 people. An airplane was spotted, and as it circled the field a splotch of red could be seen in the plane. The plane landed in the center of the park, the reindeer and Eskimo trotted out to meet Santa, then he was enthroned in the sleigh and a grand tour made around the grounds.

Santa's entry into Portland, Oregon, was on October 26, the earliest of any American city. The first full-page Christmas advertisements appeared in the Oregon *Journal* on November 5, which meant an advance of Christmas shopping by thirty days. This pageant brought joy to the children, increased good will and advertising lineage in the newspaper, developed a feeling of reality in the spirit of Christmas, and strengthened parental discipline. Visits were made to schools and hospitals where the reindeer could be petted by children. They paraded the streets and were seen and enjoyed by millions of people. Similar programs were held in the various cities throughout the country.

Cities, businessmen, railroads, and bus lines all recognized the unique value of having Santa and his reindeer in their areas and co-operated fully to make the gala event long remembered.

Typical was the way the San Francisco *Bulletin* introduced Santa's Christmas Eve appearance at a great celebration in the City Auditorium, which was filled to capacity on Christmas Eve. Shortly before midnight Santa came on stage, with his reindeer and sleigh, to tell the eager audience about his life and thank them for their fine hospitality. As twelve o'clock approached, the lights of the hall suddenly went off. In the darkness could be heard the clatter of reindeer hoofs, the jingling of bells, the squeal of departing runners, and Santa's fading voice calling out:

"A merry, merry Christmas to all, and to all a good night!"

The lights came on. The stage was empty. Santa and his reindeer had vanished, gone up into the blue dome of heaven to return to their home at the North Pole.

18.

LATE IN May 1929 I arrived in Seattle in time for the sailing of the first steamer of the season to Nome, the S. S. *Victoria*. This was a nine-day trip, and with me was my bride.

Laura Volstead was an only child. When her father was elected to Congress from Minnesota in 1902, she went to Washington with her parents. Andrew Joseph Volstead was the author of the Farmers' Co-operative Marketing Act and the Volstead Act, the Federal Prohibition Act passed by Congress in 1919.

During the twenty years her father served in Congress, Laura spent most of her life in the nation's capital city, and graduated from George Washington University Law School. In 1912 she attended Stanley Hall in Minneapolis, a boarding school for girls. There she met my sister Helen, also a student, and they became fast friends.

Some years later, when I went to Washington on business, I paid my respects to the Volsteads and met their charming daughter. It wasn't long before I was smitten by Laura's many attractions. But I was hesitant about asking her to marry me.

My business was highly speculative, to say the least. I was on the move the year around: in the summer to Nome and our scattered reindeer herds; to New York and Washington, D. C., in the winter. I could offer very little home life to a young lady who had grown up in Washington and enjoyed its social activities.

However, after a lot of hemming and hawing, I finally

proposed to Laura Volstead and, to my astonishment and delight, she accepted. On October 30, 1928, we were married at the House of Hope Presbyterian Church in St. Paul, and left immediately thereafter to spend the winter in New York.

When the lighters put us ashore at Nome in mid-June the whole population, white and Eskimo, were gathered at the water front to meet the first steamer and greet their friends. I introduced my bride all around, and she was immediately accepted by the community, entering into a strange new life as if she were born to be "Mrs. Sourdough."

The marking season for the deer was not far off and we were soon preparing for the trip to Choris Peninsula, just below the Arctic Circle. This was the location of our corral system for handling the Kotzebue herd. A few days after arriving in Nome we took off for camp with one of the bush pilots. It was a 250-mile flight and marked my first experience in flying to a roundup and marking.

Laura was dressed in leather breeches, wool skirt, leather jacket, and Eskimo skin boots. A couple of parkas, sleeping bags, soap, towels, a kit of toilet articles, and my brief case completed our luggage.

Bright sun and a cloudless sky made it easy to pick out the narrow strip of land that was to be our home for several days. The characteristically deep-blue water of the Arctic Ocean stretched as far as we could see. Wild flowers were in profuse bloom everywhere. Pale yellow poppies swayed with the breeze. Clumps of dark purple iris proudly raised their heads. The songs of birds and the lapping of the waves on the pure-white sands were all that broke the silence of that beautiful warm day in the Arctic.

Our Eskimo friends erected a tent for us. I noticed a couple of old rusty bedsprings being brought up. This was a special treat in deference to my bride, as I was accustomed to laying my sleeping bag on the ground. An empty orange crate and a tin washbasin completed our living quarters.

Laura entered enthusiastically into all the activities of the camp. The Eskimo, as I have said, are a kindly people with a good sense of humor, and soon she was talking and laughing with the women, exchanging neighborhood gossip as women do the world over.

The camp was short of certain supplies, especially fresh food, for there had been no boat from the "outside" since October of the year before. There were no eggs, of course. However, Leo, the Eskimo cook, provided good hotcakes, toast, oatmeal, canned fruit, and coffee for breakfast. There was plenty of reindeer meat and some dehydrated vegetables.

One morning Leo told Laura he had some eggs ready for her. Knowing that the camp had no eggs but thinking one of the Eskimo women had saved a few from last fall and sent them to her, she could not refuse, and Leo brought her two of the largest eggs she had ever seen.

"These are crowbill eggs," said Leo. "Try them. One of the boys got them from the nests in the cliff."

Laura attacked the eggs hesitantly but, to her surprise, found them excellent.

At the summer marking a number of fawns are always butchered for parka skins. Laura watched the Eskimo women skinning for several days when one of them looked up and said to her: "You skin fawn." Laura turned to our Lapp friend, Mike Nilluka, and asked him for his sharp skinning knife, which Mike handed over with the admonition: "No matter how long it takes, a parka skin must have no holes in it." Laura tackled it gingerly while the Eskimo women went into peals of laughter. She was no speed artist, but in time she produced a good parka skin. In chorus the women exclaimed, "Ahregah!" which meant approval.

Laura and I were gone from Nome twenty-eight days. From Choris Peninsula we traveled by boat to Kotzebue and stopped at Igloo Point for another marking before returning to Nome.

Living as we did, there was no such thing as a bath. Much of the time Laura slept with her clothes on, usually for warmth, but there was little or no privacy and the night was as light as day. Though we went bathless, there are often greater hardships in the northland, and we were happy and content.

My brothers and I were much interested in the progress of aviation in Alaska, appreciating that the airplane would bring great changes in our northern territory.

During the spring of 1919 I had returned from Washington en route back to Alaska. Brothers Ralph and Alfred, recently discharged from the Army, were in Seattle. A few days prior to my arrival they had flown with Eddie Hubbard of the Boeing Company, and I found them tremendously enthusiastic and insistent that I make a flight. The boys had been among the first group of four to fly "commercially" with the Boeing people, Alfred holding their flight certificate No. 3 and Ralph No. 4. Arrangements were soon made and I took off with Eddie as "Flight Passenger No. 86." Following my fifteen minutes in the air we landed and went to the Boeing factory with Hubbard, where we met the executives of the company. We discussed costs of planes and the proper type for use in Alaska. We could visualize the great possibilities of the airplane in the reindeer industry for locating herds on the vast ranges and carrying supplies to the herders. Then there would be the great saving of time in moving from herd to herd, compared with slow boat travel that often took several days, even weeks. But to purchase a plane in those early years was far beyond our means.

Colonel Carl Ben Eielsen became Alaska's pioneer pilot. He organized the first Alaska airplane company. I was honored to be appointed a member of his first board of directors, along with Juan Trippe, later to become president of Pan

American World Airways and one of the airways' greatest executives, and Colonel John B. Hambleton of Baltimore. My connection with the new company was due only to my Alaska residence, as I could offer no financial assistance.

In the first ten years of our reindeer operations we had traveled to the herds by dog team in winter and small motorboats in open weather. Completing the work at the herd in summer, we were sometimes forced to remain two or three weeks awaiting transportation. During these periods we strengthened our friendly ties with the Eskimo. We told stories, played games with them, and engaged in foot races and other sports, in addition to discussing the work we were all interested in—reindeer.

Then came the era of the airplane. Instead of days, it required merely hours to reach our most remote camp. From the air we could spot a herd that would formerly have taken days to find. With radio we could instruct the herders to have the main herd at the corral at a certain time. Completing our work, we could telegraph or radio for a plane. This made it possible to mark several herds prior to the mating season.

I was greatly surprised one summer to be told by an Eskimo deer man that "you Lomen boys don't like us any more. You used to come and spend much time with us, play games, and have races. Now you come and when herd has been handled you go."

I explained that there were other herds to handle and we had to leave as soon as possible; that in the earlier years we were forced to wait for the "mailboat." This the Eskimo understood, and were therefore satisfied.

Colonel Eielson was the man who blazed the Arctic trails that others followed. Ben was liked and respected by all who knew him. He soon became manager of Alaskan Airlines, Inc., a subsidiary of the Aviation Corporation of America.

During the fall of 1929 the M.S. *Nanuk,* with Olaf Swenson and his daughter, Marion, on board, froze in at North Cape,

Siberia. Colonel Eielson was commissioned to proceed to North Cape and transport passengers and the cargo of valuable fur to Nome.

On October 30 Colonel Eielson and his mechanic, Earl Borland, left Teller, Alaska, for North Cape, Siberia, in an all-metal Hamilton plane, and made a successful flight to the ship, returning to Nome with passengers and fur.

On November 9 Ben and his mechanic left on a second trip, carrying a heavy load of gas and oil, coffee, bacon, eggs, and other merchandise for the *Nanuk*. The weather was bad, the Bering Strait banked in by dense fog. The fliers did not reach the *Nanuk* on schedule, but no concern was felt for them. Once before, Ben had made a forced landing on the Arctic ice pack, when with Sir Hubert Wilkins. On that occasion they were obliged to abandon their plane and walk back to the north coast of Alaska. It was a grim trip, though Ben treated it as a lark. He had also been Wilkins' pilot on his Antarctic expedition and that epic flight from the north coast of Alaska across the Arctic to Spitzbergen.

With the passage of several weeks, and still no word from the missing men, Alaska Airlines went into action, as did the people of Nome and Teller. The United States Air Corps, when appealed to by wire, reported they had no planes suitable for such a mission. On November 29 Joe Crosson, chief pilot of Alaska Airlines, arrived at Teller in a Waco, followed shortly by Frank Dorbandt from Nome. On December 10 pilots Barnhill and Moller showed up in a Standard; the next day Ed Young in a Stinson and Harold Gillam in a Stearman; and on December 18 Matt Nieminen and A. Cope arrived at Teller. Clark Bassett came in as a mechanic to assist with the planes, and Canadian pilots came to take part in the search.

By this time the entire country was aroused. I was in New York and met with the officials of the Aviation Corporation, Mr. Grosvenor, the president, and Colonel Bain. Soon after, brother Alfred was appointed by the Aviation Corporation to take full charge of the rescue operations. Alfred proceeded from Nome to Teller, where search headquarters had been established. His first act was to brief the pilots and check all clothing and equipment. Jack Warren, the superintendent of our reindeer operations and trading post at Teller, was invaluable in locating fur clothing and necessary supplies for the protection of the pilots. Alfred secured Gus Masik, who had been with Stefansson and spent years in the Arctic; he was engaged to teach the pilots the art of building a snow house for shelter in case of a forced landing and other techniques of Arctic survival, also to act as interpreter to Siberian Eskimo. Olaf Swenson provided headquarters on his ship, the *Nanuk,* for the pilots. His wide experience as a trader on the Siberian coast proved of inestimable value. He flew with the pilots and also took part in the search by dog team.

Now started the greatest privately conducted aerial search ever known, bucking the toughest of all odds, the elements—extreme cold, ice, snow, and fog, with the dreaded Bering Strait to cross.

We in New York were doing everything possible from that end. During the Christmas holidays, Mrs. Mabel Walker Willebrandt and Dr. Vilhjalmur Stefansson were our guests one evening. All angles of the search were discussed. Federal action was important. Our Government had not at that time recognized the U.S.S.R., and it was as though they did not exist. The Russians could prove very valuable in the search. Mrs. Willebrandt offered to return to Washington that night to secure help. There she immediately contacted Senator Borah, who obtained a promise of assistance from the Russians.

On December 19, with low fog and poor visibility, Joe Crosson and Harold Gillam, in two planes, took to the air to reconnoiter the Bering Strait. They found a hole in the fog and crossed safely but were later forced down on the Siberian coast, Gillam reaching the *Nanuk* the twentieth, Crosson on the twenty-first. These two were to base at the *Nanuk* and carry on the search from there.

As gasoline was a big factor, Ed Young and Victor Ross flew in what they could from Nome when weather permitted. It was generally a period of foul weather, of driving winds and heavy snow, two to three hours of daylight, and temperatures ranging to fifty below zero. Meanwhile, three Fairchild 71's with crews were on their way. One was washed out in taking off at Fairbanks, and one was forced down some thirty miles north of Unalakleet, Alaska, having lost part of one wing. Temporary repairs were made and the ship flown to Nome where she was put in condition, then flown on to Teller by T. M. (Pat) Reid with Bill Hughes as mechanic. Ed Young brought the third ship with Sam McCauley, mechanic.

These intrepid fliers were in the air every day, weather permitting, and at times when conditions were extremely hazardous. In such extreme weather, and in so vast a country, there is a great sense of helplessness when men fly away and fail to return. In the frozen Arctic even the smallest injury can sometimes prove fatal, since it ties a man down to one spot where there may be no food and usually no shelter.

Hope continued strong that Ben and Earl were still alive. The men participating in this search took many chances with death. They knew, had they been reported missing, Ben Eielson would literally have "flown the wings off his plane" to find them. They did likewise.

Soviet planes now arrived under the leadership of Commander M. T. Slipnev. They assisted in the search and spared neither men nor expense. Their one thought was to find the missing men, and they never asked for remuneration.

On January 25, 1930, a message was received from Joe Crosson. He and Harold Gillam had found the Hamilton plane, wrecked and partially buried in snow and ice, about ninety miles southeast of North Cape, Siberia. The cockpit of the plane was entirely torn away but the cabin was intact. Though they searched for a long time, there was no sign of either of the men. Could they have managed to leave the plane and still be safe?

Crosson and Gillam returned to the *Nanuk* for help. Planes and dog teams were dispatched to the scene of the wreck. Digging deep into the hard-packed snow turned up scattered tools. A week after the digging started, Borland's helmet and mittens were found at widely separated points, and then they knew that the men had met their death.

It was not until February 12 that Earl Borland's body was found, and on the eighteenth, Colonel Eielsen's. They were first taken by Commander Slipnev, by plane, to the Russian ice-bound steamer *Stavropol,* where the ship's doctor prepared the bodies for their last long flight together. Then they were flown to the *Nanuk.*

With the two bodies in the Fairchilds, Ed Young, Sam McCauley, and Joe Crosson left the *Nanuk,* homeward bound over the frozen, silent wastes of Siberia, across the windswept Bering Strait and thence to Teller; they were accompanied by Commander Slipnev and mechanic Fahrig, arriving March 3.

Thus was the hazardous search ended. The pilots had lost a great buddy. His undoubted courage, fearlessness, and faith in aviation had been an inspiration to those who risked everything under the toughest possible conditions to find him. It was a sad farewell as Ben was borne away on wings from the country he loved so much, to be laid to rest at his home in North Dakota.

The expedition was not yet completed. Gasoline borrowed from the Soviets had to be returned, there were planes on the Siberian coast to be brought back to Alaska. This took many crossings and weather delays. *Finis* was written on May 11, 1930, to one of the longest and most complicated search expeditions known to aviation up to that time.

19.

FROM 1928 to 1930 we conducted our largest, most ambitious operations in the North, shipping to the States in that period some 30,000 carcasses of meat and thousands of reindeer hides for the manufacture of gloves. Our selling price was twelve and a half cents per pound for the carcass, F.O.B. Seattle.

People often took the trouble to warn us, "You can't make a paying business of the reindeer!" Yet in the face of many difficulties we had developed large herds, acquired and installed modern equipment, corral systems, abattoirs, and cold-storage plants in the North, refrigerated ships to transport our products to the States, at the same time creating a demand equal to our output at the peak of our shipments outside.

When the great depression burst on the country in 1929, meat prices toppled. It became the common experience of cattle and sheep men in the United States, shipping carloads of animals to the stockyards, to receive less money in full payment for their shipments than was required for just the railroad freight bills. We also failed to recover the butchering and shipping costs for our products. At the same time we had confidence that the depression could not last forever, and the time would come when meat prices would go up again.

My old Lapp friend, Sam Balto, once remarked to me, "The reindeer business is the only enterprise I know of where a man can be drunk all the time and not lose his property." Even that type of reindeer owner could still make money in the reindeer industry today. In 1953 reindeer meat sold at the Golovin herd for fifty-five cents per pound, retailing in Nome for seventy-five cents.

During the depression we were the largest employers of Eskimo labor in the world, having on our pay roll 579 full- and part-time Eskimo employees in 1929.

With increased employment and larger pay rolls, resulting from the expansion of the industry, the purchasing power of the Eskimo herders and other Eskimo workers had increased, as did freight shipments and supplies of all kinds from the States. Reindeer-meat shipments from the north tended to lessen that most difficult of transportation problems, the furnishing of south-bound cargo. Of necessity freight rates to Bering Sea ports were high.

All this while the industry was widely publicized. The word "reindeer" has romantic associations, and the American press, though sometimes inaccurate as to facts, was generous with its space. Such headlines as "A new meat to supplant beef," "Reindeer, a competitor for beef and mutton," and similar phrases scared livestock producers. Actually, sales of reindeer meat in the United States did not reduce the sale of packing-house products. On the contrary, the development of the new Alaska industry opened up a great country and created an enlarged market in the north for the livestock and packing-house products of the United States.

However, with increased reindeer shipments from the north, hostile opposition developed in the States from live-stock producers, cattle and sheep organizations, meat packers, farmers, and others. In Kansas and Nebraska, boycott measures were adopted by local livestock interests when it was learned that two carloads of reindeer meat had been shipped to chain markets in those areas. Full-page ads in some papers urged people not to buy reindeer meat. The chain markets, fearing to antagonize some of their customers, requested to be released by us from firm orders. We complied, ordering the two carloads of meat that were in transit shipped to Chicago and placed in cold storage. We were more eager to retain friendly relations than to force the delivery of meat.

Livestock interests in the Middle West regarded the entry of reindeer meat into their section as an "invasion" of their market. Our position, however, was that the situation was comparable to that of one livestock-producing state objecting to interstate shipment of meat by another state. The pioneers engaged in developing the reindeer industry were simply Americans who had traveled north to Alaska, just as pioneers of the cattle and sheep industries were Americans who had traveled West.

During the late summer of 1930 the Department of the Interior brought south, on its vessel *Boxer,* reindeer meat from several Eskimo herds. Being without a sales organization, the Department circularized 200 cities of the United States through Chambers of Commerce and other civic organizations:

The U.S.S. *Boxer* will arrive in Seattle about December 1st with a cargo of Alaska reindeer meat. It will consist of 550 dressed and thoroughly frozen carcasses, weighing approximately 71,550 pounds. Will you please advise if you know of anyone in your city who would be interested in purchasing the entire cargo? In the past we have received as high as 17¢ a pound for this meat. However, this year, in order to make a quick sale, we are offering it for 9¢ a pound, F.O.B. Seattle.

This bulletin was signed by the purchasing agents and office manager of the Department of the Interior, Seattle, Washington.

Here was a new and disturbing situation. We were devoting the efforts of our organization to develop a market for reindeer meat in the United States, had opened offices in Seattle, San Francisco, Los Angeles, and New York, and established agencies in many other cities as well. We had some 24,000 carcasses of meat in storage in the United States.

We were not furnished with the Government circular, but through a meat dealer we saw a copy in Minneapolis some weeks later. Our price for reindeer was twelve and one-half cents per pound. Now the Government made public that its price was nine cents per pound—three and one-half cents under ours. We learned that the shipment the Government was attempting to dispose of actually consisted of only 137 carcasses. This publicity had the dual effect of causing the cancellation of a number of orders we had received and establishing a fixed price on reindeer meat throughout the United States.

We suggested to the Secretary of the Interior by telegram and letter that the attempted effort on the part of the Department to enter the domestic market with reindeer meat from Eskimo herds that lacked all equipment necessary for the proper dressing of meat would destroy the markets in the States to the detriment of Eskimo and white alike.

Nevertheless, the Department brought south a shipment on the *Boxer* at a freight rate of $5 per ton, while the tariff on commercial vessels was $42 a ton.

Early in 1931 two gentlemen called at our Seattle office to try to interest us in a stock-selling plan. Leonard Baldwin was visiting Seattle at the time. His suggestion was that we see the gentlemen but shoo them off as quickly as possible. Following a half hour's visit, Mr. Baldwin became nervous while waiting and joined us. He was immediately asked by one of the callers: "Did you ever consider the great advantage your company would have with small stockholders scattered up and down the Pacific Coast, who would prove potential boosters for your products?"

Mr. Baldwin pulled up a chair and answered: "Amplify that statement. You interest me."

The result of the visit was the organization, by our visitors, of the Interstate Sales and Publicity Company, and their purchase of 45,000 shares of preferred stock and 45,000 shares of common stock in our Alaska Livestock and Packing Company.

We stated our purpose as follows: "In line with other livestock and packing companies, the Alaska Livestock and Packing Company desires to secure a number of stockholders in each community in order that a more general interest may be created in its products and a better knowledge established in local markets of the value of reindeer meat as a staple food. To bring this about, in lieu of a general advertising campaign, its stock is offered in small blocks to a large number of people."

The stock-selling campaign proved successful and with it came increased sales of the company's products.

A complaint that our stock-selling plan was unfair to the purchaser was made to the Securities Division of the Department of Licenses of the State of Washington. But at the hearings, held in Olympia, it was shown that the Lomen Reindeer Corporation had surrendered all preference rights in stock held by it in the Alaska Livestock and Packing Company, its subsidiary.

"This, in my opinion," wrote the Supervisor of Securities, "is a demonstration of good faith with the purchasers of their stock, and certainly is more than fair to the public, who have already purchased preference stock of the Alaska Livestock and Packing Company. If more corporations would adopt such attitudes of square dealing with the public who are investors in their securities, it would be less difficult to secure public co-operation in financing the development of our resources."

In 1932 the Department sold a shipment of reindeer meat to a San Franciscan. Though the sale was only 400 deer, the check bounced, marked "NSF." Again the Department sent out circulars. This time it was to the hotels, meat markets, and cafés of California, by circular under Government postal frank. The prices given were:

½ deer	4¢ a pound	
Whole deer	3½¢	"
Saddles	5¢	"
Fronts only	2¢	"

This, be it noted, was less than the freight rate from Alaska.

The result of this "brilliant deal" on the part of the Department of the Interior was far-reaching and disastrous. The circulars came to the attention of the stock raisers of California and a reinterpretation of the California law was secured "prohibiting the importation or sale of any meat raised without the borders of the state in counties of more than 27,000 population, unless said meat bears a federal inspection stamp."

Reindeer meat was not included in the Meat Inspection Act of the United States, so it was impossible for the Alaskans to comply. We had offices in San Francisco and Los Angeles. We offered to pay the expenses of a state inspector of meat to proceed to Alaska to inspect our output of meat in order to allow us to remain in the California market. But the California officials contended that their inspectors would be without jurisdiction in Alaska.

We closed our offices and shipped to Seattle all reindeer meat in storage in California. After ten years of business in the state with full approval of the business interests we found ourselves shut out because of federal interference in a commercial enterprise its agents did not seem to understand.

Reindeer herds neighboring ours were Eskimo-owned. Each herd had its own range (public domain), and all concerned knew the boundaries of the ranges. We realized that the herds were growing and the time would soon come when some ranges would be crowded. Boundary disputes would then naturally arise. We appreciated that, lacking proper laws, the Eskimo would hold a preferential position. Therefore, we decided to request grazing legislation from Congress before disputes arose so that all owners would be protected.

I suggested to both Agriculture—through the Bureau of Biological Survey—and Interior, as well as to various members of Congress, that grazing legislation should provide that the boundaries and acreage be determined by the Biological Survey, since that Bureau was making a scientific study of the grazing areas involved and the total acreage required per animal. I also suggested that Interior grant the leases, under the General Land Office. Shortly, following my suggestions, three grazing bills were introduced, two by Interior, one by Agriculture. The legislation proposed by Interior was written by people unfamiliar with the industry, and its provisions would make it impossible for the industry to function, should it become a law.

Immediately I protested to an official of Interior but was told that the longer the legislation was held up by the opposition the more drastic it would become. The bill was before the Public Lands Committee of the House and I requested to be heard.

"In opposition?" inquired the chairman.

"Yes, in opposition."

I didn't know any member of the committee, so selected one from a "livestock state" and secured an appointment. I explained to him why the legislation proposed by the Interior Department would prove a detriment to the industry. He made no comments. When the committee met, Interior's solicitor, Judge Finney, presented the bill and urged its adoption.

The member whom I had visited put a technical question to the solicitor, who could not answer but suggested that

"Mr. Lomen is present and he probably could answer the question." This happened several times.

Later Judge Finney asked me what amendments I considered necessary. I stated them, and he answered, "Why, I will offer those amendments myself!"

He did, but these changes were later nullified by another amendment adopted in executive session of the committee. As far as I know, no lease was ever granted under the law, certainly not to any white reindeer owner.

Several years later I was calling on the solicitor when he stated: "I now see where we made many mistakes in the Alaska Grazing Bill."

"Yes, Judge," I replied, "and I was there trying to point them out."

There was little or no co-operation between Interior and Agriculture. Perhaps it was asking too much to expect a federal department, which itself lacked the information necessary in preparing legislation for an industry it had jurisdiction of, to obtain that information from another agency of the Government that did. This legislation was one of the first steps on the part of the Government in what later proved to be practically the destruction of the reindeer industry.

In 1929 jurisdiction was transferred from the Bureau of Education of the Department of the Interior to the Governor of Alaska, whose office is under the Secretary of Interior. The Governor resided in Juneau, and the Alaskans felt that he would be in closer touch with many problems confronting the reindeer work and in a better position to lend a helping hand when necessary.

Shortly after the transfer of jurisdiction, one of the Seattle papers gave space to alleged injustices practiced by the Lomen Reindeer Corporation in its dealings with the Eskimo and his reindeer. In effect, the Lomens were charged with taking deer belonging to the Eskimo and depriving him of his ranges. It was predicted in the newspaper article that the company would own all of the reindeer in Alaska within three years.

We requested the Governor of Alaska to make an immediate investigation of these charges. Not only was our integrity involved, but we believed the situation to be an example that would prove the advantage of jurisdiction of the industry residing in Alaska rather than in Washington, D. C.

Having been an employee of the Department of the Interior for many years, the Governor was prone to follow the old pattern of avoiding direct action, referring the matter back for the Department of the Interior to pass upon at Washington.

The source of the press charges was one C. L. Andrews, formerly a teacher and also a supervisor of reindeer. He had resigned his position with the Government and moved to Seattle. In his criticism of our business he exhibited the enthusiasm of the zealot, electing to appeal to the general public of the United States through church bodies and missionary societies to help "straighten out the Lomens." He made his protest through letters and a publication that he issued to church organizations and to the Indian Rights Association of Philadelphia.

This association published a monthly periodical, *Indian Truth*. Its issue of January 1932 carried an editorial maliciously condemning the Lomen family, and this was followed by a similar editorial in the next issue. Both were not only unjust but grossly untrue, and we were not given the courtesy or opportunity of correcting misstatements prior to publication.

Andrews' appeal fell on fertile ground. The office of the Secretary of the Interior, as well as offices of many senators, was deluged by veritable floods of mail.

Soon after the outburst in *Indian Truth,* a periodical called *Women and Missions,* published in New York City, came to our attention. Picking up the editorials from *Indian Truth,* it enlarged on the subject matter, appealing to all good women to write to the Secretary of the Interior and to their senators, condemning this family that was preying on the Eskimo people of Alaska. The Secretary of the Interior received more than 500 letters of protest against the Lomens from women and women's organizations throughout the United States; likewise, many United States senators built up quite a file on the Lomen family, largely adverse.

However, even before this, Secretary Ray Lyman Wilbur of Interior had determined to get to the bottom of the charges and countercharges, attempt to clear up some of the inequities, and try to place the industry on a sound footing. Accordingly, in 1931 he appointed a Reindeer Committee.

For chairman, the Secretary selected the Hon. John B. Kendrick, United States Senator for Wyoming, the outstanding authority in Congress on livestock and animal husbandry, and one of the largest cattle owners in the country. This committee held public hearings in Washington in February and March 1931, hearing witnesses both from Alaska and the States. At the conclusion of the hearings Senator Kendrick said:

"I do not believe that the record has established anything in the way of serious criticism of either your company or others connected with the raising of reindeer. To me it has revealed just the ordinary controversies that arise in connection with such an industry."

The Seattle *Times,* interesting itself editorially in the investigation growing out of the Andrews-inspired crusade, said among other things:

... The inquiry cannot fail to show that there would be no reindeer industry at this time but for the initiative and enterprise of the Lomen brothers who form the company. From the time the first few reindeer were set down in Alaska by Dr. Sheldon Jackson, it has been demonstrated that every condition was favorable for virtually unlimited enlargement of the herds. Reindeer were established in Alaska for the primary benefit of the natives. Native herd owners could eat but few and had no means of marketing the constantly increasing surplus of their stock. Not until the Lomens took hold was there any sign of solution for the problem of what to do with the deer. The Lomens not only organized sufficient sources for a dependable supply, but also organized the market and found the means of transportation. Of recent years, gradually and intelligently, they have extended the market, so that Alaska reindeer meat is now procurable in almost every part of the country. The *Times* knows nothing about the intimate business methods of the Lomen Reindeer Company; but it is no more than fair to say that it created a real industry where there was none, nor any early prospect of one. To the extent that they have been successful, the Lomen brothers deserve the credit commonly given to those who pioneer in a field of usefulness to others as well as to themselves.

The Reindeer Committee recommended the establishment of a Reindeer Council of five members, to be selected as follows: the Governor of Alaska, chairman; the chief of the Alaska Division, Office of Indian Affairs; the General Reindeer Supervisor, Alaska Reindeer Service; a representative chosen by and from among Eskimo owners; a representative chosen by the Lomen interests.

In the view of the Committee, the Reindeer Council should have general executive and administrative control of the reindeer industry. In actual practice, following the discharge of the Reindeer Committee, the Department saw fit to delegate only advisory responsibility to this body, so once more the industry found itself back under the control of bureaucrats in the Department of the Interior at Washington.

The meetings of the Council were held in Nome, the first in June 1931, and the second and last during August 1932. The most noteworthy action taken at the first meeting was the adoption of new range rules, subsequently approved by the Secretary of the Interior.

At the second meeting the Lomen representative brought

to the attention of the other members of the Council the alleged misrepresentations of unfair range practices by the Lomen Company that had been so widely circulated for several years, together with a resolution by the Northwestern Alaska Chamber of Commerce, commending the corporation. It was felt by the corporation interests that one of the most important matters before the Council was to iron out the many controversies inimical to both Eskimo and whites, and restore the harmony so necessary to effective operation. The Council, however, took no action, and the resolution died.

We had found ourselves fighting innuendo, untruths, inaction, and sheer stupidity—but we refused to quit an industry into which we had poured our strength, our hearts, and everything we possessed.

20.

IN THE summer of 1932 the Secretary of the Interior sent north two Department investigators, Captain Trowbridge and Mr. Gilman, to assist the Governor of Alaska and the Reindeer Supervisor in the reorganization work suggested by the Kendrick Committee. The investigators met with all interested parties; in so far as the work of our corporation was concerned their findings were favorable.

One costly mistake was made by the Government agents in Alaska that year, however. The Buckland herd was a mixed one—with Eskimo, Lomen, and other white-owned deer. The Government agents insisted that, instead of on July 15 or 20, as formerly, the Buckland herd be handled and marked on July 1. From experience we knew that that was too early; the summer grasses not having had enough time to grow, the animals would have insufficient pasturage. Also, the fawn skins that the natives required would not be prime by that time. Notwithstanding, it was insisted that the herd be handled then.

Seven Government men attended the handling, including the reindeer superintendent, the Unit Manager of the Buckland Unit, the local reindeer superintendent, Captain Trowbridge, and Mr. Gilman. With me was Mr. Daly, a member of the Swift meat-packing organization from Chicago. Mr. Daly's work was to make estimates of livestock for the Swift company in various parts of the world.

More than 20,000 reindeer were brought to the pasture by

the herders—a far greater number than could possibly be handled under feeding conditions.

"The first thing I would do," I said, "is to turn out about half that herd. There isn't feed enough here."

"No!" the Government men declared.

"What would you do?" I asked Mr. Daly. "This is going to be terrible before we are through."

"Let them go," he said. "They are going to suffer just as much as you are, and it is the only way to teach them."

"How about the poor deer?" I inquired dubiously.

"Let them go to it," he answered.

Each day of the marking I called a meeting and inquired: "What do you think about it now?"

The answer was always the same: "We can handle the deer. The Eskimo want to handle them because some of the adults are not marked."

I noticed during the last days that every deer coming through the chute walked as though intoxicated, some even falling on their faces before they got through the chute. Still the Government men insisted on continuing the work.

After the marking was over, the same group of Government men walked about a quarter-mile out in front of the chute and counted more than 800 dead reindeer lying on the ground —they had starved to death. One night a couple of thousand deer, desperate for food, broke away from the main herd and swam the Buckland River to freedom. I was glad to see them go. Had the Government men walked five miles out in front of the corrals they would have counted several thousand dead reindeer.

Laymen and the inexperienced often argued that there should be a separation of white-owned and Eskimo-owned reindeer, that wherever mixed herds occurred, the reindeer belonging to white interests should be transferred to other ranges.

Separation of reindeer on a basis of ownership is impossible. Reindeer have a homing instinct and will return to their home range if they can. The cost of confining deer on a strange range would be excessive, as day and night herding is required; the maintenance of that type of herding on a boundary line fifty to a hundred miles in length would be a hopeless task.

At the Kendrick hearings the Lomen interests suggested to the Committee that they would willingly withdraw from ranges held in common with Eskimo deer men "providing they would be given other deer, of like kind and number, together with compensatory range." Our thought was to exchange deer but not to attempt to move deer; Lomen deer mixed in one herd would be exchanged for the Eskimo deer in another mixed herd, thereby cleaning both herds.

However, during the summer of 1931 the Government and Eskimo alike had requested permission to drive the Lomen deer from the Buckland (Lomen, Herbert, Eskimo, Nilima range) to the Kotzebue (Lomen) range. Reluctantly the Lomens consented but stipulated that they would not be responsible for any part of the expense.

The first winter, under the direction of the federal unit manager, 7,000 Lomen deer were transferred to the Kotzebue range. The following year the percentage of Lomen ownership in the Buckland had decreased approximately one per cent. During a four-year period some 18,000 Lomen deer were moved, with the result that at the marking of the Buckland herd at the end of the period, the percentage of Lomen deer in the Buckland herd was just about the same as it was prior to the attempt to separate. This information is from Government records.

The Eskimo were guided by and followed the recommendations of the Government. To separate the deer of the various owners took several months and required the services of many more men than those who tended the herd. The pathetic part was that the work of separation was performed during the winter when the Eskimo should have been busy trapping to augment their income. Consequently, in those four costly years very little fur was taken by them on the Buckland Range.

The Lomen corporation never ceased to study ways of broadening the industry by utilizing more of the animal. In so doing they increased employment and added to the income of the business.

The manufacture and sale of reindeer clothing—parkas, fur pants, mukluks, mitts, socks, and caps and reindeer sleeping bags—was a side line we opened up. The hides were supplied by the Lomen corporation, the Eskimo women did the work, thus adding income for the Eskimo.

Fur clothing for the first two Byrd Antarctic expeditions, as well as for Byrd's North Pole flight, was supplied by us; it had publicity as well as income value, and we received many orders for fur clothing from leading sporting-goods houses in various parts of the United States. When made in the proper manner, reindeer clothing and sleeping bags are the warmest and most desirable items of the kind known to the Arctic and other cold centers. We also developed a new type of flying suit that was found by aviators to be excellent in warmth and flexibility as well as light in weight.

The work of reorganizing the industry in conformity with the recommendations of the Kendrick Committee went on. I realized the importance of bringing livestock people into the industry and took the trouble to visit members of the congressional committee, recommending an amendment to the Interior Department appropriation bill making mandatory the selection of men trained in animal husbandry for appointment to the reindeer service. The amendment was adopted and the service was much improved. Though I didn't realize it at the time, even the stenographers had to have animal-husbandry training!

In a strange way the reindeer got tangled up with the Alaska native school system. The Bureau of Education, Department of the Interior, had charge of native schools for Alaska. Married couples were preferred as teachers. Upon arrival at their posts the teachers often found many duties other than teaching thrust upon them, such as caring for the sick, counseling the natives in their domestic life, instruction in sanitation, and other matters. Teachers in reindeer country found themselves also "Superintendents of Reindeer," with Eskimo deer men looking to them for guidance. Unlike the stenographers, no actual training of teachers for reindeer work was required, with the result that very few were able to be of much help to the deer men. Inasmuch as department personnel in Washington in charge of reindeer matters were equally unacquainted with husbandry, confusion resulted all around, sometimes with disastrous consequences.

Pioneering with a new industry in a vast territory requires substantial investments of money, and, too, groping a way along unmarked paths over countless obstacles requires patience and imagination as well as money. Had we not had boundless faith in the enterprise and its future we would have given up in the early stages.

The reindeer industry was the only one in northwestern Alaska in which the Eskimo was an important factor. It gave him opportunity for development, permanent employment, and assured independence. Over the years the Lomens furnished employment to hundreds of Eskimo reindeer men, paying them hundreds of thousands of dollars. We made a point of familiarizing ourselves with the characteristics of the Eskimo, and it became the policy of our corporation not to give to them, but rather to make it possible for them to secure those things necessary for their livelihood. In other words, we helped the Eskimo to help himself.

Federal paternalism toward the native people, on the other hand, invariably proves detrimental to Eskimo character and welfare. Here is one angle the teachers and others in the federal reindeer service seldom perceived in their approach to the problem. If Eskimo are so poor that reindeer must be given them by the Government, then they are also too poor to herd them properly. They cannot tend reindeer in the storm-swept hills without supplies and equipment. Eskimo and their families need oil for lights, salt, matches, ammunition, flour, sugar, milk, tobacco, and many other things which our advancing civilization has taught them to use. Income obtained from hunting and fishing provides at best a meager supply of these items. Native reindeer associations, with only local markets for their reindeer, lack the funds to support the herders. By providing employment for Eskimo deer men, our company made it possible for them to purchase necessary supplies for themselves and families, and at the same time care for their own deer, which were mixed with ours. Thus the industry insured to the Eskimo a more stable economy.

In the eyes of the American public, Will Rogers was the eternal Connecticut Yankee at King Arthur's Court, smart as a New England Yankee, and as unreconstructed as a southern rebel. Americans instinctively love a cowboy, and he was one of the best; he was really an expert with the lariat and delighted in demonstrating his ability. But as famous as he became, despite the astringency of his wit, he always remained a plain man, without a mean streak in him anywhere. He used to say that he never saw a man he didn't like, and that if he could make up his own epitaph it would read that he never hit a man when he was down.

In the summer of 1935 Alfred, who was in Nome, received a wire from Will, sent from Fairbanks. "Expect to be in Nome in a few days; want to rope me a reindeer."

Alfred wired back, "Will have herd of 12,000 reindeer at Golovin for you, but bring your own rope."

A few days later International News Service wired to

Alfred, "Charter a plane, engage photographer, and secure pictures of wreck Post and Rogers plane near Barrow, Alaska, and fly them to Seattle."

When the wire arrived no plane was available at Nome; but one of our bush pilots, Chester Brown, was at Golovin eighty miles southeast. Alfred telephoned, asking him to get back to Nome immediately for a flight to Barrow. The weather was unfavorable, but Chet arrived, and they set off the same day for Barrow. Crossing Seward Peninsula to Kotzebue, some 300 miles, they "picked flowers all the way," that is, they flew under the fog. At Kotzebue they gassed up and took off over the fog. They ran low on fuel after some hours of flying and Chet suggested turning back.

"We can't turn back," Alfred remonstrated. "Find a hole in the clouds and get down under this fog."

They flew on and providentially an opening appeared in the clouds. The pilot banked steeply and slid down through it. There, just a short distance from where they broke through, was Post's plane. They landed, being fourteen miles from Barrow, the top of the North American continent. No white men, but some 200 Eskimo were gathered at the scene of the wreck. The photographer immediately took the desired photos.

The Post-Rogers plane was as thorough a wreck as they had ever seen, being nothing but a huge mass of twisted and broken wood and metal. A portion of the plane cabin had to be torn out before the body of Post could be removed. The engine had been forced back into the cabin, pinning him as in a vise. Rogers had been farther back in the cabin and partially protected by the baggage they carried, but he, too, had apparently been killed instantly.

Alfred asked an Eskimo to move in a little bit in order to include him in a picture, but the Eskimo stepped back instead. Alfred realized the situation at once. Charlie Brower, that famous old resident of Barrow, who was "king" of the area, had cautioned the Eskimo not to pose for pictures if anyone showed up with a camera.

Deciding to have a bit of fun, Alfred offered the Eskimo $10 if he would appear in the picture.

"No!"

"One hundred dollars."

"No!"

"One thousand dollars."

"No!"

"Five thousand dollars."

"No!"

"Ten thousand dollars."

"No!"

The photographs were taken and, though the Eskimo would not be bribed, the photographer was able to catch him in the pictures taken.

Finishing the photographs, they flew into Barrow where they met, in addition to Charlie Brower, Joe Crosson of Pan-American Airways, one of Alaska's outstanding pilots, who had arrived to carry the bodies of the fliers to the States.

Alfred was in a predicament. His pilot had never been to Barrow before and had never made the flight between Barrow and Fairbanks, 600 miles to the southeast, the course they must take on their return. It was a dangerous flight, as the 10,000-foot altitude of the Endicott Range had to be crossed by a pilot unfamiliar with the passes. In addition, they had no aviation gas for a return flight. Alfred and Joe were friends of long standing, but Joe had photographs to carry to the States, too. Alfred requested passage for himself with Joe to Fairbanks.

"Can't do it," Crosson answered. "I have a load."

"Will you permit us to take sufficient aviation gas from the PAA supply here to get us to Fairbanks?"

"Can't do it—we may need it ourselves."

"Will you carry a package to Fairbanks and mail it for me?"

"I'm going over to Charlie Brower's to lie down for awhile," Joe replied.

A half-hour later Alfred heard a plane take to the air. It was Joe Crosson with the two bodies off for Fairbanks.

It was important to get our pictures to Seattle first. With no aviation gas available, it was unwise to take the direct route for Fairbanks, so they gassed up with ordinary gasoline obtained from Charlie Brower and headed for Kotzebue. Arriving there, they took on a load of aviation gas and headed for Fairbanks, where they landed some five hours after Joe Crosson.

Here again Alfred tried to have PAA carry a dummy package for him, figuring that if Joe thought he had Alfred's pictures he might not be in such a hurry. But PAA was not to be fooled. Chester Brown flew back to Nome. Alfred secured a small single-engine plane with two pilots, Noel Wein and Victor Ross, and took off for Whitehorse, landing a few hours later. After registering at the hotel, Alfred stepped over to a restaurant and perched himself on a stool alongside several men. He then learned that the topic of conversation all over town was the Barrow flight; that the man seated next to him was the radio operator at Whitehorse, and that great excitement had been created by the airplane "race." Alfred was not known to the men in the restaurant.

"How is the race going?" the cook inquired of the radio operator.

"PAA are down for the night at Kluane Lake and the pilot says that sport, Lomen, thinks he will be the first in Seattle."

This brought a laugh, since Alfred's chartered plane was fifty miles an hour slower than the PAA plane.

Alfred slipped out, found his pilots, and said: "PAA are down for the night at Kluane Lake. They have the organization and equipment, but I think we have the guts. Let's go!"

Dropping out of the window of the hotel, they hurried to the airfield and took off for Seattle over the high mountains of

Yukon Territory and British Columbia. Alfred was perched on top of several cases of gasoline and spent most of the night pumping gasoline into the wing tanks. Several times they rounded the shoulders of gigantic snowcapped peaks. Alfred told me later he never realized what a great institution daylight was until it broke that morning.

Brother Ralph was in Seattle. The manager of the news service called him late the evening after the planes had taken off from Fairbanks. "Does your brother realize that he is in a race?" Ralph, who had received no more information than had the manager, replied: "Yes, Alfred knows that he is in a race, and don't worry, for in all his life he never yet has lost one."

The following morning Ralph hurried downstairs for the morning paper. On the front page he read: "Mystery plane over British Columbia."

"That's All!" exclaimed Ralph—and it was.

Finally Alfred spotted a town.

"What place is that?" he inquired.

The only map they had was one issued by the Alaska Steamship Company, which, naturally, was not interested in aviation. Not certain where they were, they landed.

The town proved to be Prince George, British Columbia, and they then discovered they had no right to land there without permission, it being foreign territory. They spent an hour with customs, then Alfred wired Ralph to Seattle: "SHOULD ARRIVE 2 P.M. TODAY," and took off for the last lap. A tail wind pushed them along and they landed at Boeing Field, Seattle, an hour ahead of schedule.

As Alfred stepped out of the plane, forty-nine hours out of Nome, a group of newspapermen and photographers rushed to him. "How about the photographs?"

"Any other plane in from the North?" queried Alfred, considering that a more important question.

"No. You are the first one to arrive."

"Well, I have some photos, but they are for International News."

"And I'm International News," spoke up one of the group. "Here's your brother Ralph to verify it."

The films were rushed to the *Post-Intelligencer* office, where they were processed.

All the papers were clamoring for pictures of the wreck and those taken turned out to be perfect. Two planes were standing by waiting for them, one headed for Salt Lake, the other for Los Angeles. This feat was pronounced the greatest scoop ever in photographic journalism.

One might suppose that as charges, opposition, and investigations increasingly assailed the Lomens, we would be discouraged from continuing business operations in Alaska, particularly in the light of mounting Federal Government domination from Washington. However, our family was a truly co-operative group; we discussed everything around the family table; we were usually in agreement and not easily turned aside. We found our work with reindeer romantic and adventurous, as well as interesting business, and nobody in the family was inclined to give up after so much of the groundwork had been laid.

Early in the game we brothers had appropriated the slogan of the Three Musketeers, "All for one, one for all." In more than twenty years of co-operative effort there had never been a financial settlement made between us. As one of the boys wrote me at a time when the future looked very black, "If the bubble bursts, think of the fun we've had!"

Whatever happened, we always tried to hold onto our sense of humor. The Lomens had health, they had many fine friends and enjoyed them immensely. The trips we made in connection with our work, both winter and summer, were invigorating, absorbing, and filled with unique experiences and adventures.

All of us took an active part in the reindeer business. We traveled up and down the coast in our small gasoline boats to visit the herds; even Helen was a "gate tender" one summer at a big marking on Choris Peninsula, and always took a keen interest in everything her brothers were trying to do. One result of her enthusiasm was a book she wrote for young people, *Taktuk, an Arctic Boy,* an authentic story of a young Eskimo boy's life in reindeer country, published by Doubleday, Doran & Company in 1928.

Father and Mother also worked with and for us. Mother and Helen were the gracious hostesses in our home where many friends, including Lapps and Eskimo, always found a hospitable welcome. Father kept the fires of research burning; being a linguist, he translated reindeer reports from both the Norwegian and the Swedish, carrying on correspondence with several foreign countries with reference to the subject in which all of us were so intensely interested.

After Father retired from the bench, he and Mother visited Egavik, an Eskimo village 200 miles southeast of Nome. One evening a group of Eskimo men and women came up from Unalakleet, fourteen miles distant, to pay their respects. The Eskimo of the two villages arranged a little meeting, and in addressing Mother and Dad, the spokesman said that the Eskimo people wished to express their thanks for the numerous acts of kindness shown them and their people for many years by Judge Lomen and his family. The meeting continued with the singing of hymns and Eskimo songs by excellent male and female native voices. The sincerity with which these kindly people expressed regret at the approaching departure of my parents from Alaska was most touching, and as Dad thanked them for their tribute there were tears of appreciation for the Eskimo people he had known and respected for so many years.

21.

EGAVIK was one of our most scenic stations, located at the mouth of the Egavik River. Here the coast runs north and south. There is no harbor, but twelve miles to the westward lies Besboro Island where there is some shelter for small craft. On the north bank of the river there was a small Eskimo village; to the south was our station, consisting of trading post and warehouse, with an apartment for the superintendent on the second story. There was an abattoir and cold-storage plant, several cabins for employees, a cookhouse, and, a hundred yards distant, the large corral system.

Our Egavik reindeer herd, numbering some 25,000 animals, grazed over a half-million or more acres, with the Shaktoolik native herd to the north and the Unalakleet herd—Lapp, Eskimo, and Lomen—to the south, with the Unalakleet River the boundary line. Egavik was on the United States mail trail between Nome and the States during the winter months, and in the open season for navigation—June to October, inclusive —a port of call for the mail boat and other small craft. With the advent of the airplane, a small landing field was constructed, sufficient for our experienced bush pilots with smaller planes, and an emergency field for larger planes. As the station was isolated, visitors were always most welcome.

Our Egavik superintendent left us in the summer of 1932 and that camp became a major problem through lack of leadership. We considered our brother George, then living in Seattle, and wired him, "We need you." He accepted immediately, arriving by the next steamer, with his wife Bertha following on our ship, the *Sierra*. But fall storms delayed the *Sierra* and by the time she had discharged at Nome, slush ice was forming in the sea and it was necessary for all shipping to be southbound.

The *Sierra* sailed for Egavik, nevertheless. It got within sight of Egavik but a storm and the slush ice prevented the ship from reaching her anchorage.

Brother George could see the ship that carried his wife and all their merchandise and supplies for the winter, together with household fixtures and furniture for their apartment, and realized it was just another case of "so near and yet so far." Fearing that ice conditions might become worse, the *Sierra* returned to Nome without discharging, and Bertha, after two tries by plane, finally made a safe landing at Egavik some ten days later.

The following winter was one of shortages at Egavik. Food was shipped from Nome by parcel post, but there was a limit to what the mail team could carry. George and Bertha spent the winter with furniture made from boards and packing cases, but there were no complaints as they were both good sports.

Toward spring an epidemic of influenza struck the Eskimo village and practically all the inhabitants were bedridden. Bertha cooked food and George packed it to the village, a quarter-mile distant, and fed the sick. This went on for many days.

George told of one of his first visits to the native village:

"All the people in the first house I entered were stricken with the flu with the exception of an old woman, undoubtedly a grandmother. The only heat in the house came from a small seal-oil lamp over which simmered a stew, a mixture of willow bark and dried fish.

"Scattered around the floor on piles of skins were a middle-aged man, his wife, and three children. All were very sick and looked more dead than alive. They didn't even seem to be interested in the food I had brought. Nevertheless, I busied myself doling out a portion to each of them, then sat back to watch the grandmother, hard at work splitting sinew."

At this village we had contracted with the Eskimo to make up a large quantity of skin clothing and the old woman was one of the most expert seamstresses on the coast.

George was reminded of those lines written by our friend, Walter Shields:

> Behind the rest on heaped up skins
> The oldest hag crouched on her shins.
> Her teeth were worn down to the gums
> And rawhide thongs had scarred her thumbs.
> She split a sinew strip in two
> The scraps she dropped into the stew.
> Between her sunken, oozing lips
> The stringy strop of sinew slips.
> She mumbles it 'twixt tongue and jaws
> As through her mouth each strip she draws.
> She rubs it with her greasy claws
> Until each soft and moistened shred
> Becomes a long and pliant thread
> Rubbed round upon her cheek.

George and Bertha knew the Eskimo from former years spent in Nome and understood their ways. Through firmness, kindness, and good example, the camp was soon restored to an efficient working unit.

The Egavik Eskimo were a fine people. Many had attended the Mission School at Unalakleet and had been taught cleanliness, although sanitation was practically unknown. During early summer, flies and mosquitoes became great pests. George made a practice of collecting tin cans, coffee cans, and others of comparable size; into these he poured crude oil and hung the cans on willows for a radius of a quarter-mile about the station, as the area was swampy and dotted with stagnant pools. Rains kept the cans full and the oil floating on top would spill over with the swaying of the willows and cover the surface of the pools with a thin skim, thus preventing the mosquito eggs from hatching.

He then took wheelbarrow, rake, and shovel and spent days raking and burning the refuse on the spit where our station stood between the winding river and the sea. The native boys watched all this very intently. Finally they asked for the loan of the tools and tons of refuse were gathered together and burned in the village area.

The mail teams were a great blessing to the people of the North during the seven months Bering Sea was closed to shipping because of ice. The teams were composed of great dogs and great men, Eskimo and white. One winter's day Misha, an Eskimo with a large northbound team, stopped at Egavik for a meeting with George and inquired about the trail ahead. He had his choice of following the land trail for fifteen miles, crossing five high divides, or going over the more dangerous but fairly level sea ice. Misha, although he did not like the looks of the weather, nevertheless decided to take the sea ice, reporting to George that a second mail team driven by John Kotongan, an Eskimo, was following, as the week's mail was a heavy one.

Within a couple of hours John Kotongan pulled in. "Which way did Misha go," he asked, "over the hills or out on the sea?"

"The sea trail," George replied.

"He must be crazy!" John exclaimed. "He's apt to be carried to sea with this offshore wind. I'll follow him to make sure he is not in trouble."

With a command to his dogs, he swung the team down to the beach and over the rough shore ice, crossed it, and proceeded out to smoother sea ice, following Misha's sled tracks.

Steep, high bluffs form the shore line of Egavik for twelve to fourteen miles, and the teams travel a considerable distance offshore. Leaving Egavik, Misha made good time riding the sled. Always alert, he suddenly noted a black streak between himself and the shore. The floe he was on had broken away from the shore ice and he was drifting out to sea. Quick action was necessary. Misha stopped, fastened his team to a large block of rough ice to anchor them, then ran toward shore and the open lead he must cross. He found a small dislodged cake of ice that was large enough to support his body. Carefully he spread himself at full length on this ice boat and, using his hands as paddles, propelled it for two hours until he reached the shore side of the open water. His clothes were wet and he was eight miles from Shaktoolik. He must travel fast to keep from freezing. It was imperative that he reach Shaktoolik and organize rescue parties to locate and save the United States mail and his dog team.

John Kotongan's concern for Misha was well founded. A few miles north of Egavik he noticed open water to seaward. Did Misha make it through or was he adrift? He forced his team, finally arriving at Shaktoolik. There he found Misha safe but learned his team was adrift at sea. A dog team had been dispatched to Egavik and Unalakleet "over the hills" to advise those camps to get help.

Brother George was very upset following the departure of first Misha and then John. It was not until the arrival of the team from Shaktoolik the following day that he learned that the two men were safe and Misha's team had been carried to sea. George suggested to the Shaktoolik driver that, upon arriving at Unalakleet, he make sure a message was telephoned to Nulato on the Yukon, where there was a wireless station, that Nome be notified to send a plane to spot the team on the ice and report its position to Shaktoolik.

George dispatched one of his men with a dog team to Shaktoolik to assist in any way possible, and then kept a lookout with binoculars for any signs of the lost team at sea. Within a matter of hours Unalakleet teams hurried by, Shaktoolik bound, and with but a wave of the hand passed through Egavik. The entire coast was on the alert.

Nome received the wireless message and a plane was dispatched to the rescue. The team was finally sighted to the westward of Besboro Island. Dog teams and umiaks were shortly under way; the sleds carried the umiaks over the ice floes and the umiaks carried the sleds over stretches of open water. Knowing its approximate location, the rescuers reached the team in a few hours.

The dogs were known fighters, but apparently they had sensed their danger and remained quiet, for none was injured. Misha carried a bundle of dried salmon for dog food that the dogs managed to reach. The team and mail were safely landed and again took the trail.

This was another tragedy averted by quick thinking and intense concerted effort.

One marking season at Igloo Point an Eskimo came to me in the corral with a day-old fawn in his arms. The mother had been badly injured. The little fellow was a beauty, its silky hair a dark brown.

"Why don't you take it home?" suggested the Eskimo, knowing my love for the animals.

"Why not?" I thought.

I carried the young fawn to camp and used one of our tents for a stable. I warmed canned milk and, holding the fawn in my lap, dipped my fingers in the milk. Soon the fawn was sucking my fingers. Then I filled a bowl with milk and left it on the floor. Returning shortly, I found the bowl empty.

The fawn soon adopted me as its mother and I found that it was not necessary to confine it. It followed me as a dog would; when I called, it answered with a grunt. We had completed the marking and the next day we made a forty-mile trip by launch to Keewalik and then a 200-mile flight by air to Nome. "Igloo," as I had named the fawn, was to be my surprise to my wife.

Laura was at the field to meet the plane. I stepped out, gently lowered Igloo to the ground, then set off at a run, knowing that the fawn would follow right at my heels and that I could not outrun him. Laura fell in love with Igloo at once, taking him into her arms and fondling him.

Igloo was immediately at home with us. A gunny sack near the door served as his bed. About six in the morning we would hear little hoofs clattering about the warehouse and grunts signifying the demand for food. A baby bottle of warm milk satisfied him and allowed us to get another wink of sleep before starting our day.

This cunning little fellow with large brown impish eyes and wobbly legs clung to us devotedly. There was no response to the stroking of his tawny, fuzzy coat, but when spoken to, he was all attention. During the daytime Laura left the kitchen door open and soon Igloo's hoofs were heard slipping and sliding over the linoleum. He was curious to know what was going on inside and seemingly wished to assure himself he was not alone.

In ten days we were off by plane to attend a reindeer roundup and marking of a large herd. Igloo accompanied us. We had become very much attached to our pet but felt the little fawn should be returned to his normal life of roaming the tundra with the other deer.

At Egavik our destination, George, Bertha, and the natives of the village were very much surprised when I lifted Igloo from the plane. No one had seen a reindeer pet before. Everyone followed us to the store, amazed at the friendliness of the little animal and his apparent unconcern at being among people.

"Ahregahs!" filled the room.

"What a fine way to secure sled deer!" I told the Eskimo.

"Get a few fawn, make pets of them, and in a year you will have well-trained deer to pull your sleds!"

The following morning, according to schedule, a herd of some 10,000 deer were driven into camp. We were off to the corral nearby for the marking. Igloo followed close behind. As we neared the marking chutes filled with grunting deer, we noticed that Igloo paid no attention to them.

I took Igloo into the corral with hundreds of milling animals, adults and fawns. Turning my back, I started for the fence. In a few minutes I heard a grunt at my heels. There was Igloo. It was quite apparent that Igloo now belonged to us. Of course, we were overjoyed for the moment, but we knew we had to part with our fawn, as we would soon be leaving for the States.

George and Bertha were intrigued by Igloo. George made a corral especially for him, and we later learned from Bertha that Igloo took walks with her and her dogs along the beach, and soon found out how he could get candy and cookies from her pocket.

Igloo lived happy and contented at Egavik for the rest of his days.

Sled deer were important to the deer men, and always I advocated to them the adoption of young animals, training them as pets, since then they could be more easily caught and broken to sled use. The Lapps had long ago adopted this policy, and their driving deer were superior to the ones the Eskimo used.

Through the busy years I was often away from home but I was always glad to get back to the other members of the large and still-growing Lomen family.

One summer we lived in a house formerly occupied by my brother Alfred and his bride. Originally it had been just a small cabin but room after room had been added at the rear

243

of the building to accommodate their five children, who were born and raised there.

When we took over, one of the larger bedrooms contained, in addition to the bed, a huge bathtub and a washbasin with running water. In Nome in those days this was considered most luxurious.

Arthur Baldwin was our house guest that summer and we offered him his choice of bedrooms. After examining the numerous sleeping quarters, he selected the one with the bathtub. Being a well-to-do New Yorker, he was accustomed to handy bathing arrangements. But the principal reason for his choice was that the windows in the room were small and high in the wall and readily covered to keep out the light at night. There was actually so little difference in the light around the clock in the summer months that people unaccustomed to it found it difficult to sleep. So for double protection against the light we provided Mr. Baldwin with a pair of goggles covered with silk and stuffed with cotton to wear while he slept.

Crystal-clear cold spring water from the low mountain range four miles back of Nome was carried to town in surface pipes and provided excellent water from early June until late September or early October. In the fall the newspapers announced the date of the shutting off of the water. In fact, by that time it was already frozen in the pipes in many parts of town.

For the winter the water man took over. Every home had a tank of some kind for water storage. The delivery man brought in water in a five-gallon bucket; eight buckets for a dollar. There was little of the precious liquid wasted during the cold months.

Our homes were built on the frozen ground. Even in summer the frost was no more than a foot below the surface. A summer thaw of a few inches would often affect the construction of the houses. The floors heaved and the siding sagged.

Each year the inside doors had to be readjusted and the windows calked.

Over a period of years one neighboring log cabin had moved of itself three feet back from its original location. One house we lived in was set on four 12" x 12" timbers forty feet in length. In the early summer, when the building started to get off balance because of the thaw, a foreman with a gang of Eskimo helpers would jack up the timbers and put in blocks to level off the house.

An old-fashioned cookstove equipped with an oil burner was a great convenience in the kitchen. An oil stove in the living room warmed the rest of the house, though not to the degree demanded by apartment-house dwellers in the States. However, we managed to keep cozy and comfortable—in the far North one never hears complaints about the severe cold.

The busy season for the businessmen of Nome began upon the arrival of the first boat from the States in the middle of June. The ice is out of the roadstead then, though there is still considerable snow on the hillsides. Upon the discharging of freight, the stores took on a new look. Shelves were replenished with dry goods, canned goods, and the many other items required by a community of 1,500 population, about half white and half Eskimo.

Weekly food supplies were dispatched by air to miners in the outlying districts. Tugs and barges carried supplies to the small villages and mining camps up and down the coast. The Lomens, meanwhile, were off to the reindeer herds for the marking.

Though we were living in a pioneer country, the social amenities were observed and many formal dinners were given. On such occasions, the table was complete in every appointment, including a centerpiece of flowers flown in from Seattle. Seven courses were usually served. The menu always included our famous Alaskan crab, and the *pièce de résistance* often was brant, a game bird of exceptional flavor. To complete the dinner, ice cream was topped with a sauce made from wild Alaskan blueberries.

The grocery stores of Nome carried the finest brands of canned goods and many delicacies. Meats were of the highest grades but, of necessity, were shipped in frozen as everything came by boat and the trip from Seattle took nine days in fair weather. Today Nome enjoys air-borne fresh vegetables and fruits, as well as some fresh meats, the year around.

Each summer Laura hired an Eskimo girl to help with household duties, usually on a part-time basis, as required. One girl had black hair that was curly rather than straight, like the Eskimo. Laura learned that her father was Negro and her mother an Eskimo. Since she had been brought up by her Eskimo mother, she abhorred conventional cooking and much preferred dried fish and seal oil.

Another girl who helped in the house was a full-blooded Diomede Island Eskimo, born near the Arctic coast of Siberia. She had been orphaned during the flu epidemic in 1918 and, along with many other Eskimo children who lost their parents at that time, she was taken to the Catholic Mission school at the Hot Springs near Teller, ninety miles from Nome. There she was given a practical education and turned out to be an excellent cook and housekeeper.

Our home was open house from morning until night. Our family was so large and our business interests so far reaching that guests—expected and often unexpected—were the rule rather than the exception. But Laura took it in her stride— just as my mother did—and the welcome mat was always in front of the door.

22.

VAST HERDS of caribou once roamed the unending wastes of northern Canada. Using the primitive bow and arrow, the Barren Ground Eskimo depended on them for food, clothing, and shelter. But with the introduction of the repeating rifle, the Eskimo went on a rampage, killing caribou by the thousands.

White men, too, shot caribou carelessly, taking only the tongues and leaving the rest of the carcass to rot. Great as were the herds, they could not withstand this indiscriminate slaughter. As a result, the caribou were soon decimated.

Vilhjalmur Stefansson realized the seriousness of the situation and in 1922 persuaded the Hudson's Bay Company to introduce reindeer into Canada's north country. Negotiations were entered into and reindeer purchased in Norway were brought to Baffin Land.

When the expedition proved a failure, Stefansson asked me to write to the Hudson's Bay Company, pointing out the reasons for the lack of success. My judgment was based on the belief, as I have mentioned before, that reindeer are possessed of the homing instinct.

These reindeer from Norway were landed on the southwest coast of Baffin Land. The bewildered animals would, therefore, naturally head eastward toward their homeland. Reaching the interior of Baffin Land, they undoubtedly would become absorbed by the caribou and lost. My recommendation was that Canada should be stocked with reindeer from Alaska in the west and driven on the hoof to the areas to be stocked.

The Canadian officials were most anxious to have domestic reindeer introduced into the Arctic wastes of their country. The Department of the Interior of Canada contacted us and we exchanged many letters. Finally, Mr. W. W. Cory, Deputy Minister of the Interior of Canada, came to New York where we had numerous conferences. Canada wanted the deer, but how to secure them and how to transport them to the areas where they were needed were the big problems. These talks continued off and on for a period of more than two years. Much valuable time was being lost.

"I'll make you a sporting propostion," I finally said to Mr. Cory. "You tell us where you want the reindeer and we will deliver them and you pay for the number we deliver."

I expected my generous offer to be snapped up immediately, but governments move slowly. The Canadian Interior officials secured the services of two botanists, brothers named Porsild, then residing in Greenland, and requested that they come to Ottawa. They accepted the commission to proceed to the Canadian Arctic, following visits to Washington, D. C., conferring with officials of the Biological Survey, then to Alaska, where they visited two of our herds to learn as much as possible about the reindeer. They then went to the Mackenzie Delta, traveling via the Arctic coast by dog team, to make a reconnaissance of the grazing conditions and report back to Ottawa. Two years later the Porsild brothers made a favorable report as to the suitability of the Canadian Arctic for reindeer and recommended that mother stock be secured in Alaska and driven overland.

Negotiations were reopened between the Canadian officials and our company and on May 8, 1929, in New York, an agreement was entered into and executed by the Deputy Minister of the Interior of the Dominion of Canada and me, as president of our corporation. We agreed to deliver to the east shore of the Mackenzie Delta 3,000 reindeer for $195,000. The gamble would be ours—we were to be paid for what we delivered at a pro rata of $65 per head. The Canadians assisted us in financing the expedition by advancing $112,000 on the purchase price, to be returned should we fail to make delivery.

We were undertaking to drive a herd of livestock from western Alaska to northwestern Canada through unmapped and largely unexplored country. We could find no record of any human, Eskimo or white, ever having traveled the route we planned for this drive. The route would be north of the Arctic Circle in its entirety with mountain ranges to cross and without maps to guide the drive through little-known and unsettled country.

How to organize the drive? How long a time would be required to move a herd of deer over an air-line distance of some 1,200 miles? What contingencies to provide for? What course to follow? These were some of our problems.

Our first consideration was personnel. We needed men with expert understanding of the animal, experience in Arctic travel, patience, loyalty to the job, and courage. We wanted no white men on the drive as we knew none with the patience of either Lapp or Eskimo. Each man must be equipped as an independent unit to insure safety. Each must have rifle, ammunition, compass, sleeping bag, food, change of clothing, knife, and snowshoes, and both winter and summer garments.

Living near Seattle were several of our former Lapp employees, all expert reindeer men, who had retired from reindeer work after they had sold their herds to us. They were now affluent citizens. I returned to Seattle to confer with my brothers and also to consult with my Lapp friends.

I explained to the Lapps the great good the importation of reindeer into Arctic Canada would do for an entire people—providing them with food and clothing, making them independent, and abolishing the specter of starvation.

The Lapps listened intently. Finally Andrew Bahr, who had been our first employee with the acquisition of our original herd back in 1914, looked up and asked: "Why don't you offer me a job?"

This was a surprising question from a man past sixty years of age who had retired a year or two before and had a bank account of some $60,000.

"Would you accept a job?" I asked.

"I guess so," he replied.

"Andrew," I told him, "you are hired right now to lead this expedition."

Some men of sixty find it difficult to get out of bed in the morning under their own steam but Andy, with his powerful stubby frame and years of clean living, was still as strong as they come. His skin was brown and as furrowed as a walnut. Knowing, honest eyes gleamed from his rough-hewn face. He was slow and sparing of speech, methodical and, above all else, fearless.

Andrew Bahr was a man of great self-confidence. It was not conceit, but rather a realization of his knowledge of conditions in the North country, of trail travel, care of the person, equipment, and clothing, and of the reindeer, gained during a lifetime, for Andrew was born at a reindeer herd in Lapland.

Once on a long winter trip to the Buckland village Andrew encountered a severe blizzard. He plodded on, at times leading his reindeer. On downgrades he rode the sled. Visibility was nil. After hours of travel he suddenly stopped. "I should be there right now," thought Andrew. Knowing that it was futile to proceed, since he had covered sufficient distance to have reached the village, he tied the deer to the side of his sled, crawled into his sleeping bag, and went to sleep. Some hours later he was awakened by the Buckland school bell. Andrew was in the village.

During another severe storm one of his Eskimo boys came to him and shouted, "We are lost!"

"Can you see me?" asked Andrew. "Yes," said the boy.

"Well, as long as you can see me, you are all the same as home."

The Kotzebue herd was brought in for marking one summer and was to be driven across a narrow neck of land onto Choris Peninsula. A score or more herders followed the animals, but the deer became frightened and continued to break back. Finally Andrew ordered the men to get out of sight of the herd. He decided to move the herd of more than 10,000 animals across the neck of land—alone. He carried a long stick in each hand. Advancing slowly and quietly, with his arms spread out, moving one stick and then the other toward some unruly animal, he went forward step by step until the leaders reached the point where the land widened. There they suddenly broke for the peninsula with the entire herd following. Such a man was Andrew Bahr.

For second in command we chose M. I. K. Nilluka. Mike had been superintendent of our Golovin herd. Though not blessed with a winning personality, he was a man who always delivered the goods.

Months of preparation were required before the reindeer drive could get under way. Forty hickory sleds were ordered and built in Seattle, with canvas tarpaulins to fit. Fur clothing, parkas, fur pants, socks of various kinds, fur and woolen, mittens of fur, wool, and canvas were ordered. Special containers were made square rather than round to pack more closely in the sleds.

Both Bahr and Nilluka proceeded to Nome soon after the opening of navigation and were flown to Choris Peninsula, Kotzebue Sound. During the summer they perfected all the necessary equipment, acquiring additional fur clothing and mukluks, making harness for the sled deer, and attending to many other details.

Andrew Bahr arrived at our camp at Nabachtoolik during early November 1929 with a crew of nine reindeer men.

Here the reindeer corral was rebuilt and enlarged. Assisted by an equal number of men from our Elephant Point plant, a roundup was made of our Kotzebue reindeer herd.

All during November and December the stormy weather kept slowing down the work. Finally a herd of 3,442 reindeer, selected from the youngest and best of our stock, was gathered and held while the herders commenced training wild deer for draft purposes to haul equipment and provisions for the drive.

A. E. Porsild, representing the Canadian Government, was at Nabachtoolik. He approved the selection of deer made by our men as he knew they were more experienced than he was. Besides, he realized that it was good sense on our part to select nothing but the best stock to insure the success of the drive.

Including Andrew Bahr, the reindeer drive comprised twelve men, each chosen for his fitness to endure the rigors of the trip, as well as for his ability and knowledge in handling reindeer. One dog team was taken a short distance to help haul supplies. We furnished all personal equipment, including medical supplies and everything else that could be anticipated for use on the trip.

The drive started from Nabachtoolik December 26, 1929, as the herd was driven eastward toward February Mountains. Two days later the entire camp moved on with fourteen heavily loaded sleds drawn by sixteen half-broken sled deer. The first days were a turmoil with the sled deer causing trouble and the entire herd constantly trying to turn back to its home range.

A drive of the magnitude of this one had never before been attempted, so we had no previous experience to draw on. Driving several thousand reindeer along the rim of the Arctic, through swamps, rivers, and blinding blizzards, was not a pleasant prospect. We knew the homing instinct reindeer always possess would cause them to make frequent breaks for the home range. But our encouragement to attempt the drive was in the realization that here was a humanitarian adventure which, provided we could get through with the herd, would be of inestimable value to the Eskimo of northern Canada.

We also realized that should we fail in making delivery it would be necessary to organize another drive, as the advance made to us by the Canadians would have been spent and we would not have the $112,000 to return to them.

Three of the twelve men who started out would return after reaching the boundary of the home range, as the start was the most difficult part of the drive. Andrew Bahr would then be left in charge with four Lapps and four Eskimo.

Each herder was given a dog of the Lapp or collie type, trained in the handling of reindeer. These dogs all understood their work so well that they saved their masters many miles of travel.

As the drive really got under way the herders found they had their work cut out for them. The first time they encountered brushy going the herd balked. While the drivers were attempting to force the herd through, several hundred deer escaped and ran many miles on the back trail. The men had to turn the entire herd and retrace their steps until they caught up with the runaways. To regain a small bunch of stray deer it is easier to drive the main herd to them because the strays will run to join the larger number when they come in sight. Just as the herd was brought together, they were caught in a blizzard.

The wind howled and battered at them, flinging icy particles into their eyes, freezing the eyelids almost shut. The temperature ranged from 40 to 50 degrees below zero with never a letup. Merely caring for themselves out in the open at a time like that is a twenty-four-hours-a-day job, but they also had the reindeer to think of.

It is characteristic of reindeer to travel against the wind if left to their own devices, which made it doubly hard for the herders. Attempting to travel against such a demoniacal wind is a man-killing task. The wind forces the snow and cold into every tiny crevice in a man's clothing. He can actually freeze before he realizes that he is getting cold.

It took a whole year to organize and cover the first 200 miles to the juncture of the Kobuk and Hunt rivers, where a fresh supply of food had been sent ahead and cached by us. Though travel during the summer months was desirable, with the snow gone it was next to impossible to transport the necessary supplies.

By the spring of 1930 the herd was on the Kobuk River. The Eskimo called that camp the "Camp of Too Many Mosquitoes." All that summer the herd was covered by a black canopy of shimmering, dancing mosquitoes, warble flies, black gnats, and nosee-ums.

The reindeer had always been accustomed to summer on the coast where they could wade into the salt water, and where the wind along the sea kept the insects at a minimum. Now they were forced to live under a blanket of constant tormentors. As a result, about a thousand reindeer stampeded and headed for their home range. The herders simply could not stop them and they were lost to the drive. But the fawning season added a large crop, so the deserters were not needed.

As winter approached, temperatures fell, and for weeks the little band of men and their herd experienced weather of 50 to 60 degrees below zero. Driving deer along in such bitter cold was an eerie sight as clouds of steam hung above the animals in a woolly fog. Most of the time, one 14 x 16 foot tent was occupied by all the men, since fuel was scarce and clothing had to be hung up to dry each night.

Soon herds of caribou were encountered. Since a really large herd of caribou would engulf the small herd of reindeer as a river swallows up a mud puddle, the herders had their hands full keeping the reindeer and caribou apart. It was not easy, but the ever-faithful reindeer dogs did the major portion of the work.

Andrew wrote us in December, 1930:

It was hard to get through the Kobuk Mountains, very rough traveling it took us month to make Noatak steep mountains all the creek and Rivers overflowed and clear ice bad feeding deep snow and no moss this country is very Poor feeding for deer very little Reindeer moss nothing but Brown moss (house moss) sled deer we have tied a month ago Plaid out and some of the deer in herd Play out. Now we are crossing the divides between Noatak and Colville the weather been bad now for three days and is snowing and blowing today I expect to have better traveling after we past the Colville Range. Som of the boys been very cranky but they are getting better.

My brothers and I, without local knowledge of the terrain, had mapped the route the drive should take through the mountains to the Colville River. Getting word of the herd's position and the possible dangers confronting the party, we sent Robbins, pilot of the Alaska Airlines, accompanied by Dan Crowley, our field superintendent, to help Andrew. Flying over the range with Andrew aboard enabled Robbins to chart his course through a pass in the mountains and on across the Ambler River. The route we had chosen was found to be impassabie because of deep canyons where deer could not travel or find food. That winter was spent negotiating the passes of the Brooks Mountains and traveling over the vast stretches of tundra that lay between. To save the sled deer, we contracted for dog teams to transport 4,000 pounds of supplies at twenty cents per pound across the first range.

In March of 1931 an epidemic of diphtheria broke out at Barrow, Alaska, and Alaska's famous pilot, Joe Crosson, at Fairbanks, was commissioned to fly serum to Barrow, 600 miles distant. After completing his mission, Joe wired from

Barrow to brother Alfred—then in Juneau, Alaska, serving as a member of the territorial legislature—that en route to Barrow he had passed over our drive on the Colville River. Alfred wired back: "Will pay you $300 for a letter from Andrew Bahr." On his return trip from Barrow, Joe located the herd, dropped down, and landed on the snow near the camp and remained long enough for Andrew to write the much-wanted letter. It was the first word we had received in many months.

Andrew advised us he would require more food by May 1. The only possible way to get it to him was by airplane. We arranged with Alaska Airlines to send Joe Crosson north to deliver the required supplies. Dan Crowley flew from Nome to Fairbanks to accompany Crosson on the flight and discuss with Andrew in what other ways we could be of help to him.

On April 9, 1931, Crowley was advised by Alaska Airlines that the plane could not possibly take off with more than 1200 pounds and, as he weighed 200 pounds, they could handle but 1,000 pounds of food supplies.

Crowley wrote us a detailed account of the trip. Mountains and fog were hazards. They picked up the Anaktuvuk River. After following it some miles, the fog commenced to lift.

Soon after leaving the mountains they began seeing caribou tracks and small herds of caribou, digging up moss and feeding on it; the surface of the snow was broken as though it had been harrowed, so it was easy to trace where they had been feeding. From an airplane, snow is bluish in color; footprints, appearing pure white, can be seen for long distances.

Finally they sighted the reindeer herd on a small creek about a mile from the Colville River. Three tents were pitched on the snow, the reindeer sleds drawn up in front.

Joe made a landing on the river directly in front of the camp. After greeting them, Andrew explained that they were not as short rationed as we had feared. He had begun rationing out the grub in February, when some things began to get short, and had it so divided that no one would have suffered if they'd had to get along another month. What they had when the new supplies arrived would last them well into June. They had also killed three moose the day before so, with the grub Joe and Dan brought, they were now well supplied.

Andrew said he figured the drive would stay where it was until after fawning and the breakup, then move down toward the mouth of the Colville, to be closer to the source of supplies, and also because feed would be better in the summer nearer to the coast. He would range the deer between the Colville and the Kuparuk rivers during the warm weather.

Andrew intended to send a dog team to Beechey Point, where there was a trading post, to find out if they had sufficient stock to supply his wants. He would also send messages to Point Barrow as often as he could, to be telegraphed from there to the office at Nome so we would be kept informed of his plans, activities, needs, and so forth.

Morale at the camp seemed to be good. When we got to the coast, Andrew planned to try to hire extra men to replace a couple who didn't suit him.

After their long trek the deer were quite poor and would not be able to go much farther the balance of the year. For the past month, Andrew said, they had been making only about five or six miles a day and not moving at all some days. Nilluka said about 250 to 300 deer had been lost during the winter from weakness; as they couldn't keep up they had been left behind. Andrew estimated that the herd at present was close to 3,000 animals, a figure with which Nilluka agreed. As it was still some 400 miles from where they were to the mouth of the Mackenzie River, it was doubtful if the drive could be completed next winter. On the other hand, because they would have no mountain ranges to cross, and having more sled deer than before, they could make an earlier start and better time. Nilluka said that the past winter they had broken in more than fifty sled deer. Andrew thought he could reach the Mackenzie fairly early, perhaps in March, but figured that the deer would be too weak to stand a hard drive at that time across the mouth of the river. He was optimistic as to the outcome, though, only regretting that it was costing so much money. There seemed nothing they were particularly in need of and he gave Joe and Crowley the impression that they were getting along satisfactorily.

One "family note" cropped up. The Eskimo Woods boys expressed a great desire to have their families join them that summer. Andrew said the boys were the best men he had and that it wouldn't be a bad idea to have the families come.

This was the sum and substance of Crowley's report to us and it relieved our minds.

In July of 1931 we received a wire from Andrew that punctured our complacence.

Foggy Island via Barrow Alaska. We camped fawning season east banks Colville below Anaktuvak River. Bad feed no moss deep snow. Snowstorms most all time. Our herd is very poor. Lots of fawns lost stillborn freeze ded. June 15 we start moving herd overland using pack deer. July 6 reached Foggy Island starving and tired footed. Mr. Smith [a trader] did not have any grub or footwear. I send him Beechey Point. After five days he return with his power boat. Brought a little flour and sugar. This store and natives here got no mukluks nor material for mukluks. We are holding main herd yet. Would need half dozen herders sent up if possible. Can get no herders here. Let me know by wire.

As suggested by Andrew, we would try to have the families of the Woods boys join the drive. We arranged for a small schooner to pick up the families at Kotzebue, take them to Barrow, and then to the eastward. Some time later we learned that the boat had passed Point Barrow. It was not until two years later that word came to us, by wireless through the Signal Corps station at Barrow, that a child had been born on the drive, and it was only then that we knew that the wives had met up with their husbands. Such was communication in the Arctic.

Andrew wrote us from Foggi Island, July 21, 1931:

Last fall in September was four feet snow and iced on top. North of Noatak Mountains was very deep snow and hardly any moss all the way down to coast. Lots of deer played out, starved and left on the trail while others died. Hundreds of them lost that way. Lots of females had stillborn fawns all spring.

We spent the fawning season east bank of Colville below Anaktuvuk River. We had poor fawning season, cold and snowstorms, poor food and no shelter. Poor females could not take care of their young ones, lots of fawn freeze, and starve dead. Here along the coast is very poor feed even in summer, no moss and too cold to grow any grass or leafs. Low land, nothing but lakes, swamps, full of water.

June 15 we start move straight toward Foggi Island using pack deer, had awful hard times on acct of the continual bad weathers, cold, snowing sleeting, raining and foggi. We had two of the Colville boys working for us but they quit and went home, they did not stand the hardship. And Mr. West was lost and he lost all three of his pack deer too, and he left all his stuff someplace tundra. He track our herd, and that way he found us after ten days lost. Mike left to camp place to sleep and was lost but he happen to find us too. We lost quite a few deer while moving to coast, lots of mothers and fawns they turn back and gotten left and go with caribou. July 6th we reached to Foggi Island, grub all gone and all mukluks worn out.

Some months later came another wire from Andrew:

While I was at Foggi Island 24 hour round trip boys was bucking and lost big bunch of herd. I sent men after he was there 5 days but he did not find and now I could not get boys to go. So I have to send Mr. Smith east to Flakeman Island to try to get mukluks there. We are holding main herd but very hard, the boys all getting tired.

Our herd has been very poor all winter spring and right now cannot find deer that is eatable. We been living almost on caribou.

This store got nothing and no fish in the waters. Starvation. I am fright our herd will get sickness such as footrot, the country is too low wet swampy and poor food.

Appreciating the fact that there were now insufficient deer in the herd to complete our contract with the Canadians, Andrew determined to travel back to the Colville River to pick up some of the lost deer. Knowing that he would be unable to drive a few strays, he divided the main herd, leaving half in charge of his most-trusted Eskimo helper, Tommy Wood, in the vicinity of the Shaviovik River, and taking the other half to use in picking up any strays he might find.

During the winter of 1931–32 we were without any word from Andrew. In April 1932 we received a wire via Barrow from Tommy Wood ordering new supplies and closing with the message, "We are all well and deer doing well fawning in good place."

The following month came word from Andrew:

We have five months roundup trip. Six men. With eight hundred reindeer one dog team and seven sled deer. Have traveled four hundred miles. Found four hundred of the stray deer. But we lost most of the deer on this trip by starvation killed by wolves. Now we are fifty miles from Peter Woods our main camp on Shaviovik River. Will be around Canning River this summer. Shortage of grub east Beechy Point.

It is virtually impossible for people living in temperate climes to appreciate what Andrew and his helpers were up against on this great trek. In summer the country was too wet and soft to transport their supplies; the winters were long, cold, and stormy, the sun dropping out of sight below the horizon during mid-November, not to reappear until late January. During severe blizzards the men were forced to take to their sleeping bags for the duration. Often they were miles apart. When they emerged from their bags again, the herd would have disappeared. They knew the direction of the winds and duration of the storm and, knowing that the deer would travel against the wind—not drifting as cattle do—and knowing the approximate speed of the animals, they could judge quite accurately where to find the herd. The period of travel was during the winter months, but this time was shortened because of the fawning season, which began late in March and extended into late May. It was heartbreaking work for the men on the drive and a great strain on my brothers, associates, and me, who were responsible for the undertaking. Fortunately, there was no loss of human life.

We did everything to render aid. We established unlimited credit for Andrew with the several trading posts scattered along the Arctic coast of Alaska and with the Hudson's Bay Company within the Canadian Arctic. We were assisted by the air lines that made occasional trips into the Arctic, by the United States Signal Corps, the United States Weather Bureau, the Northwest Mounted Police, and the Canadian officials at Ottawa, Aklavik, and Herschel Island. The entire north country of Alaska and the Northwest Territory of Canada were interested in seeing the drive a success.

We brothers traveled with the herd in spirit, if not in fact. It was a tremendous undertaking, and there was little that we could do to assist the boys on the trail. The expense of carrying on averaged $30,000 a year. We had estimated that it would be possible to make delivery to the Canadians at Kittigazuit in two years' time.

An ordinary drive of equal distance in more settled portions of Alaska would not be difficult, but this drive involved exploration to prevent the possibility of driving into an area where forage would be hard to find, or of following a blind lead where backtracking would become necessary.

In September 1932 came word from Andrew: "Can we deliver less than 3,000 deer to the Canadian Government?" That told us a story. Andrew did not have 3,000 deer in the herd, but there was the possibility that he could backtrack and pick up some lost deer. We must be very careful what instructions to wire, knowing that Andrew would attempt to carry them out.

Our answer read: "Our contract calls for delivery of 3,000 reindeer. Every animal less than 3,000 will cost us sixty-five dollars per head. You must decide whether to try to regain lost deer."

Andrew, as we later learned, thoughtfully and wisely decided that it was more important to push ahead than to hunt for lost deer.

23.

IT WAS heartening to realize the friendly co-operation and help given us by the many varied interests of the Arctic, in both Alaska and Canada. Familiar with the severe conditions we faced, these people understood that the task we had undertaken was a tremendous and dangerous one which, if it could be accomplished, would eventually improve the lives of thousands in the Canadian Arctic by assuring a permanent food supply, skins for clothing, and by establishing an industry in which native people could play a major part.

However, because of misunderstandings, jealousies, or simply the mistrust of our organization occasioned by adverse publicity, certain elements did their utmost to handicap our efforts. As an example, a friend in charge of the Weather Bureau at Barrow, Alaska, sent my brother Alfred a clipping from the *Northern Cross,* published by the Mission there. It was headed "Lomen's Deer" and stated that the Lomens had sold a big bunch of deer to the Canadian Government, driving them through a pass in the Endicott Mountains and, after getting them far to the eastward, had on one plea or another deserted them. The piece went on to say, "Now, if in time they send men to round up these deer, and if they discover, as is likely, that their deer have joined other deer, or taken unto themselves double, triple, or quadruple their number of deer belonging to the natives of this coast, will the Lomens claim the entire number? Loudly it is whispered that this is their scheme ofttimes worked to the south. However, it is not impossible that even the Lomens may learn that the northern Eskimo is of another stripe, not at all so docile and non-combative as is his southern brother, so long domineered over and harassed and browbeaten by the white man. The north-coast Eskimo is honest and wishes to be treated fairly and honestly, and will be so treated or will know the reason why."

In addition to that "friendly statement" by the local missionary, the Department of the Interior schoolteacher at Barrow addressed letters to the several Eskimo herds along the coast instructing them not to bother with any stray deer that might enter their herd, not to care for them, to beware of the drive, to watch their herds closely, or the Lomens would take them, and to extend no courtesies to the Lomens.

These suggestions created unfounded suspicions and naturally prejudiced the natives against us.

All reindeer selected for the drive to Canada bore our earmarks. Those born on the trail en route to Canada could not be handled for marking, so the herd was eventually made up of reindeer carrying our mark or the unmarked offspring. The reindeer in all Eskimo-owned herds bore the marks of their owners so that they would eventually show up should there be stray deer other than our own when delivery was made in Canada.

Earmarks are as readily read and recognized by the Eskimo herders as are printed words to anyone who reads, or brands to a cowboy. Any strays would soon be detected.

Many of our deer were lost. Many reached Eskimo herds and none were ever recovered by our organization.

These trying years were complicated by investigations that were being carried on by the Department of the Interior. We were in difficulties over a loan from the Reconstruction Finance Corporation, and with inspectors of Interior's General Land Office, who were investigating our several ranges of grazing lands. I spent many winter months attending hearings relative to reindeer, and testifying before committees in Washington; and my brothers and I had to put in much of our summer time preparing material for departmental investigators sent North.

The Canadian officials had secured three Lapp reindeer men in Norway who were to be employed at Kittigazuit to take over the herd on its arrival. Because of delays occasioned by storms, wolves, lack of supplies, and other causes, and realizing that the Canadian Lapps were awaiting the arrival of our deer, we recommended that Canada instruct their Lapps to proceed westward until they met the herd, then travel with Andrew and so learn the American technique of handling the animals. Since there were many differences between the methods employed in Alaska and those used in Lapland, we felt the suggestion would prove beneficial both to us and to the Canadian Government. This was done.

In midsummer 1933 we received word through the Canadian representative in the north that Andrew was failing mentally and physically, and should be replaced. We were well aware that Andrew had lived a rugged life, particularly in the three years of the drive and, though we knew he would continue doing his best, human endurance had limits, and the reports probably were accurate. What to do?

Our thoughts turned to our former field superintendent, Dan Crowley, now living in San Francisco. We telephoned him, explained the situation, and asked him to proceed north to join Andrew and help him in every way he could. Dan responded willingly, rushed north as fast as train and river steamer could carry him, to remain until the drive would be over and the reindeer delivered to the Canadians.

He wrote us after talking the situation over with Andrew that no serious obstacles appeared and, with a little judgment, patience, and hard work he felt sure the drive would be completed in December. Fortunately the deer were in excellent shape. There was good food for a distance of forty miles eastward; from there on it wasn't so good, but fortunately they wouldn't have to go much farther if they took the island route. Andrew intended holding the herd on this good feed till they were ready to make the final dash for Richard Island.

Residents of the section advised them not to take to the ice before mid-December. They were going to start at the earliest possible moment and ten days later should see them at Kittigazuit. They would decide on the exact route when the time came, out across the islands or across the lowlands. Both routes would be gone over by dog team and the better one selected. The survey trip should take only a week, ten days at most, and could be done in November. Already the Lapps had been on some of the islands and reported a little feed. Across the lowlands the hazards would be underbrush, willows, and possibly glare ice. The latter would probably not be encountered on the island route.

Dan reported that, contrary to rumor, Andrew's mentality was as good as ever. He had the situation well in hand and Dan found his management excellent. If he suffered from anything it was too much help, especially through the last summer. But that was being corrected and would cut down expenses, a good thing as grub was very expensive in the region.

The Canadian Lapps kept pretty much to themselves but Andrew had no difficulty in handling them. Besides Andrew, there were six men, three natives and three Lapps. As the herd had to be watched night and day because of wolves, that was about as few as could take care of the job. Only a couple of days back one of the Lapps had discovered the wolves sneaking on the herd.

The weather was cold and disagreeable so they were fortunate in having plenty of beach wood for fires. Between there and Barrow there were three herds. The first one coming east from Barrow was owned by a native named Totpon and numbered about 1,500, located near Beechey Point. The next numbered about 400 or 500, owned by Tom Gordon. A native named Richmond Clohak had 200 or 300. Gordon's herd was near Barter Island. Clohak's near Collinson Point.

Dan wound up his report saying, "The Arctic is full of ice floes as far as the eye can see."

Andrew, being in full charge of the drive, accepted orders from no one but my brothers Ralph, Alfred, or from me. Possibly this irked some who did not agree with him on how and when to move the herd and undoubtedly had instigated the tales about his poor health and failing mentality.

The drive arrived on September 15 at King Point with all their camp equipment. In early December the sea froze over and enough snow fell on the ice to keep the reindeer from slipping and falling. Andrew had sent ahead to obtain the services of Oliver, an Eskimo guide, who was said to know the Mackenzie Delta country well from having trapped and hunted over it for years. On December 6 Andrew had the herd brought close to camp, intending to move them out to sea, across the ice, the following day. But it was the day before Christmas before he finally got them moved to Shingle Point, because from December 7 to Christmas Eve there were terrific windstorms the like of which they never had seen.

To make sure they had all the deer, the day after Christmas all hands went to the hills for a general roundup. This took several days. When they had finished, Oliver the guide arrived. The next step was to check on ice conditions of the delta. Andrew sent Oliver and Michael, one of the Lapps, out on the ice. They returned that evening and Michael reported conditions fairly good—some glare ice but only small patches that could be circled.

Again Crowley reported:

The boys and herd got away for Richard Island the morning of January 3. I thought it was all over but signing on the dotted line. I never dreamed of anything going wrong. They probably would have got through if they had had a good guide, but Oliver evidently became confused and, according to Andrew, led them around in a circle. They traveled all that day, that night and the next day, stopping occasionally for a bite to eat. The second night they came to a low island with no feed on it, just marsh grass, and stopped to cook some food. The deer showed a tendency to want to rest so they thought they would be all right for a little while. Andrew says he tried to get some of the boys to watch, but they were all so tired and hungry no one wanted to take it on. After eating, Andrew sent out a couple of the boys to see about the deer, only to find that the animals had gone back. The boys set out with skis and dogs to try and overtake them; after following the trail for six hours, they gave up and returned to camp. As soon as they were rested, Andrew told the Eskimo to take a little grub and follow the deer back to the mainland and he would follow along. The next day the boys set out to cover the fifty miles on foot with nothing but a primus stove and a little grub. It took them twenty-four hours. Fortunately, they had good weather until the last two hours, when it stormed badly, but they made it. They were in bad shape, faces, hands, and feet being severely frostbitten. One of the boys is still limping. This all happened when we were having only about five hours' daylight out of the twenty-four and the temperature about 40 degrees below zero.

After the boys had returned from their futile attempt to over-take the deer, Andrew asked Oliver how far they were from Kendall Island. He wanted to get some supplies and hire another dog team to help haul the outfit back to the mainland, the sled deer being too weak to make the trip. Oliver said about three or four hours' journey from the island, so they started out. After going four hours, Andrew asked how much farther. Oliver thought about three hours more. After another three hours, Andrew again asked how far. Oliver thought about two or three hours more. This kept up for twenty-two hours. Andrew thought they were lost and wouldn't ever reach the island. When they finally got in they were frostbitten, numb, and weak from exposure and hunger. Andrew says if there had been five miles further to go he thinks they couldn't have made it. The dogs were played out and about ready to quit.

The reindeer were too weak to attempt another drive across the delta that winter, so 1934 found them again on the banks of the Mackenzie.

When spring arrived that year and the sun commenced to shine, it beat down with a white heat known only to the far North and the equator. The river ice started to rot. Broad sheets of water were soon sliding out from under every snow-bank, causing them to crumple from the bottom, and in an unbelievably short length of time the country was a dead brown, flecked here and there with the deeper snowdrifts that still kept slumping down.

The sudden change from winter to summer is awe-inspiring in the far North. The sterile, deep-frozen land changes almost overnight. Tiny moss flowers appear in every tuft of tundra moss, very small but perfectly shaped and of many colors. A restlessness sweeps over the land and even imbues the phlegmatic reindeer with a strong desire to return to the home range.

Each morning the herders put on dry mukluks but before noon they would be soaked through. The lower half of a man would be very nearly frozen while the upper half roasted in that blazing sun that poured down twenty hours out of the twenty-four. The herders still clung to their reindeer-skin parkas, for the mosquitoes and flies hung like a shimmering veil over the land now. They arose from the tundra in such great numbers that sometimes a man became panicky, fearing he would not be able to breathe.

Even with the parkas on, those devilish insects worked themselves under the herders' shirts and bit and bit—never stopping until so sated with blood they would burst or be crushed by agonized hands pawing at them. There simply was no way of evading them. Within the herd area itself they were even worse—hanging in clouds so thick it seemed as though an ever-moving curtain was spread over the frantic animals.

It is sheer torture to stop for meals when the insects are so thick. Almost every spoonful of food holds its quota of insects, while occasionally a herder will choke and gag as an unwary insect travels through his nose and down into his lungs, tickling as it buzzes and struggles to escape. It is the most fiendish type of torture—and there is no escape from it.

Dan Crowley reported:

The study of the island route should commence this spring in April. There are many islands to be examined, some with moss and some without, some hard to approach and some easy. Someone should go there in April when the days are long and the weather fairly mild, visit these different islands, and select the one closest to Shingle Point, which has sufficient moss to graze the herd for a day or two, get the exact compass direction for there and estimate the distance as closely as possible, which I imagine will be about fifty miles. That is about all that can be done this spring. During the summer fifty stakes [small spruce trees eight to ten feet high with the upper branches left on] should be ordered and brought to Shingle Point by boat.

If the delta route is found to be unfavorable, the trail to the Island should be staked starting about November 15, and the ice examined to determine its fitness. One stake to be placed every mile. There would not be much expense attached to staking the trail and I think that by so doing many miles of travel might be saved by the herd. Trying to follow a compass course when you are walking is very hard, especially at night. Also I am sure everyone would feel much safer and sure of the fact that they were going to the right island.

Halfway across, a tent should be set up and plans made to serve a hot meal and have it ready when the herd arrives. A relief crew of four men should be stationed here. They could leave the shore about ten hours ahead of the herd and be ready to take up the drive when the others arrive. The first drivers could rest for about six hours and then catch up with the herd. Also a camp should be established on the island to which they are going, instead of these tired, cold, hungry men having to make camp and gather wood after they get there. The things that I mentioned could practically all be done by our own men so that the cost would be very nominal. Whichever route is selected, camps should be made halfway across and at the terminal, and meals to be eaten en route planned before leaving the base camp. None of the things I have mentioned above were done on the drive just attempted which failed.

During the summer of 1934 the herd was closely watched. As soon as ice conditions permitted, the trail across the delta was staked and every precaution taken against possible mishaps. The Dominion government officials were becoming restless because of the many delays, and we were rapidly approaching the end of our resources.

We in the States knew that the attempt to cross would be made in December. The start would be a day or two before the full of the moon to get the benefit of its light, the sun being below the horizon during the entire twenty-four hours of the day at that time of the year.

Came December and the time of the full moon. "They are now out on the delta," we said. Then I learned there was to be a total eclipse of the moon in the region of the Mackenzie Delta. What would that mean? Would the superstitious natives abandon the herd when they saw the moon beginning to dim? We were not long in doubt. Chinook winds had struck, the snow on the river had melted, and the drive, of necessity, postponed. They would try again during January. Still no snow covering the ice. February would be quite late and we feared that another year was lost.

In mid-February came a wire:

Arrived Richard Island twenty-first. Very successful crossing sixty hours en route stormy tough trip but account preliminary work done and sheltered route no mishaps. Deer came through fine shape but weak now. Carrying many deer on sleds today. Necessary remain here one week before proceeding Kittigazuit. Expect transfer about March sixth. Due Aklavik fifteenth probably. Advisable take mail plane leaving twenty-fifth due Seattle April first. Signed Crowley.

We were thrilled and greatly relieved. We had performed the impossible and Canada was to have a new industry.

On March 6, 1935, the herd was passed through the chutes of the corral at Kittigazuit and counted. There were 2,382 deer checked, including twelve sled deer left on Richard Island. The herd contained but 10 per cent of marked, or original, deer, 90 per cent of unmarked, or deer born on the trail during the five-year and three-month period of the drive. Within a few weeks 811 fawn were born to the herd. This would have constituted clear profit could we have held the herd until after the fawning season—nearly $53,000 at $65 per head. But we had considered our original offer to the Canadians as a "sporting proposition" and we felt that we must deliver the herd upon its arrival at Kittigazuit, unless to do so would prove dangerous to the does then heavy with fawn.

Shortly after delivery I proceeded to Ottawa with Arthur Baldwin to complete settlement with the Canadian Government officials. One of the department officials—of whom there were many present—stated at the conference: "I was in on the capture of a general during the Boer War; I had my fling in the World War; but never in my experience have I been connected with anything that held the romance, the excitement, and interest of this drive during these five years from Nabachtoolik in western Alaska to Kittigazuit in our own Canadian Arctic."

We had expended in excess of $150,000 in making the drive; had earned $154,830 for 2,382 reindeer at $65 per head, from which was deducted the $112,000 advanced to us and $9,588.39 covering certain expenses incurred, including wages, bonuses, supplies, dog hire, and other items guaranteed by the Dominion Government and to be paid by us prior to final settlement.

We were proud of our achievement and happy that we had undertaken it. It was a great accomplishment, made possible by the leadership of Andrew Bahr, Dan Crowley, and their loyal helpers. The city of Seattle celebrated Andrew's return by designating the day of his arrival "Andrew Bahr Day."

Now, a quarter-century after the start of the great trek, delivery of an equal number of reindeer could be made at much less cost, with smaller loss of the herd and less suffering on the part of men and animals. Today young stock would be selected and could be flown across the northlands in large transport planes.

In the years that have passed, thousands of reindeer from this original stock have supplied the Eskimo and the missions of Arctic Canada with food and clothing. And in addition, the herds have multiplied threefold. The Lomen brothers feel privileged in having played a part in the development of this fruitful enterprise.

24.

SHORTLY after New Year's day of 1933 I had been called
from Los Angeles to New York for a conference with Leonard
Baldwin. When I arrived it was to learn that he was under-
going surgery; a few days later he passed away. His death was
a great blow to me personally, to our family, and to our corporation. A finer friend we had never known, nor would we
ever meet a more kindly counselor.

It developed that everything was held in common by the
Baldwin brothers, using one pocketbook, share and share
alike. Hence Leonard's death automatically tied up all Baldwin funds. Testifying a year or two later before the United
States Senate Appropriations Committee, Arthur Baldwin explained it this way: "My brother and I had an arrangement
which we made when we were young boys. I think the first
record is in a diary I kept. I noticed that I sold my first skunk
for one dollar and gave him fifty cents." Senator Elmer
Thomas put in that he got his first dollar by catching a
skunk. Senator Adams of Colorado remarked with a grin,
"Well, you fellows certainly started in a smelly business."

In addition to the Baldwins' stock interest in our corporation, for which they had paid $1,200,000, they had been our
bankers, loaning us $410,000. Leonard Baldwin had suggested
to the Kendrick Committee that our corporation required
a further investment of $50,000 a year for another five years
before it could function fully.

In view of the fact that the Baldwin funds were tied up as

a result of Leonard's death, I was advised that it would be necessary for us to apply for a loan to the Reconstruction Finance Corporation. Papers were accordingly prepared and I proceeded on a new venture to Washington. At the time former Senator Pomerene of Ohio was Chairman of the R.F.C.

Our application was approved by the Board of the R.F.C. in the sum of $247,500. One hundred thousand dollars was paid over to us immediately, the balance to be available as soon as certain certificates could be secured from the court in Alaska and filed with the R.F.C. The order of approval for our loan was issued early in 1933, one of the last acts of the old board prior to the incoming of the board appointed by President Roosevelt.

Harold L. Ickes was appointed Secretary of the Interior. When he assumed office he found a massive record covering various investigations and hearings on the reindeer industry. In this connection it is interesting to note that investigations of the industry, and more especially of the Lomen Company, became the order of the day as far back as 1927. From then until 1938 there were some ten investigations and sets of hearings.

Mr. Ickes appointed within the Department of the Interior a "Reindeer Committee" of five. The first two meetings of the new committee were held eighteen months apart. During that period I saw various committee members but there was no committee action.

In midsummer 1933 Secretary Ickes learned of the loan to the Lomen Corporation. He requested the R.F.C. to suspend the loan, pending results of investigations he was making.

This turn of events came at a time when my brothers and I were in Alaska proceeding with developments that had been made possible by the promised R.F.C. loan and essential to the progress of our work. Our herds now numbered a quarter-million animals, our equipment was valued into the hundreds of thousands of dollars, and our total assets bordered on $5,000,000.

News of the suspension of the loan was a fearful blow. We had already made commitments, and the thought that the funds—though already fully approved by the R.F.C.—might not be forthcoming was alarming, to say the least.

This coincided with the time when Secretary Ickes assumed the role of "hatchet man" in the Roosevelt regime. As for the reindeer problem, he tackled it with all the subtlety of a bulldozer.

A propaganda smoke screen thrown up by the United States Department of the Interior was out of all proportion to the importance of the reindeer question. Into the melee charges of stampeded herds and fake roundups were hurled, to make it sound like the cattle rustling of an earlier day in the West. Once more all the old charges already disproved by the Kendrick Committee were dug up, and new ones added. Commotion and confusion rose to a high pitch.

The reindeer industry now assumed the quality of a nightmare. The new charges stirred a distrust in the minds of the Eskimo that seemed likely to affect permanently the best interests of the industry. What little lingering interest the natives had in reindeer evaporated like dew under an August sun. In the bureaucrats' eagerness to gain power, they were wrecking the entire industry.

The death of his brother had greatly afflicted Arthur Baldwin and he was not well. Leonard had devoted a large part of his time to our company, even to a certain degree directing policy.

Generous as always, during December of 1934 Arthur Baldwin addressed the following letter to Secretary Ickes:

DEAR MR. SECRETARY:
This letter is to confirm the proposition I made to you this day: REINDEER.

Northwestern Livestock Corporation parent company has issued and outstanding 12,000 shares of preferred stock, $100 par value, and 24,000 shares of common stock, no par. It owns all the stock of (1) Lomen Commercial Company; (2) Arctic Transport Co.; (3) Nunivak Development Co.; and (4) over 90 per cent of the common and preferred stock of Alaska Livestock and Packing Co.

Lomen Commercial Company owns the warehouses, dock and lighterage equipment at Nome, Golovin, Teller, Egavik, and Candle; stores and trading posts at Egavik, Golovin, Nome, Candle, Teller, and Baldwin, with necessary merchandise stocks at all of those trading posts. It also owns stocks of coal, lumber, hay, and other merchandise at Nome.

Arctic Transport Company owns the steamers *Arthur J. Baldwin, Sierra,* and *Silver Wave,* the former two known as refrigerated ships.

Nunivak Development Company owns the herd and trading post at Nunivak Island with necessary stocks of merchandise. Alaska Livestock and Packing Company owns the herds, estimated at above 250,000 reindeer, corrals and abattoirs, herding equipment, cold-storage plants, etc., located at Egavik, Golovin, Nome, Teller, and Baldwin.

I desire in behalf of my late brother, Leonard D. Baldwin, and myself to create a trust for the benefit of the Eskimo and natives of Alaska, and for that purpose I propose to turn over to three trustees—namely the Secretary of the Interior, the Secretary of Agriculture, and the Governor of Alaska, stock of the parent company, the Northwestern Livestock Corporation, as follows:

13,996 shares of common stock and 8,000 shares of preferred stock. I desire these trustees to take full charge of the Northwestern Livestock Corporation and of all its subsidiary companies and devote the income they may receive from such securities to welfare work among the Eskimo and natives of Alaska, whether in the form of schools or hospitals, or such other welfare work as to them seems advisable.

If this proposition is suitable to you, I will take immediate steps to carry it out.

Sincerely yours,

ARTHUR J. BALDWIN

After studying this proposal for some time, the officials of the Department of the Interior stated they could not accept this generous and selfless offer.

During the early summer of 1934 I was with the Reindeer Committee when Mr. Chapman said, "Lomen, why don't you make us an offer?"

"Along what lines are you thinking?" I inquired.

"Well, we want to control the deer."

"You want to own the deer?"

"Yes, we would like to buy your deer."

"You want to buy our corporation?"

"No, but we might want some of your equipment."

"Well," I replied, "that's a big order. I will want to consult with Arthur Baldwin in New York."

"All right," he said, "have a letter on my desk Saturday morning."

This was on a Thursday. I caught a midnight train and was in Mr. Baldwin's office the following morning. When he heard my story, he asked what I thought of it.

"What do I think of it?" I said. "We graze our herds on the public domain, as do the Eskimo deer men. We have been notified by the General Land Office of the Department of the Interior that we will be charged a grazing fee—which we will be unable to pay. It looks as though the Department is anxious to secure control of the herds and that we must play ball with them or have our herds confiscated."

We had applied to the General Land Office for grazing areas. In fact, we were the first to apply for such leases under the Grazing Act of 1927. It was now 1934 and still none had been granted.

"What do you suggest?" he inquired.

"I recall the evening when you and your brother invested $1,200,000 with us. I would suggest that we offer to sell to the Government all of our reindeer, wherever found, except-

278

ing the deer we are still driving to Canada for the Dominion Government, and all of the equipment, corrals, range equipment, cold-storage plants, abattoirs, and everything else that has anything to do with reindeer, for $1,200,000."

We prepared a letter to that effect and I placed it on Chapman's desk Saturday morning.

The following week Mr. Baldwin came to Washington on invitation of the Committee. When he joined me at my hotel, I suggested that he meet with the Committee alone and, should I be wanted, telephone me. I was sent for in a matter of minutes.

As I entered Chapman's office, Mr. Baldwin spread his arms out and laughingly said, "Carl, I have been generous with your money!"

"In what way?" I inquired.

"I have cut off a quarter of a million from our price, bringing it down to $950,000!"

"You know that whatever you decide is all right with me," I answered.

Mr. Chapman spoke up. "That is just what we have wanted."

I considered that now my work in Washington was done, that I could return home shortly and devote my time to other matters. Here was a spendthrift administration, passing out huge sums of money, and now they had a worth-while business that would benefit many thousands of government wards, secured at a price less than a third of its value. To wind up such a deal seemed a simple matter.

In late July 1934 Mr. Burlew of Interior telephoned, informing me that Mr. Ickes had approved the recommendations of his committee and would send an auditor to our Seattle office to make a complete check of our properties. In itself, this required several months, and it was now more than a year since the loan of $247,500 to us had been approved by the Board of R.F.C. We were in dire need of funds.

The summer dragged on. On September 17, while I was still in Washington, tragedy struck Nome. Fire! Eighty per cent of the town was destroyed. I received many telegrams urging me to consult with Government officials and secure immediate relief. Through Emergency Surplus Relief, $50,000 was credited to Alaska's governor. Quick action was imperative, as the city would require building materials, food, and fuel; otherwise it would be necessary to evacuate a large part of the population. And in late October navigation with the port of Nome would close.

On October 8 I appealed to the R.F.C., requesting a short-term loan of $30,000 to our company, with which to purchase lumber and coal. This was granted. The papers covering the transaction were not completed, however, until October 20, but as soon as I learned that the loan had been approved, I telegraphed my brothers, who purchased needed supplies dispatching a chartered vessel to Nome.

It was only when the papers were finally placed before me that I learned for the first time that, in order to secure the $30,000 loan, I would have to agree to cancellation of the $147,500 balance due on the loan of $247,500 awarded us a year and a half ago—and which had never been paid over to us!

Here was a fine kettle of fish indeed. We had already obligated ourselves for $30,000 through purchases of lumber and coal in Seattle.

It was obvious that both R.F.C. and Interior were making use of this fortuitous smaller loan to bail themselves out of an embarrassing position in that the original loan had been withheld, at the request of Secretary Ickes, for more than a year after approval. But there was no alternative, and I signed the papers. The check for $30,000 was delivered to us on November 1.

In addition to these difficulties, the R.F.C., although they already held all collateral of the parent company, demanded all the unissued stock of one of our company's subsidiaries. I explained that though all stock of this subsidiary was owned by the Lomen Company, it had never been issued.

"Then issue it!" was the retort.

We did.

Some weeks later we were advised by the Internal Revenue Department that we were indebted to them in the sum of $2,940 stamp tax for the stock issued. We paid this sum; I am glad to report, however, that years later it was credited back to us.

Such was the experience of the Lomens with "high finance" in Washington.

Short of funds as we were, I instructed my brothers to cut down the herd crews to skeleton basis, as the money now spent in herding would be lost to us when transfer of the reindeer was made. I prepared to leave for the West but was requested by the Reindeer Committee not to go at that time.

Three months later, while I cooled my heels in Washington, Mr. Slattery called me to his office to inform me that the Department of the Interior had failed to secure the approval of the Bureau of the Budget. That prevented the introduction by the Interior Department of its proposed legislation in Congress to provide for the purchase of all white-owned reindeer and necessary equipment. One more delay to an already ravished industry! It was first necessary to have a bill passed by Congress to authorize an appropriation, and a second bill to carry the appropriation.

I secured a copy of the Department's bill, and later was able to persuade Alaska's delegate to Congress, Anthony J. Dimond, to introduce it in the House. In the Senate a similar bill was introduced by Senator Elmer Thomas, chairman of the Senate Committee that had investigated the reindeer industry in Alaska.

Finally the bill passed both houses of Congress, providing for $2,000,000. It was signed by the President and became law on September 1, 1937.

The Act authorized and directed the Secretary of the Interior to acquire, in the name of the United States, by purchase or other lawful means, including exercise of the power of eminent domain, for and on behalf of the Eskimo and other natives of Alaska, reindeer, reindeer-range equipment, abattoirs, cold-storage plants, warehouses, and other property, real or personal, the acquisition of which he determines necessary to the effectuation of the purposes of this act. It provided also for condemnation proceedings.

The reindeer industry was now to become purely an Eskimo business, with whites, Lapps, and others forever barred.

The Lomen Corporation had fully demonstrated its constructive aims. It had expended large sums of money and furnished employment to hundreds of Eskimo, as well as to Lapps and whites. It had purchased hundreds of surplus male deer from the Eskimo deer men. It had developed improved methods for handling the deer. It had introduced reindeer meat and reindeer by-products to the people of the United States, and had created a substantial demand for them. In one winter season alone we shipped out of the port of Seattle fifty-one carloads of reindeer meat, each of approximately 30,000 pounds.

In this connection, it is an interesting sidelight that five years after our separation from the industry, in 1945, Mr. J. Sidney Rood, General Reindeer Supervisor, wrote as follows:

A few white owners attempted to make money by shipping reindeer products to the United States. A few made a gesture at herding with hired help. One of them installed efficient butchering equipment, set up general stores which also served as herd commissaries. It developed lighterage equipment, and even operated ships to convey products to the States. This concern undertook management of some herds, wherein native reindeer were mixed. It applied for grazing rights to ranges adjacent to good shipping points. It shipped and sold a large quantity of reindeer meat and skins; it really created a substantial demand therefor. It taught many natives and government officials important things about processing equipment and accounting procedures. During the course of its aggressive efforts it became involved in much persistent conflict with Reindeer Service officials and with native reindeer owners, particularly those whose animals became mixed with its own. Other whites, some of whom had commercial or personal trouble with the concern, fanned the struggle against it over reindeer problems. The conflict suggested that the native people were anxious to herd and manage their reindeer efficiently, but were prevented by this white operator from doing so. Later, when the government had extinguished ownership, it was perceived that this was an illusion.

In a forty-one-page document written by Dr. Carson W. Ryan, Jr., director of the Division of Education of the Bureau of Indian Affairs, the author paid our family the indirect compliment of quoting Leonard D. Baldwin's characterization of the action of his brother and himself as "an investment in the Lomen family rather than in reindeer. The father, the Judge on the bench, and the wonderful wife with five boys and a daughter, and grandchildren about him, are as worthy an institution as can be found in this country. I have dealt with them. I lived with them in their home. They have been in my home, all of them. I have been through their books. I have put accounts through them. On account of the charges, unwarranted, prejudiced, political, largely of suspicious people without character as far as I know, I feel that such a statement from me is not only warranted but called for." To which Dr. Ryan added, "So much of what has been said from time to time against the Lomens sounds prejudiced that one needs to use every precaution to be fair to them. Others besides the Baldwins have paid tribute to their qualifications. It is partly, of course, a matter of interpretation and the individual's own philosophy. What some people would call a 'monopoly in the region of the Seward Peninsula created by investment and energy,' others would characterize by harsher terms." This despite Dr. Ryan's misinterpretation of the situation in other phases of the proceedings!

During the ten investigations of the industry there was no proof offered that could be substantiated that the Lomens ever acquired any reindeer illegally or had been unfair in their dealings with the Eskimo. At the hearings Government men, Eskimo, and whites all had the opportunity to testify.

The never-ending conflict between the officials of the Reindeer Service of the Interior Department and the Lomen Corporation, in reference to Eskimo-owned deer that ranged in our herds, suggested that the Eskimo were anxious to herd and manage their own reindeer, but were being prevented from so doing by the action of the Lomens. Nothing could have been further from the truth.

There was another complication. Suddenly there appeared a great enemy of the reindeer, the wolf. For a number of years that great scourge of the North had been drifting westward, approximately forty miles per annum, from central Alaska. During the late twenties it started to filter into reindeer country.

The wolf was new to Eskimo reindeer men and they did not know how to combat the menace. They thought only of the value of the wolf skin as the fur was very desirable for a ruff about their parka hoods.

But one night on the Noatak a wolf attacked an unguarded reindeer herd, killing more than twenty animals. The local Eskimo hunters began preparations to hunt the wolf down but the herd owner warned, "No, that is my wolf!" Its hide would be worth forty dollars to him, whereas he had no market for reindeer meat. Though his herd continued to suffer, he failed to find the wolf.

At first the extent of the damage caused to the herds by this new pest was unrecognized. Some hunters saw an occasional wolf; a few dead deer were found. I once came across a fine large buck with its tongue missing, and later I learned that the tongue of the reindeer is considered a delicacy by the wolf, which will take out the tongue and leave the rest of the carcass untouched.

The wolf that now drifted into reindeer country had followed the caribou for centuries. It found the reindeer easy prey. As reindeer do not migrate from one part of the country to another in the manner of caribou, the female wolf had a handy food supply while raising her pups. The result was that more pups were raised, female wolves making a habit of raising the litters within range of a herd, where they were sure of food.

Prior to the advent of the wolf, we had had difficulty at our Egavik herd with brown bears. Unlike the wolf, the bear hunts for food only. To combat its ravaging of our herds, we offered a fifty-dollar bounty on bear. Within a matter of a few weeks we had paid out $500 as the bounty made it worth while for the Eskimo hunters to search out the bear. Encouraged, we gave notice that we would pay a bounty of $150 on wolves caught on our ranges.

Some time later one of the Eskimo boys at Unalakleet ran across a wolf's den. There were eight pups, one of which he managed to capture. His plan was to raise the pup and breed with his dogs, knowing that the cross would be a larger and stronger animal.

I recommended that the entire village go out and hunt down the rest of the litter, as well as kill the captured pup, for otherwise the Unalakleet Eskimo would lose hundreds of their reindeer.

The timber wolf that preys on the reindeer is the largest

of the wolf family and weighs upward of 150 pounds. A family of wolves usually travels together, and they cause tremendous damage to the wild life of a country. For years these vicious animals were protected in McKinley National Park, the territorial government paying a bounty on all killed outside the borders of the park. The theory was that the "balance of nature" must be maintained.

Man, as we had proved with the reindeer, can intelligently control the balance of nature to the benefit of mankind and the welfare of the animals themselves.

25.

IT WAS in 1934 that the Government first suggested that our reindeer be disposed of by sale to the Department of the Interior. We made our offer in writing, and the terms, as amended later by Mr. Arthur Baldwin, were acceptable to the Department, through Assistant Secretary Chapman and other members of Secretary Ickes' Reindeer Committee. However, the Department was blocked when the Bureau of the Budget refused to approve the appropriation for enabling legislation to acquire the deer. It is worth noting here that our offer of $950,000, covering our herds and equipment, was considered a fair one in 1934.

An authorization of $2,000,000 was enacted in 1937, as I have said, for the purchase of all non-native deer and equipment. Then in 1938 the reindeer item in the Appropriations Bill was deferred by the House for one year. The Senate amended and passed the bill; the Conference Committee agreed to an investigation of the matter, appropriating $50,000 for expenses.

A committee of three was selected to proceed to Alaska, investigate the industry in all its phases, and report back to Congress.

This Committee spent some time in Washington, studying records and reports made by previous committees, then proceeded to Alaska, arriving at Nome on June 22. Of their fifty-eight days in western Alaska, thirty-six were spent in the field studying the situation as to both reindeer and their owners. The Committee made a lengthy report to Congress, showing location of equipment recommended for purchase, and setting forth the number of deer it was thought necessary to purchase. An arbitrary figure of 180,000 animals was decided upon.

In estimating the value of various equipment, committee members were none too generous. For instance, on the Golovin range we had constructed a seven-mile fence across Darby Peninsula forming a holding ground; some ten miles in length and five in width, it was built of spruce poles and two-strand twisted wire, to serve the Golovin herd when marking and butchering. The Committee placed a value on the fence of $250.

For the corrals and cabins at Nabachtoolik, used in selection of the reindeer purchased by the Canadian Government, "Value: buildings, corral and fence, $175." Our Choris Peninsula property, $75. Our natural cold-storage plant at Elephant Point was rejected entirely, even though it would be of no value to us following sale of the deer.

The report fell far short of what we had a right to expect but we approved it, nevertheless. Obviously we had been as "hamstrung" by the Government as the reindeer were by the wolves—two-legged as well as four-legged—through investigations, departmental, senatorial, and congressional, in the years since 1927, to say nothing of the departmental competition on sale of meat and hides in the United States.

This was too much for any industry, especially one in northwestern Alaska. The Government clearly wanted total ownership and control of the deer, with elimination of non-native ownership, which, as with the Eskimo, had only public domain on which to graze its herds.

We felt that we had done a good job. We had built up large herds through study and hard work, had introduced new and scientific methods of handling the animals, exchanged bulls from one herd to another to build up the stock, devised new corral systems, and freely passed on to the Government and Eskimo alike these innovations, which proved a betterment to the industry.

We had a right to expect rapid action.

What happened?

The Rachford Committee reported to Congress, following which an item of $1,070,000 was included in the Department of the Interior Appropriations Bill. The item was stricken from the bill on the House floor on a point of order "because of inclusion of legislative matter in item." Amendment was offered and rejected. The Senate reinstated and passed the bill. Conferees agreed to submission of the item to a vote of the House. But it was rejected by the House.

Secretary Ickes addressed a letter to Senator Hayden:

Much has been said concerning the alleged concealed purpose of the 1937 act to "bail out" the Northwestern Livestock Corporation (Lomen). The Interior Department does not subscribe to the theory that the Lomens or anyone else are being "bailed out." The Department has taken the initiative in this matter because of the apparent dissatisfaction of the natives and their growing suspicion that they were being overreached by non-native owners. Investigation and investigation has been made in the Territory and numerous suggestions have been made as to what should or should not be done. The only way in which the Interior Department can acquire full control of the reindeer industry in Alaska is to acquire all livestock of non-native owners and all equipment that has been used by them in connection with their activities.

With the rejection of the bill, I called on the administrative assistant to Secretary Ickes, Mr. Burlew—an official I respected highly for his honesty and co-operation—to let him know that I now intended "taking my coat off" and calling on as many of the House members who had voted against the bill as I could make appointments with.

Mr. Burlew cautioned against this action so strongly that I

inquired in what way I could harm the bill, since it had already been defeated. There seemed no clear explanation.

Through the following two months I tramped the halls of Congress. I met 103 members, all of whom had opposed the bill, and told them my story. Mr. Taylor, chairman of the Appropriations Committee, urged me to carry on. Later he included the item in the Deficiency Bill and it was passed.

I was requested to appear before the Appropriations Committee of the Senate. The day following my appearance I met the clerk of the Committee leaving the committee room carrying an armful of papers. When he saw me he said, "I suppose you'd like to know what the Committee did with the reindeer item."

"I certainly would," I assured him.

"Well, they kicked it out."

When I survived that body blow I knew at least that my heart was sound, otherwise I would have expired right then and there.

There were but two more days of Congress. I rushed to the Senate lobby and called out Senator Henrik Shipstead. When he heard what I had learned, he said, "It will be impossible to bring up any item before the Senate now, no matter how worthy. We will not bring up the reindeer item. It will be forced to go to conference. The House will stand pat, the Senate will recede, and the item will pass."

The bill passed Congress and was signed a few days later by President Roosevelt.

By 1939, when the appropriation finally passed Congress, it had been whittled down to $720,000. Mr. Chapman then stated to me that, whereas our offer of $950,000 covering our herds and equipment had been considered perfectly fair in 1934, now the reduced appropriation—to "buy out" not alone our interests but all other "non-native" interests, numbering some fifty owners who had filed "declarations of ownership" to more than 200,000 reindeer—was insufficient to carry through the real purpose of the departmental plan.

In mid-October of 1939 I was advised that Secretary Ickes had appointed Charles Burdick, an employee of the Forestry Service stationed at Juneau, to negotiate with all non-native owners, and to acquire—either by purchase or condemnation —their reindeer for the Department of the Interior. Being told also that several months would be required by Interior to perfect its plans, I returned to my office in Seattle, after an absence in Washington of more than a year.

On November 25 Mr. Burdick called at our offices and after our greetings stated: "I have an offer to make to you, good only for today." My associates were in Nome and New York and there was insufficient time to communicate with them, even had the offer been acceptable to me, which it was not. I refused.

Mr. Burdick left for Alaska within the next day or two. I learned he was clothed with full and final authority to consummate the purchase of all non-native reindeer and equipment and that he planned to handle the herds during January and February in an effort to determine the numbers of reindeer on the several ranges. This we knew could not be done with any degree of accuracy. We were of the opinion that in view of the situation our figures on reindeer would be some indication of our holdings. Subsequently many telegrams passed between Mr. Burdick and myself.

We protested the plan of attempting to corral reindeer during January and February, being too close to the fawning season, when it was dangerous to corral the females heavy with fawn. We were fully aware that winter handling was beset with cold and storms, that drifting snow often obscured the ground from observers in a plane. Another real objection was that corrals for handling the animals were in nearly all instances located near the coast, where there would not be proper food at that time, and that long drives would be necessary to reach the corrals.

I went to Washington in an effort to secure an extension of time limit of the appropriation as it would expire at the close of the fiscal year, June 30. This would permit a summer count of the deer that would be far more accurate than any estimate, even our own.

The telegrams received by me from Mr. Burdick through the United States Signal Corps in Washington, D. C., were most alarming, for they clearly showed that they came from a man inexperienced in the work he was attempting to perform.

Referring to our first meeting in Seattle and the one-day offer, Mr. Burdick wired:

"Our discussions in Seattle were preliminary only. It was not a standing offer. It was based on how I would negotiate with you at that time. Investigations so far have proved to my satisfaction that three dollars less costs of preparing condemnation suits would be highest courts would award and this factor considered in arriving at my offer."

Again a wire from Mr. Burdick:

"Based on conditions found here large number of deer are without commercial value except for skins with market value approximately one dollar each."

By this time the Lomen Brothers were boiling mad. But we gave Mr. Burdick permission to use our corrals and necessary equipment at all our herds, free of charge, and made various recommendations for procedure based on our long and wide experience with reindeer.

Came another wire from Mr. Burdick:

"From personal experiences other types livestock and limited knowledge reindeer am of opinion July handlings would cause fawn loss through trampling in corrals."

That suggestion came from a man who admittedly had little or no experience with reindeer, to me who had handled tens of thousands of reindeer, most of them during the month of July. During one July handling of more than 12,000 reindeer at our Teller herd, the only accident was one broken horn of a single fawn.

The correct period to corral reindeer should be determined by many factors—advantages and disadvantages—then selecting the best time, weather conditions and other lesser details being taken into consideration. Any time a herd becomes frightened and attempts to turn against the mill, deer will be injured, no matter what time of the year. Our objections to winter handling of the deer continued.

Mr. Burdick wrote me under date of February 6, 1940, following citations of summer handlings that showed a high mortality of animals handled. He concluded with this paragraph:

I would be very glad to receive copies of any statements by experts in these matters which bear on this subject. To have any value whatever the statements would need to be based on sufficient research to justify conclusions by a scientist. An opinion not based on fairly conclusive factual data would have little value in any case.

Under the same date I received a letter addressed to me by Dr. Seymour Hadwen, director, Department of Pathology and Bacteriology, Ontario Research Foundation, Toronto, Canada, a scientist of the first order. In answer to my questions, he wrote:

Why do I prefer summer roundups? In the first place, the weather is usually good. The deer are easy to drive and they are generally close to the marking corrals on the coast in July and August. This is because they come down to the sea to escape the flies. The proper time to corral the deer is toward the end of the fly season, during the last part of July and the beginning of August. At this time the velvet on the horns is becoming less vascular, and the rutting season has not started. The castration of calves and bulls is safe also because the weather is turning colder. It is possible to work late and early this time of year, thus shortening the period required for marking. As regards the herders and others who assist at the roundup, they can work better in good weather. It must be stated that the corraling and handling of deer must be carefully done at any period of the year and that rough methods in catching the animals, lack of food and water, injuries of all sorts can generally be avoided under proper management.

Will the does lose their fawns if driven for long distances, or suffer from being corraled and handled during a roundup in February? It is probable that the does will not lose their fawns or show visible ill effects after being handled. In March, however, I am of the opinion that the does would suffer noticeable after-effects from driving, corraling, and shortage of food. If the animals are at all wild the effects will be greater. One important objection to corraling the deer in February and March is that the days are short and storms and bad weather frequent. Usually the winter ranges are many miles inland from the permanent marking corrals, which would necessitate long drives to and from the coast. The only way to avoid the above would be to build corrals or else use the brush enclosures which were made for the purpose of separating mixed herds in January on the winter ranges.

My objections are then that the does will suffer adverse after-effects if they are driven and handled in their last period of pregnancy, that is, in March and the first half of April. The weather is uncertain and the days are short in February and March. If the coast marking corrals are to be used for counting the animals, it will necessitate driving the deer to and from the winter ranges and they may thus suffer from lack of food. Personally, I should not like to be responsible for ordering large roundups in February and March in view of the damage which might be noticeable later on, causing weak fawns and debilitated does. The hazards due to stormy weather and short days should also be considered.

It would be most difficult for one not familiar with the entire situation to appreciate fully my reaction to the attitude of a Government official in dealing with a private corporation that had operated legitimately for more than a quarter of a century in a worth-while venture. To be told that we must sign certain papers by a specified date or condemnation proceedings would be instituted sounded to me harsh and un-justified.

The first offer made to us by Mr. Burdick following his arrival in Alaska was three dollars per head for 20,000 rein-deer in our mainland herds: Kotzebue, Buckland, Teller, Golovin, and Egavik. But we knew that in 1934, when nego-tiations with the Government for the purchase of our deer began, we had at least 250,000 reindeer, and I had made declaration of ownership of such numbers. Since the deer were no longer herded, we could not point our finger and say: "There are so many deer in this herd or that herd." The animals in all herds were scattered the width and breadth of the reindeer country. That would not so much matter to the Government as it would to private ownership, for the only ownership of reindeer would hereafter lie in Government and its wards, the Eskimo. We knew that our animals had strayed but, harassed as we had been over a period of several years, we no longer had the funds to maintain proper herding.

Mr. Burdick settled with all non-native owners by purchas-ing 82,442 reindeer, in full settlement. Of this number the Lomen Company received payment for 25,000 in their main-land herds and 17,500 in the Nunivak Island herd.

This was an amazing climax to a long-drawn-out problem. Mr. Burdick and his assistants did not see 82,442 reindeer in their attempted roundups and counts of reindeer during the winter period of 1940. That was simply the number the Gov-ernment settled for. The area over which the reindeer belong-ing to non-natives ranged was entirely too vast to be covered during a few months of the winter season.

During the twenties, prior to the time our herds reached the 100,000 mark, we brothers, in our interest and enthusiasm, worked on many problems respecting the herds. We knew that well-cared-for herds doubled in numbers every three years. Nineteen twenty-three saw our herds jump to 40,125 head with 10,928 new deer marked during the summer season.

That was a 37 per cent increase to the 29,197 reindeer in our herds prior to the fawning season.

Three years later, in 1926, we marked, by actual count, 23,212, which brought our herds to an estimated 85,867—again a 37 per cent increase. During the four markings, 1923 to 1926, inclusive, we marked, by actual count, 61,772 new deer in our herds.

Following the Kendrick hearings in 1931, the Department of the Interior in its report made the following statement:

"The small number of reindeer brought to Alaska many years ago (1,280) as a means of furnishing the natives with food and clothing have multiplied perhaps a thousand fold."

That estimate would mean a million-and-a-quarter deer.

During the negotiations for the taking over of our property, brother Alfred was in Nome. After the Government vouchers had been completed he wrote me, under date of June 15, 1940, about his adventures in trying to recover something for property we had in the field, various cabins, winter and other corrals, and so on. Some of our cabins were on the direct winter trails, but Burdick seemed to think that although the usual Government policy was to furnish shelter cabins, it was up to our corporation to supply them. Our alternative, therefore, seemed to be either to deed our property to the natives living adjacent to it—who were very friendly to us—or let it go to public domain.

There were innumerable minor details, and it annoyed Alfred when he and a couple of attorneys were kept haggling all day over a matter in which fully five dollars was involved. However, Mr. Burdick held all the cards and was not inclined to be generous. "He has cut every corner possible," Alfred wrote. "I do not believe I have won one single argument with him or gained one favor. I did not win a round with him but I have done my best." Alfred concluded, "Our policy here is to take our defeat gracefully, forget the reindeer deal, make no enemies, and carry on our commercial interests as best we can."

I myself had no desire to continue the fight. I had fought and worked for the industry for many years, both in Alaska and at Washington. I was about played out. To me there was no alternative but to accept the Government offer and kiss the reindeer good-by.

At this time we were indebted to our private bankers in the sum of $410,000, and to the Reconstruction Finance Corporation for another $125,000. The R.F.C. was certain of receiving payment in full, though the private bankers were not. The company stockholders would receive nothing—nor the Baldwin family for their more than a million-and-a-quarter dollars, the Lomen family for their labor and earnings during a quarter of a century, and the other stockholders who had invested tens of thousands of their money.

There was only one bright spot in the dismal picture. Following the acquisition of our reindeer herds by the Government, the Baldwin family, as a protective measure, took over the remaining assets of our company. Both Leonard and Arthur Baldwin had since passed on. But the younger generation were anxious to carry through, in so far as possible, the concept of their parents. I met with Donald Baldwin, son of Arthur, and with the approval of Leonard's son Franklin they turned over to my associates and me the lighterage business on the most generous of terms, thus permitting us to continue to be actively identified with the north country where we had spent so many years and the Alaska we had learned to love.

So ended our reindeer adventure. With our withdrawal from the industry, we could think only that it would be interesting, and doubtless not a little heart-rending, to sit back and watch how the Government would deal with the problem.

Under date of December 22, 1953, the Bureau of Indian Affairs, Alaska Native Service at Juneau, wrote me:

This will acknowledge your letter of December 9, 1953, in which you requested that we furnish you with the latest figures on the estimated number of reindeer now in the herds in Alaska. The last report which we have was prepared about six months ago and shows an estimated total of 26,157 head of reindeer in Alaska at that time. This number has been reduced some since that time by butcherings and death losses.

When we were forced to quit, most of the Eskimo followed suit, although they were now the only ones permitted to own reindeer. Wolves entered the grazing lands and killed thousands of reindeer. As the Eskimo no longer had assured markets for deer meat, they killed the animals and used the carcasses for dog food and as bait for fox traps. One village alone destroyed 3,000 reindeer in a single year to provide food for their dogs. Unherded and uncontrolled, tens of thousands of reindeer traveled eastward and joined the caribou. Thus has a great industry with incalculable possibilities been reduced to a ghostly specter of its former importance.

Hundreds of millions of dollars have been spent in Alaska by the United States in recent years in the construction of Army and Navy installations. In view of the type of neighbor we have across the waters of Bering Sea, this was necessary. More millions will be spent as a protective measure in future years. General Billy Mitchell once made a statement that has since become famous. "He who holds Alaska rules the world." With development of long-range planes, the truth of that statement becomes increasingly clear.

In Korea, the American Army rediscovered that the lowly mule, which had been discarded as of no value in modern war, was just about the most perfect means of packing large amounts of supplies through the mountainous country where it was forced to fight.

In Alaska it would seem only sensible that the Army, following the example of the Russians just across Bering Strait in Siberia, should make use of reindeer as draft animals. In Siberia, tax collectors, guards, and others who must travel long distances in winter are trained in the use of sled reindeer.

During the Russo-Finnish War, just prior to World War II, the Finns used many small companies of infantry, trained in the use of reindeer, as reconnaissance troops. The deer were used in several ways. Some traveled with the conventional sled, others pulled troopers on skis, with the soldier's pack lashed on the back of the reindeer. With this light equipment soldiers traveled as much as a hundred miles in a day; and the Finns had a fast-moving screen of reconnaissance troops to act both as "eyes of the Army" and as Arctic cavalry.

The Finnish Army selected white or almost white reindeer and used white-painted sleds. Wearing light white drill parkas over their fur clothing, the troops drifted like ghosts across the snowy Arctic wastes; appearing out of nowhere, they struck lightninglike blows at strategic spots and then quickly retreated.

The fluidity of the movement of the Finns under conditions that would normally hamper all troop movements was amazing, forcing the Russians to shorten their lines and be ever on the alert. The Finns even mounted artillery on heavy skis, using large teams of reindeer to haul the guns. Such maneuvers should appeal to officers of the American Army, since teaching in all of its command schools has of late years been concerned with fluidity of movement.

The rebuilding of the reindeer herds in Alaska should no longer be regarded as a purely commercial enterprise. The United States Army has given much thought to developing the interest of the Eskimo in guerrilla warfare ever since the end of World War II. The Army has gone about this type of work along conventional lines, patterned after procedures already known and accepted.

The Eskimo like these war games. In fact, they like them so well that they sometimes neglect their hunting in order to take part in the maneuvers.

A comprehensive program of rebuilding the reindeer herds, plus training by the herders of large numbers of reindeer for draft purposes, would prove one of the most worth-while accomplishments the Army could attempt in Alaska. Visualize, if you will, specially trained troops using reindeer for transportation, with good equipment, a vast reservoir of reindeer from which to draw for replacements—and in case of necessity, for food—scouting the Arctic in the event of war. With this type of highly trained troops on which to depend, a constant source of information could be had from the Kuskokwim River in the south to the International Boundary Line to the north and east.

Compare this picture with that of the average army—one that must be supplied with everything it uses. Army transport is expensive in the Arctic. Exceptionally cold weather plays havoc with machines. Tank tracks crack and break under Arctic conditions.

In this day of the atomic bomb and the jet airplane the average person, without knowledge of conditions in the Arctic, would consider the airplane the answer to Arctic reconnaissance. Such is not always the case. Along the rim of the Arctic, in winter, a "land fog" conceals the ground much of the time. This is caused by fog or a "ground blow"—a blinding sheet of wind-driven snow forming an effective curtain through which observers from an airplane cannot see. Sometimes this veil of fog and snow covers the land for days at a time. Enemy movements during such periods would be safe. Such conditions would prove no deterrent to the reindeer, for they could still maneuver.

In case of need, an army fighting in the Arctic and hard

pressed for food would most certainly welcome a dependable meat supply. The primary objective of any Arctic traveler or explorer is to live off the country. It is thus only logical that the reindeer herds be rebuilt on a sound basis and kept on a level consistent with the grazing possibilities of Alaska.

With the transfer of our herds and equipment to the Government, the general impression was that the Lomen family and other company stockholders had enjoyed a handsome profit.

"Why," people exclaimed, "we understand that you made more than a million dollars!"

Their estimate is never less than that figure. It reminds me of the story of Tom, Dick, and Harry.

"I haven't seen Harry around lately," Tom remarks. "What's he doing?"

"Haven't you heard?" Dick replies. "Harry made four hundred thousand in four months in the jewelry business in New York."

"Impossible!" Tom scoffs. "I don't believe a word of it!"

"Wait a minute," Dick says. "I'll phone Bill and ask him. He knows the whole story."

Whereupon Dick phones Bill and after some talk, hangs up and turns back to Tom.

"Well," Dick explains, "it's just like I said about Harry making a killing. Only it wasn't in New York; it was Chicago. And it wasn't the jewelry business; it was the cement business. And it wasn't four months; it was four years. And it wasn't four hundred thousand; it was four thousand. And just one more thing—Harry didn't make it, he lost it."

Today Laura and I live in Seattle. Father died in 1934 and Mother in 1951. Dad was in his eighty-first year and Mother in her ninety-seventh, bright and active to the end. Brothers

George and Alfred have also passed away. My sister Helen lives in Seattle with her own family.

With my brother Ralph I am actively engaged in the interests of the Lomen Commercial Company. We go to Alaska on business and always look forward to seeing some reindeer, though it is a rather wistful occasion. We hope that someday others may take up the challenge where we left off.

We are convinced that the reindeer industry can once again prove of great value to the people of Alaska and the far North. A domesticated animal that can live without shelter in the Arctic the year around and feed itself, that lives free of disease and furnishes fine meat and beautiful skins to make the warmest garments ever developed for Arctic wear, is certainly worthy of further serious study and development by both government and private industry.

For our own part, we are deeply thankful to have had the opportunity to add a few chapters to the history of that magnificent animal and good friend of man, the reindeer.

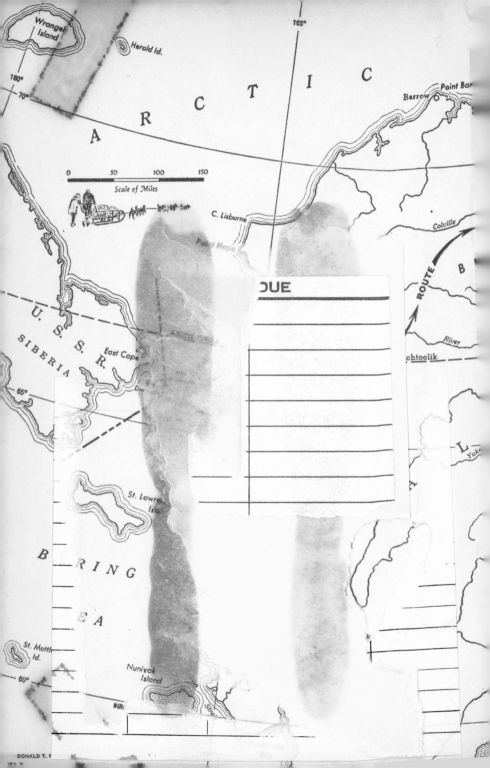